ALL MY FLASHBACKS

ALL MY FLASHBACKS

LEWIS GILBERT

Writing Associate: Peter Rankin

Reynolds & Hearn Ltd
London

For Hylda,
who lived most of this book with me

ACKNOWLEDGEMENTS

Thanks to Bob and Annie Kellett, who were in at the beginning, and to Cornel Lewis for the cover photo

All other pictures are from the author's collection, and are used with grateful thanks to the relevant production companies and distributors

First published in 2010 by
Reynolds & Hearn Ltd
61a Priory Road
Kew Gardens
Richmond
Surrey TW9 3DH

A CIP catalogue record for this book is available from the British Library

ISBN 978 1 904674 24 5

Designed by Chris Bentley
Printed and bound in Malta by Melita Press

Contents

1
Reality vs Fantasy

In the 1880s Joseph Griver, my Jewish grandfather, took his two sons and fled the Russian pogroms to establish himself as a cabinet-maker in London's Brick Lane. His wife, having refused to leave Russia, was gradually erased from his life, to be replaced in due course by a young woman sent over by his family. She arrived in London never having met her future husband and speaking no English. A year later my mother, Ada Griver, was born, and as soon as Ada could walk she could dance. At the Lyceum Theatre, aged 12, she won an open competition – her prize, with Christmas coming, was a huge turkey. It had been plucked of its feathers but its long, dangling neck and its head were still attached. Thrilled with herself and the turkey, Ada took it home on the bus in the rush hour. Her fellow passengers were not so thrilled. At home Joseph, who had always disapproved of his daughter dancing in public, was so angry at seeing a non-kosher turkey in his home that he threw it out of the window. Some passer-by must have had a welcome, if unexpected, dinner that Christmas.

The next day a woman turned up at the flat, saying that she had seen my mother win the prize at the Lyceum and was most impressed. The woman was Louisa Gilbert, one-time music hall performer, now variety artiste manager. She was Irish, full of blarney, and once she started to talk nobody could resist her. The acts she managed were in fact her own ten children. Who the father or fathers were, no-one knew. To Louisa, wedlock had not been important. Now she wanted Ada to join one of her acts, if Joseph would allow it. He was furious. There was no way he could let anyone take his 12 year-old daughter out on tour round the country. Ada had to go to school and that was that. "But this is much more important," said Louisa, "and, in one of our acts, she'll have a better education than she'll receive at any school." After half an hour of Louisa exerting her extraordinary Irish personality, Joseph finally agreed. For him to do that was amazing. For Ada, it was exactly what she wanted.

The act was called The Four Juvenile Kemptons, so Louisa suggested that Ada change her name from Ada Griver to Renée Kempton. Joseph didn't seem to mind, while Ada was delighted. She needed a partner to dance with, though, and for that job, Louisa chose her youngest son, the 14 year-old George Gilbert.

Thrown together on tour, Ada and George gradually fell in love. What they saw around them in that very adult world and what they got up to who knows, but after four years they decided it was time to get married and strike out on their own. Louisa was not that dismayed and even allowed the name of the act to go with them. As it was going to be four adults though, the word 'Juvenile' had to be dropped. The entire act, consisting as it did of a tango, a charleston, a waltz, a highland fling and so on, was billed as 'The Four Kemptons, Dancing Round the World'. The other two Kemptons were frankly whoever Ada and George could find to join them. Ada danced well enough but George was the one who shone. He was the one who had personality.

Soon after they set out on their own, Ada and George had a

child, Renée, my sister, and three years after that another one, me. I was born on the 6th of March 1920, in a trunk. By the time I was four years old there was little about variety I didn't know, because every night I would stand in the wings and watch the different acts. The knockabout ones I loved, and when they were throwing flour over each other you could not move me from the side of the stage. I never liked the two people who sang love songs. To me that was terribly boring. The patter acts and quick-fire stand-up comedy I didn't really understand, but I was still interested because I knew where the laughs came. I'd look out at the audience and wait and think, "This is it. Laugh," and they did. They all laughed. That feeling of knowing more than the audience was wonderful. However, as I stood there every night I was filled with experiences not only wonderful but also strange. Still, they exercised my imagination.

There was the ventriloquist. Of course I knew he was manipulating the doll and that, in some way, his voice was the doll's voice. I understood that. It wasn't hard but then there came a moment in the act when he threw the doll back into its box, slamming the lid down and the doll kept on talking. "What are you doing? Let me out! This is terrible! Why won't you let me out?"

"Keep quiet in there!" the ventriloquist would say.

"Shan't!" the doll would retort and on this went until the curtain came down with the audience applauding wildly. Afterwards the ventriloquist would take the box, its lid still locked, and push it to the back of the stage. This really terrified me. I knew he manipulated the doll up to a point but he didn't manipulate it when it was in the box. In the box the doll had a life of its own. It had to have because it answered back. That I could not understand and I would never, ever, go near the box.

In fact, I would go out of my way to go round it.

I had several experiences like that. We were doing *Little Red Riding Hood* and the actor playing the wolf, his wolf's head under his arm, came to wait for his cue next to me in the wings. He chatted away. "When are you going to school? Do you like being here? Do you think you'll be dancing like your father and mother?" and really he was very nice to me. When his cue came he put on his head and went out on to the stage. "Grrr!" he exclaimed and started to behave like a wolf. The characters drew away from him in terror. A nervous rustle went through the audience, particularly among the children, and then he came off, walking towards me with his head on. I was terrified. Only two minutes before I'd seen him put that head on but it made no difference. When he walked past me to his dressing room I shrank back into the shadows. As a small child it was very difficult to differentiate between fantasy and reality.

When I was six it was still going on. By then my parents were performing in Cine Variety, where short films and variety acts were interleaved. During the First World War variety had done extremely well but now, in 1926, people's economic situations were beginning to change. I loved those films and, if I could, I watched them twice a day. They were usually Westerns, which were very popular at the time. However there was one thing I could not understand. Why would an actor – and I knew that actors appeared in films because I had already been in a couple myself – why would an actor playing a cowboy or an Indian allow himself to be killed? Why would he let someone fire a gun at him or shoot an arrow through him? I couldn't understand that at all but I didn't want to ask. One day the answer hit me. I went to the green room, the place in a theatre where performers go to relax, and found three or four of them sitting around, talking and smoking. "You know those people who get killed in a film," I said, "I know how they get killed and why they get killed." They all stopped and looked at me.

"What do you mean? They're actors."

"I know they're actors," I said, "but what actor would want himself to be killed?"

"They aren't. They're acting."

"No, no. I've seen them dying. I've seen them fall off horses, dead."

"So, what do you think happens?" they asked.

"What you do," I said, "is, you go to the prison and you find somebody who's going to be hanged and you say, 'Look, if you come into our film and get killed, we will pay you some money and we will look after your family. You might as well do it our way and get paid because you're going to get hanged anyway.'"

Well of course they roared with laughter and thought that was the funniest thing they'd ever heard. "No, son," they insisted, still laughing, "it *is* acting. Honestly, it really is." But I thought, 'I don't believe that,' and I turned round and stalked out. There it was again, the inability of the child thrown into a world of fantasy to adjust to what was fantasy and what was fact.

Before that, when I reached four, something happened that remains very clear in my memory. It had a great effect on my parent's act. There was a trick cyclist who used to go round the stage on a variety of bicycles, a one-wheeled bike, a two-wheeled bike, a large bike, a tiny bike, all of them, specially made for him. Part of his act was riding off on one bike and coming straight back on, riding another. That always went down well, but then it was a good act. One day, without him telling anyone, he asked me to join him. I loved the idea. I thought that was terrific. This is how it worked. He rode off on a big bike, as usual, but, from the same spot, I pedalled on, riding a tiny bike. It looked as if the trick cyclist and his bike had shrunk. The house erupted and the manager tore down to see what was happening. In their dressing room, my parents said, "The trick cyclist's doing well tonight," before they too came down to have a look. They weren't angry. They laughed and then realised there was something in it, something they could use for themselves.

Normally, to boost applause at the end of their act, my parents would have an assistant stage manager come on with a bouquet of flowers. "For me?" my mother would mouth, pointing at herself and coyly fluttering her eyelashes, "Thank you." And how funny it was, I thought, that she could do this night after night and it always worked. The audience fell for it every time despite the flowers, that weren't even real, getting tattier and tattier as the weeks went by.

The week after the trick cyclist business, though, he having gone his separate way, my parents tried out their new idea. While the audience was applauding their act, they went off and came back on, with me and my long blond hair, in the middle, holding their hands. As soon as we were centre stage I performed a simple time step my mother had taught me, ended on a buck and wing and took a bow. The storm of applause was as loud as it was for the tiny bike appearance. 'My God, the Kemptons are going well tonight,' thought the manager in his office.

And from then on that is what happened at quite a lot of theatres, but not every night. It was usually on the ones when the act had gone down only so-so and the applause needed extra boosting. It meant, though, that I was now part of the company, treated as a member of the team and spoiled by everyone. I loved it. As for school, in those days the rules concerning attendance were virtually non-existent, not that anyone in theatre took much notice of them anyway. School was something that could be discussed later... and later... and later.

On Sundays we would travel to the next town on the variety circuit by train. Every time the ticket collector approached, my parents quickly pushed me up on to the overhead rack and covered me with coats and hats. They weren't going to waste money buying a ticket for me and the collector was too busy punching the others' tickets to look upwards. For a five year-old this was deliciously exciting.

We always seemed to change trains at Crewe Junction, the busiest station in the north and an exciting place to be. I loved the clatter of trains coming and going, the tall funnels smoking, the bursts of steam hissing over platforms, the whistles blowing and the guards slamming doors and waving flags. When we were actually changing trains, lugging our belongings from one platform to another, my parents always found friends for a chat and an exchange of news. Those Sundays were like musical chairs. It seemed that every variety act on the northern circuit was changing trains at Crewe, all of us moving on to the next booking, the next set of digs, the next bedroom.

When we finally reached our room for the week, my father had an invariable routine. He pulled back the bed covers and put a small mirror he carried with him between the sheets. If the sheets were damp, the mirror would cloud over. He had tuberculosis and damp sheets made him wary. In one room where the sheets were damp, he confronted the landlady. "Ma," he said – landladies were always called Ma – "have you just washed our sheets?"

"But of course," came the crisp retort, "my husband died in there last week." My mother, squeamish about having a corpse recently in her bed, asked for another room but no other was available, nor other sheets either, so she had to settle for a stone hot water bottle.

During the busy summer season, it was normal for performances to be twice nightly. My appearances, however, were restricted to the first performance. After our evening meal at the digs, between shows my parents went back to the theatre leaving me with the landlady. There's one particular boarding house I have always remembered. The landlady washed me, helped me into my pyjamas and put me to bed in the small room I was sharing with her three year-old daughter. For a long while I looked across at the pretty face sleeping peacefully in the other bed. I then climbed out of mine, walked across to hers, kissed her softly on the cheek and went back to my own bed filled with innocent happiness. To this day, I don't know why I did that. It can only have been the curve of the little girl's pretty cheek.

I was not always touring, and when I wasn't I stayed with relatives back in the East End, uncles and aunts usually. My sister, Renée, would be there already because she didn't care for touring. Where she most preferred to be was Joseph's place because she adored her Russian grandmother who, by the way, we called Annie. If you loved warmth and food and cuddles, that was the place to go, particularly on a Friday night when the evening meal before the Sabbath was delicious. Annie, however, was almost a stranger because she mostly spoke Yiddish and never learned more than a few words of English. A language she had no problem with was music. Renée took piano lessons and Annie loved to drop by to hear her granddaughter play. As she listened, tears would come into her eyes. I thought Renée's playing was nothing special, but then I was her kid brother.

I have no memory of seeing Annie outside her home and

neither she nor Louisa, my other grandmother, ever visited each other. Their lives were quite separate and it was up to me to react accordingly but children are quick at that. I'm wrong about Annie never leaving the house. We once went to the pictures together. It was a silent film, still quite common when I was seven. Words on cards used to come on the screen to tell the audience what was happening. Annie couldn't read English, so when they appeared, she would turn to me and I would read out, "Heart spoke to heart in the still of the night," or whatever it was. As I whispered, though, I realised there were lots of other children sitting next to relatives who couldn't read English because right round the house would go this chorus. "Heart spoke to heart in the still of the night." The piano accompanying the film was quite drowned out.

Joseph spoke a little more English than Annie but what impressed me most about him was his craftsmanship. For ages I used to watch as he and his two sons marked, sawed, turned, sanded and joined pieces of wood. What a pity that I was unable do it, any of it. My hands are the most hopeless in the world. They do not belong to me. When, later at school, my contemporaries in woodwork were carving cabinets, I was down among the juniors struggling with a toilet roll holder. Sandpaper as I might, the bit in the middle still stayed square. That sounds funny now. It was not then. The teacher, because he couldn't believe anyone could be so dense, got angry and there was only one way I could get through the lesson. Passing my other grandmother's place, Louisa's, on the way to school, I would put my head round the door and ask, "Any errands you want running, Grandma?" certain that she would say, "No," but give me a penny. With that penny, I bought a bag of sweets and so, by sucking hard on a pear drop, I managed to get by. Even so, when the teacher approached, the sweet had to go double quick as eating in class was not allowed. A sudden fit of coughing would do it and into my hanky would go the sweet. Out of this humiliating experience came one good thing, though. I discovered that, after watching someone crafting away, I could tell someone else how to do it. And when I came to films, I discovered a great relish in working with skilled artisans, all our particular talents pointing towards one end, the film itself. I also learned – and I'm thankful it happened at an early age – that my hands could never earn me a living.

I'm sorry now that neither my grandfather nor Annie ever spoke about their lives in Russia. I can only guess that it was an existence both limited and harsh. Recalling it in detail would probably have been unbearably painful for them.

At Louisa's, there was no craftsmanship, no warmth, no cuddles and no tears for sentimental tunes. The only food I can remember is not so much the stuff itself as the smell of a rather unappetising stew that was permanently on the go. And yet, hers was the place I most loved to visit. It was the talk that did it. Blarney, perhaps, but it was vivid and energetic and that fires a child's imagination. To start with, there was the nagging question of her ten children's father. Who was he? Or, who were they? I never found out but it was certain Louisa was quite the free spirit. She may have been a Catholic but I never saw her go to church. Her background, each time she described it, had a way of shifting around. Sometimes her husband was a military gent. Sometimes he was a circus ringmaster. Whatever he was, though, it was always colourful. The only sure thing in all this was that we never saw him or, for that matter, them.

"What towns have you been to?" she would ask as soon as I was through the door. "And who was on the bill with your mother and father?"

"George Formby Senior," I'd answer or "Ella Shields," both of them, big names of the period.

"Do the act," Louisa would say and I would have to do the act, the star's act. Being very young, I remembered every word, of course. It was easy, and apparently I was quite good at it because one day Louisa looked at me and said, "You're the one. You will be the one who will have his name up in lights." I suppose that was ridiculous, her saying that to a six year-old. I may have known what a name up in lights meant but how it got there, I hadn't a clue. Nevertheless, the force of Louisa merely saying those words, struck home. That moment sowed the seeds of ambition. Ambition to do what? To do well, to start with. But to do what, exactly? That would have to wait.

Although she was not what we would nowadays call touchy-feely, she was a good entertainer. I caught chickenpox once and had to be off touring and away from my parents for three weeks. To a child, a length of time like that that can easily feel like three months. In this case, I wasn't bored because Louisa, as well as telling riveting stories, played games. Most absorbing was to see her take a piece of wool, make a loop and play cat's cradle. She could weave one mesmerising pattern after another.

Her mischief was not confined to tales of her dubious past either. Two of her daughters married Jewish boys and went to live in Stamford Hill, the part of London where Jews moved when things in the East End had gone well for them. Every now and again, these two daughters would come to visit, first one and then the other. "Got everything you need, Ma?" the first one would ask, "All right for Guinness, are you?"

"No," Louisa would answer, shaking her head, and an hour later, after the daughter had left, a crate of Guinness would arrive. Straight under the bed it went. The next day, the other daughter would drop by and also ask, "Got everything you need, Ma? All right for Guinness?" and Louisa would still shake her head and say, "No." This time, though, she would glance over at me as if to add, "And don't you dare." An hour later, another 12 bottles would arrive to join the first 12 under the bed. I'm not a great beer drinker, myself, but on the rare occasions I feel like one, I find myself ordering a Guinness.

One night, when Louisa was really old and I was staying with her, she beckoned me to her bedside. "You see that trunk over there?" she said.

"Yes, Grandma," I answered.

"Open it."

I did and found all the dresses and props for the various acts she had once performed.

"I want you to have that." she said.

"But what will I do with it, Grandma?"

"Keep it because one day, you and I will get the old act out again."

What a strange couple we would make, I thought, Grandma aged 80, me aged 11, dancing round the stage. It never came to it, though. That was the last time I saw her, the old girl, as she was known. She died soon afterwards, but at least she had given me my inheritance. It was not the trunk. It was her, and when I add the whole lot up, Irish Catholic on one side, Russian Jewish on the other, I think "Unusual but not unhelpful."

2

An Actor's Life is Not for Me

When you grow up with someone who has a life threatening disease, you're used to it. You're sad, of course, because you hate to see suffering but seeing suffering is not the same thing as understanding death, not if you're five years old.

Tuberculosis was still rampant in the 1920s and my father had it. He carried on as long as he could, doing what mattered – being a father, loving his family. He even kept working. However, from my position at the side of the stage I could see that his job was becoming tougher and tougher for him. Sometimes, in the middle of a solo, he would nod to my mother and on to the stage she would dance, smiling away. As he danced off, you would have thought it was all part of the act but, barely into the wings, he would double over, racked with coughing, and when he drew his handkerchief away from his mouth blood would be on the linen. Even so, I can't say I was that frightened because I didn't think he was going to die. He was just not well and, for me, that was normal. For instance family and friends always said of him, "Poor George," so I, on once being asked his name, answered, "Poorgeorge." It meant nothing to me. In this way things stayed normal, that is as long as we kept working. With money coming in we were all right, not rich by any means but when we looked around and saw real poverty we knew we were not doing badly. There was food on the table and, for the first five years of my life, that's how things stayed. When I was six, there was a change. Times came when my father had to be off work and, while he was recuperating in a sanatorium away from the smoky East End, usually Frimley near Guildford, our savings ran out fast. Only a few weeks had to go by before worry set in.

With little to do, my main occupation in life was kicking a football around. Dribbling along, out in the street one afternoon, I was approached by a kid who seemed to appear from nowhere. "Hey, Gilbert!" he said. "Your father's just fainted up the road." I stopped and, setting off in the direction the boy was pointing, ran like crazy. Up the road, on the pavement, lay my father, people all around. "Give him air!" someone shouted. Men from the crowd picked my father up and carried him to our flat. I followed, very frightened. The men didn't have far to go – we lived on the ground floor – and once inside they lay my father on the couch. To a six year-old, things seemed strange and out of control. As I stood watching, though, I saw my father stir. This movement prompted a woman to fetch a glass of water and the rest of the crowd to drift away. For them the drama was over. No mention was made of hospital. In those days you stayed well away from there if you could. With a bit of calm restored, I felt free to go up to my father. He seemed not so bad. I gave him a kiss. He smiled. Perhaps things were going to be all right. They weren't. And over Sunday lunch one day we found out how far the rot had gone.

My mother liked to do Sunday lunch at home whenever she could. It was particularly important for us, because only then were we a complete family. Renée, my sister, as I've said, didn't like touring. In fact, she didn't like any of showbusiness and would soon go off to pursue other interests, namely public relations. Some very famous companies became her clients. That Sunday, though, it was just nice for her and us to chat away merrily, and while we were doing that my father started his lunch. He was putting some food into his mouth when he keeled over and fell to the floor, unconscious. Our first reaction was shock, but a split second later my mother leapt to her feet and called for the neighbours. In those days neighbours were a big thing in your life. As front doors were always open they were constantly in and out and a good neighbour was invaluable. We didn't have telephones, so it was a blessing that my mother could tell a lad to run to the local hospital and fetch an ambulance.

During the limbo days that followed, with no work and my mother always at the hospital, I was left to amuse myself as best I could in the back streets. I found a gate. Normally, it was shut but that afternoon somebody had forgotten to close it. Putting my hand over the lock, I swung backward and forwards. All of a sudden, the gate clanged shut.

That was a bad day for my mother. No sooner had she returned home from visiting her husband than she had to hurry off to another hospital to see her son. The tops of the fourth and fifth finger on my right hand had been sliced off. At home, she was confronted with a playmate of mine holding up those missing fingertips. Not knowing what to do with them, she flushed them down the lavatory.

A few days later I was in the playground, kicking a football as usual, when a grown-up cousin of mine called me over. "I've got bad news for you," she said. "I've just heard. Your father died today." I looked at her, bewildered. She, not knowing what to do, added, "Don't worry. I'm sure your mother will be home soon," and took four coppers from her purse. "Here, buy yourself some chocolate or something." I thought that was very kind. Buying a bar of chocolate, I could understand. Taking in my father's death was much harder. I ran off.

Later, sitting on a bench, eating the chocolate, I tried to think. When people got old they died, I knew that, and at 34 my father did seem fairly old. However, I could not take in the finality of it. Still less could I take in what his death implied. It was not long before I found out. My mother was devastated. All she knew was the act. All her life, that's all she had done. Without my father there was no act. There was nothing.

If she had been alone in the world, despair might have overwhelmed her. However she was not alone. The Jewish religion is a practical one. The haves must look after the have nots. Jews with adequate incomes are instructed to put aside money for Jews who have run into trouble. That way poverty can never be abject. My mother, barely able to think and certainly in a muddle about me, approached the Jewish Board of Guardians. To give her respite they sent me, bandaged fingers and all, to a home in Hove. Without their help we might have gone under.

At the home in Hove were six or seven other children, each with their own problem, like getting over an illness or being caught up in a messy divorce. However, my background was so different from theirs and we had little in common. Above all, I missed my mother.

Lessons distracted me during the daytime; reading and writing usually, which in my case were a novelty. At night, however, all I could do was lie there and wonder what was going to happen. It was then that it sank in that I would never see my father again. Many nights I cried myself to sleep.

Weeks passed like months. Twice a week, sometimes three times, my mother would send a postcard. In one or two, she even said she was coming down. This was very exciting and on Sunday I'd be all ready and waiting at the door. She never came. Soon afterwards, another card would arrive with an explanation. "I'm sorry, darling. I so wanted to come but I didn't have the fare." That was tough and I didn't forget it. In the film *A Cry from the Streets*, which I made 31 years later, a child waits at a gate for his mother to collect him from the orphanage. She never comes. The mother in the film is an alcoholic and that's why she doesn't show. My mother was not an alcoholic. Her problem was survival.

Each week we were given a penny to buy sweets. It must have been a very old head on my six year-old shoulders because I didn't spend any of it. Knowing that times were hard I saved the coins in case we might need them one day. After some weeks my mother, more collected by now, sent for me to come home. Things were hardly great though, and it seemed to me she could do with a cheer-up. I had those coins. "What would be a good present?" I wondered. "Perhaps a bar of chocolate?" No, too ordinary. I needed to show that I had given it a bit of thought. At Woolworths I found a miniature elephant made of stone. When I gave it to my mother she didn't say, "Thank you." She burst into tears, which was wonderful because it was better than "Thank you." After she died the elephant went to my sister, Renée, and now Renée's son has it.

It was then that one of those good neighbours of ours, seeing the jam my mother was in, proved her worth. This neighbour was a woman who worked as an extra in films. "Why don't you do the same?" she suggested. "Someone like you, who's been around theatre, you're perfect. They'd love you." 'They' was the

Film Artistes Association, which was a posh name for the organisation that ran extras. It sounded like a union but it wasn't really.

My mother joined and that was it. She was earning a living. By this simple action she set the course of my career because, at work one day, she heard that a child was needed. "I have a son," she said. "He's very keen. He was brought up in the business, you know. He'd love to do it."

As a child extra I was soon brought to the fore and even given the odd line. Casting directors noticed that I didn't muck up and began to give me little parts to play. I became known as a performer who could be depended upon, and all at once I became the breadwinner. It was rather a burden, but not in the sense that my ambition had faded. That was still there. It was simply pointing in a different direction. I'd always wanted to be a professional footballer. Eight pounds a week, which is what they earned, was fine by me. The fact that your talent had to be extraordinary to hold down that job, and that at 32 you were out, was not in my ken. For a start, 32 seemed ancient.

I can't have been that weighed down though because there was a happy-go-lucky side to my life. The school I was being sent to was up in Islington. Two old ladies ran it and it could not be said that education was uppermost in their minds. We only did mornings. Our afternoons were free so that we could be available for film work. Each day my mother would give me four pennies, one for the bus fare there, one for a bun, one for a glass of milk and one for the bus fare home. I simply hopped on the back of a horse and cart and got a free ride. If the driver flicked his whip backwards to get me off I jumped on another cart. In those days there were plenty around. At school I skipped the milk and bun and when it came to the journey home it was back on the horse and cart. The four pennies I spent on going to the pictures and that was my education.

So there I was, a child actor with parts coming in but they tended to stay small, until one afternoon came a break. A few days before I had been out in the country, on location for a film about the highwayman Dick Turpin. "Hop up on that roof," the director had said. "Dick gallops by and throws you a bag of money. Catch it and show me that you're really thrilled." And that had been fine. I had gone home and forgotten the whole thing.

Three days later I was out in the back streets choosing my team for football, I being the captain, as usual, and not bad at it either, when two men came up to me. Doug Murray and Dennis Van Thal were theatrical agents who in the past had got me a few small parts. "You have to come with us now," they said. "We've spoken to your mother and it's all right."

"Yes, but why?" I asked.

"There's a job come up. *Dick Turpin* – it's a film."

"I know," I said, "I've already been in it."

"This is another part. Now, don't argue. We've got to get to the Stoll Studios right away."

"But I can't go like this. I'm dirty."

"Get into the car. We'll run you round to your mother's. She can wipe your hands and face. That's all there's time for."

And that's what I did, at the same time wondering how on earth you could have another part in the same film. Once we were all back in the car we set off for Cricklewood to what had previously been an aircraft hangar but, with a lump taken out of it, was now a sound studio. As we went along, the two agents explained. In the film there was a rather nice character, and the part had gone to Hughie Green. I'd heard of him. He was quite well known. I'd also heard that he was obnoxious. The director had filmed with him for one day and come to the same conclusion, so Hughie had got the chop. I could see that the situation was serious. Without another boy right away the production was in trouble.

"Then, they remembered you – " said Dennis.

"But – "

"Wait. I'm getting there – and they had a brainwave. They're going to turn the boy you've already played into the boy Hughie Green was supposed to be playing. The business with you getting the money from Dick Turpin ties in perfectly."

At the studio, the director was in the middle of directing a scene. Even so, when he turned to talk to me he was very nice and I was in.

The film's star was Victor McLaglen who, in a very short time, was going to win an Oscar for his performance in John Ford's *The Informer*. What he was doing in this little English picture I never found out, but he too was nice and, more than that, he took a shine to me. During our conversations I told him that I had no father and it gave him an idea. Towards the end of the shoot he spoke to my mother who had been bringing me to the studio each day. He told her that he would like to adopt me and take me back to America. My mother thanked him but declined the offer.

The Dick Turpin film was a big break for me. It didn't make me famous, but in the business I became known as a safe kid who could deliver lines, do what the director said and behave himself. It was certainly no opportunity to become big headed, not if you take into account what happened at the next job interview. George Cukor, the Hollywood film director, came over to look for a boy who could play David Copperfield as a child. He was staying at the Dorchester Hotel and that's where I was taken. The look he gave me as I went in was kind but sad. "How old are you?" he asked.

"Thirteen," I answered.

"I thought so," he said. "We're really looking for a boy who's ten." And that was the end of the interview. Freddie Bartholomew, who lived in America, got the job and became a big child star.

I took whatever came up and that's how it went. It could be a pageboy being given a tip by Charles Farrell, Hollywood star of the early talkies. "You can have it back," was my line, "Give it to the starving Armenians." What it meant, where Armenia was, I had not the faintest idea and no-one told me.

It could be an information short. One was financed by the Temperance League and involved a day's work at the tiny Marylebone Studio. It didn't go quite as I expected. In the first scene I came into a room, found my father drunk on the floor and ran out, appalled. At that point, we broke for an early lunch. When we came back, the first assistant director told us that filming had stopped for the day and that we should be back ready to pick up the next morning. This was surprising but fine because it meant another day's pay. The next day, we reached the second scene where I walked into my mother's kitchen and she asked if I had found my father. "Yes," I answered, "but, mother, he was drunk, dead drunk." Then, we broke for another early lunch. When we got back, the first assistant told us that filming had stopped altogether. I asked the actress playing my mother why. After all, the film wasn't finished.

"The director and the cameraman can't work," she said.

"What do you mean?" I asked.

"You wouldn't understand," she said, "They're both alcoholics." And so ended the film entitled *The Evils of Drink.*

Film fees tended to come in guineas. A guinea is one pound and one shilling and the arrangement I had with my mother was that from every guinea I earned, I could keep the shilling. Many I saved but, with the first five I bought a bike. As you would imagine, at that price it was a boneshaker. I loved it though, because it gave me a sense of freedom. Once on it, I could cycle all the way to Clapton to see my favourite cousin. He was the son of my mother's sister. Jack Cantor was his name. He and I were the greatest of friends and as he too had a bike, we were able to cycle round together.

By now my lack of education was beginning to alarm my Stamford Hill aunts, the ones who had sent crates of Guinness to my grandmother. Their two sons were attending a private school, Clark's College, and that's where they thought I should go. Fees would be paid by them. At first it felt strange because I was the youngest there, but in no time I joined the football team and, despite being so young, became the captain. My experience on the streets did that. The pupils of Clark's College could only play on official spaces. In this way I became popular and was able to command respect. I may not have turned professional but football has always stood me in good stead.

Clark's College, on the other hand, only lasted three terms. It was a proper school and proper schools don't look kindly on pupils taking time off for filming. I left and went back to a place that would turn a blind eye. We were now in the 1930s. In 1929, Wall Street had crashed. If you had a job, you hung on tight.

My mother and I were well out of variety because that was dying. Film, on the other hand, was flourishing. Cinemas were opening all over the country, growing larger and larger. Eventually, they became luxurious palaces, two to three thousand seaters where you could find warmth and luxury, most welcome in those days. The main source of films, then as now, was America. Hollywood was flooding this new market. To protect British film-makers, the quota system was introduced. For every American made film, there had to be a British made one on the same bill. What a good time it was to get started in the film business. I was lucky.

In reality, the quota system was an exercise in cynicism. The films made under it were only an hour long and very cheap. Budgets, calculated at a pound a foot, usually came out at £5,000 per film, while the schedule was ten days. Quality was not important. The films didn't necessarily have to be distributed to qualify. They had to be shown but, if a film wasn't considered good enough for distribution, one showing would do. This could well take place in the morning before an audience of half a dozen people who hadn't paid, or even for the cleaners. To rich Hollywood studios, losing a few thousand on such a film was considered worth it. A big budget feature of theirs with popular American stars could absorb the sum easily, and so, 20th Century-Fox established Fox-British at Wembley Studios. From there they sent out a stream of these short films which became known as Quota Quickies. For British film companies they were a bandwagon and those companies jumped on it.

Despite the low budgets and short schedules, some Quota Quickies did achieve distribution and a few made handsome profits. So this system, cynical and cut-throat as it was, at least provided work for British crews and, better than that, a good training ground for directors, technicians and actors. The director Anthony Asquith began his career on Quota Quickies, as did another, Michael Powell. I was in one of his.

It was a typical Quota Quickie where, at the end of the ten day schedule, if you hadn't finished you either worked on through the night until you had or else you tore the unfilmed pages out of the script. This was a work-through-the-night one. Unions were weak. Unemployment was rife. You could get away with it. The title of the film was *The Price of a Song*. At the beginning a pianist is murdered, leaving the rest of the plot to be taken up with the inquiry. I was the hero's girlfriend's brother and, at the time, aged about 13 or 14. Towards the end of the last day of shooting, a very long day, I went to the only empty room I could find, the extras' dressing room, and fell asleep. At two o'clock in the morning I was woken by an assistant shaking me. I didn't know where I was. He shoved two pages of script into my hand and told me to learn them. The scriptwriter, realising that time was running out, had put in a cut and tacked the two outer bits together. This was the result. With bleary eyes I started to read only to be interrupted by another assistant. "You're wanted on the floor now," he said.

I went down to the set. Michael Powell, a difficult, hard man who didn't care if an actor was 9 or 90, snapped, "Know your lines?"

"Oh, Mr Powell, no," I said.

"What?" he shouted, "You wretched boy. Hundreds of children out there would give their eye teeth to have your job!"

"But these pages, they've only just been given to me," I said.

"God, I'll kill him!" yelled Powell and summoned the assistant who had brought them. "Do you mean to say you've only just given this boy these pages? He should have had them half an hour ago. That's when they were written. It was your job to see he got them." Before the assistant could answer, I spoke up. "Excuse me, Mr Powell, I think I could learn this in one or two minutes. I'm very quick." I read the scene through a couple of times and told him that I knew it. He didn't say, "Well done," or

"Good boy," only, "In that case, stand over there and do it."

Twenty-two years later, after I had directed *Reach for the Sky* and it had been the biggest hit of the year, winning a Bafta for best picture and making me the blue-eyed boy at Pinewood Studios, there came Rank's annual Christmas dinner. All the posher directors and actors were invited. Next to me was Michael Powell. I reminded him of that long, hard night. He didn't soften. "Now you're a director," he said, "you know what we had to put up with in those days."

Will Hay was a bit jollier, or rather his comedies were. He himself was not nearly so extrovert as the blustering chancer he played. In private life he was an astronomer who discovered a new star and named it after himself. In his films, his character was often a schoolmaster who was surrounded by the same six boys. In two of these pictures, *Boys Will Be Boys* and *Good Morning, Boys* I was one of those pupils. The principal two were the fat Graham Moffatt and the old Moore Marriott, neither of whom were real boys but that was part of the fun. Another boy was the comedy actor Charles Hawtrey. He played the swot, always being bullied by the others. I didn't forget him.

During most of the films I was in, though, I was on my own and technicians, seeing a boy, often with nothing to do, became teachers. "Want to have a peep through here, son?" the camera operator would ask. "Find out what it's going to be like on the screen?" and so I would get to look through the viewfinder. Then he would explain that what I saw was achieved by a particular lens that he and the director had chosen together. His assistant, the focus puller, would chime in by telling me why he made chalk marks on the floor during rehearsals and why he kept measuring the distance, with a tape measure, between the actors and the camera. The boom operator, not to be outdone, would explain that during the lighting of a shot his job was to make sure that the boom, the long pole at the end of which was the microphone, did not cast a shadow on the actors' faces or come into the shot. If I went out into the corridor, I'd hear, "Come and see what I'm doing." It would be the editor, frequently a woman, like many today. With that invitation, I would get to watch her run the individual takes through the Moviola and then start to splice them together, a much slower process than it is now. It involved scraping away at two frames and using a strong smelling adhesive. Even so, with patience, I was able to see how you can make film dance along and tell a story. An idea began to form in my head.

At the age of 17, which means it was 1937, I played an office boy in the film *The Divorce of Lady X*. The producer was Alexander Korda, head of London Films and mastermind of the huge, new Denham Studios. The director, an American, was Tim Whelan and the stars were Laurence Olivier, Merle Oberon, Ralph Richardson and Binnie Barnes. I was not in awe of Olivier and Richardson at all. For a start, I hadn't seen them in the theatre and when I watched them working on the set I thought they were a bit hammy. I could see Tim Whelan struggling with this. It was a situation he was not used to. The reputation of these stars in the theatre was huge, so how was he going to tell them to take it down? He didn't and nor did it help that the script was based on a stage play.

Because the film was a comedy and about glamorous people it was shot in colour. This made for a paradox. Light and stylish though the film was meant to be, it was heavy going in the making. Three strip Technicolor, the process it used, required an enormous amount of light and light makes heat. After every take we had to run out of the studio to cool down.

Towards the end of the shoot, Alexander Korda came on to the set. When he arrived it was being lit for the next scene, so it was a quiet moment. He came over for a word. That morning he had watched the rushes, the material shot the day before, and had liked my performance. I was over the moon. Korda was a god in British cinema, but then he told me that I was coming to the difficult inbetween age, no longer a child actor but still too young to play adult parts. To fill in those dead years, I should go to the Royal Academy of Dramatic Art, RADA. That was his advice. I decided not to accept it because in that moment my idea crystallized. Sometimes in life, one can think very quickly. 'Your hands are useless,' I thought, 'and your education is nil, but you know one thing, one thing that a university student does not. You know how films are made.' Nothing concentrated my ambition more than the lack of choice. Quite simply, there was nothing else I could do. "I don't want to be an actor," I blurted out, "I want to be a director."

Korda laughed. I expected that. What I did not expect, and what amazed me, was what he said. "I will talk to Mr Cunynghame. That's the studio manager. Report to him Monday morning." That was it. I was to start at the bottom of the ladder, but then if I fell I didn't have far to go. *The Divorce of Lady X* was my last film as an actor.

3

Learning the Ropes

Mr Cunynghame was not pleased when I knocked on his door. Interference from above irritated him. Nevertheless, he brought himself to tell me that I was to be third assistant on a film called *The First and the Last.* The screenplay was based on a story by John Galsworthy and it was another London Films production starring Laurence Olivier. His co-star this time was Vivien Leigh.

The reputation of the director, Basil Dean, was that of a bad tempered bully who created a tense, unpleasant atmosphere on the set. It was well earned. Everyone hated him, cast and crew alike.

We were on location in Southend, shooting a scene involving a young woman when the pretty actress playing this character fluffed her lines twice. Basil Dean flew into a rage. In his case, this came out as sarcastic jibes. Why was he cursed with such an incompetent idiot? Who was she sleeping with to get the part? Everyone was embarrassed. The actress tried again and again but the more Basil Dean shouted, the more flustered she grew and finally she burst into tears. A crowd of cockneys, out on a day trip, was watching and this was too much for them. Shouts and jeers broke out. There was uproar.

"'Ere, look what you've done!"

"Leave off!"

"The poor gel!"

"Shame!"

"Bully!"

Grabbing what we could, we moved to another location to shoot a different scene. The one with the girl was abandoned for that day.

Back at work in the studio one evening, I was delivering call sheets to the artistes' dressing rooms for the next day's filming when I saw Basil Dean walking towards me from the other end of the corridor. To avoid him, which I was skilled at by then, I dodged down a side passage and found myself behind our two stars, Laurence Olivier and Vivien Leigh. A lot of animated talk was going on, most of it coming from Vivien Leigh. It was clear that she was worked up about something, while Olivier was trying to placate her with nods. Eagerly, I eavesdropped. Vivien Leigh's well-bred tones rose higher and higher. "Larry, I swear to God, if he goes on like this, bullying us all, I'll kill the fucking man!" I was shocked. At 17 I was still innocent enough not to have heard any woman use such a word, let alone a beautiful lady.

Those days before the Second World War may seem distant but photographers and scandalmongers hovered like vultures round celebrities, just as they do today, waiting to grab a photo or a tit-bit of scandal. Rumours were racing round that Larry Olivier and Vivien Leigh, both at the time married to other people, were having an affair. But were they? They were being discreet and keeping it private, if they were. That is, until the day Olivier's wife and Leigh's husband turned up on the set at the same time. Both were carrying their spouses' babies. A deathly hush fell on the studio. The embarrassment was tangible. No longer could anyone be in doubt that the rumours were right.

The two stars retired with their families to their separate dressing rooms. It was too late. The damage was done. The scandal spread across the sensationalist papers of the day and the twin divorces made headlines all over the world. Olivier and Vivien Leigh married in America. When the film was finished, it was judged so bad that new material had to be shot before it was shelved. It wasn't until years later, half way through the war in fact, when films were in short supply, that *The First and The Last* was brought out. It had another title by then: *21 Days*. It still didn't do well.

One of the writers who worked on the screenplay was Graham Greene. From an office at Denham Studios he used to send out pages of additional dialogue to be typed and given to the actors concerned. My job was to take those pages down to the typing pool, wait for the work to be done and then take the new pages to the actors. If only I had paused before leaving the typing pool, to snatch Graham Greene's original pages from the waste paper basket where the typist had thrown them. Silly boy.

My job over on that film, I was once more out of work. A friend told me that Associated British Pictures at Elstree Studios were looking for assistant directors. Why didn't I apply? Instead of working freelance, I would have a permanent job with a regular pay packet. As this sounded great to me, I wrote off at once. A note came summoning me to an interview with the studio manager, Clarence Elder. On hearing me tell him that I had worked for Alexander Korda and with stars like Olivier and Vivien Leigh he looked impressed and took me on. This time, though, I was to be, not third, but second assistant director and my wage was to be five pounds a week. Maybe snobbery had something to do with my getting that job but I had no reason to complain. I had just turned 18. I was working in my chosen career and I had been promoted. As I reported for work on Monday morning, I was delighted.

At Denham I had been tea boy, gofer and general dogsbody. At Elstree, my main job was to look after the actors. Having been an actor myself, this wasn't difficult. My responsibility was to get them on to the set when required, made up and in the right costumes. The person who told me which actors were required was the first assistant. He never left the floor.

Even a simple task was an opportunity to learn. The dressing rooms were sometimes quite a distance from the stage on which we were shooting and, during the walk along the endless corridors, some actors became nervous. Cinema in the 1930s was still young and offering a new challenge. These actors, older ones usually, with years of experience in theatre, found it difficult to adapt. They were used to playing to a live audience, establishing a rapport and building a performance to suit a house, be it a half-empty matinee or a jam-packed Saturday night. Listening to their worries taught me, in a roundabout way, what did and did not work on the screen.

"Theatre or film?" was a debate held endlessly wherever actors congregated, be it the dressing room, the green room, the wings, the pub or the train, though it would still be interspersed with the witty, caustic, sympathetic, bitchy gossip you always got from actors. Nowadays, they are much more adept at suiting their performance to the medium they're working in, whatever it may be, theatre, film, television or radio.

Not long after I had started to get work as a child actor I had moved, with my mother, to a block of flats mainly inhabited by policemen and situated in the Charing Cross Road between Leicester Square tube station and Cambridge Circus. While that had been convenient enough for my acting work, it no longer was for my new job at Elstree. The journey took up too much time. To see the actors into make-up and wardrobe I had to be at the studio first thing. Somewhere closer was needed. Luckily, on my very first film, I took an instant liking to the clapper-loader, Max Kemp. He was ten years my senior and staying at a boarding house just round the corner from work. In his room was a spare bed. He and I could share the room and the rent. I paid the landlady 25 shillings a week, which by then I could well afford, and for that I got not only lodging but a cooked breakfast, a hot lunch and a cold supper. This gave me a new kind of independence and I revelled in it.

There are always pretty girls working at a film studio. One day, I caught the eye of a particularly pretty one just as she was leaving the canteen. I smiled at her and she smiled back. We got talking. Her name was Peggy Simpson and she was an actress playing a small part in another film shooting at Elstree. We started going out together, but sadly just as my film began hers came to an end. Still, in that short time we became very attracted to each other and it was good fun to make up a foursome, drive down to London in a friend's small car, see a show, have a meal and perhaps dance at the Hammersmith Palais. On my five pounds a week I felt like a millionaire.

As I started that first film at Elstree it was 1938 and war was looming. Neville Chamberlain, the then Prime Minister, flew to Munich to visit Hitler and returned waving a scrap of paper for the waiting cameras. "Peace in our time." Everyone breathed a sigh of relief. It is hard to imagine today how so many newspapers and so many senior politicians, including the Foreign Secretary Lord Halifax and even the Prince of Wales, thought Hitler was a splendid chap who was doing a lot for Germany. That September, with Chamberlain talking of "A quarrel in a far away country between people of whom we know nothing," we shamefully betrayed Czechoslovakia.

The film, my first at Elstree, was *Vessel of Wrath*. It was taken from a story by Somerset Maugham and its star was Charles Laughton. He was also the film's producer. He and the German director, Erich Pommer, boss of the UFA Studio in Berlin, were co-owners of the independent production company Mayflower Pictures. Laughton, after many films on both sides of the Atlantic, including *Mutiny on the Bounty*, was already a big star in Britain and America. He liked to take a long time over his make-up and was in the studio every morning at six, which meant an early call for me. The part he played was Ginger Ted, an unkempt old tramp. This was a big make-up job that could take a couple of hours.

In those days films were normally shot in the studio and nowhere else, but as this story took place on a remote desert island the exteriors were going to be shot on location abroad. This was a huge thrill for me as the furthest I'd been away from London was Southend, Cromer and Blackpool. I could hardly believe that, for my first trip out of England, I was going to the South of France and being paid for it.

The entire film unit, in a convoy of pantechnicons and trucks filled with everything we needed, moved down to Cannes. The crew stayed in small hotels at the back of the town, way back, while the cast and the big shots stayed at the Carlton where Queen Victoria had always stayed on her visits under the name of Mrs Queen. Our remote desert island was the beautiful, low lying Ile Sainte-Marguerite, perhaps a mile out into the bay of Cannes. It was famous for the grim fortress where the Man in the Iron Mask was said to have been imprisoned.

Before the war, British crews working abroad were very

conservative about food. The unions insisted that a British catering wagon had to be on hand to provide hot meals three times a day. That would be roast meat and two veg followed by treacle tart and custard or spotted dick, even when it was 90 degrees Fahrenheit. As my favourite food had always been fish and chips – it still is, to tell the truth – I was quite content with familiar British catering. On weekday nights and Sundays, though, if I'd been working late taking artistes back to the mainland on the ferry, I would miss out on the catering wagon and grab the opportunity to sample the many bistros and brasseries in the back streets of Cannes. By the time we'd finished on that location I had become a convert and a lifelong addict to French cuisine – and to Cannes, where I now live.

On our remote desert island, which in reality was about as barren as Hyde Park, we had to shoot a scene with a dog. While burying a bone he uncovers the opening of what eventually becomes an escape tunnel, so he was crucial to the plot. "Use my dog," the prop man had said back in London, "He's brilliant." When it came to it, though, would the dog scrabble away on cue? We tried everything. We even held his legs, but it was the stupidest dog in the world. Every evening, round about six or seven, when we were looking forward to going home, the director would say, "We'll try the dog shot again," but it never worked and to this day I couldn't tell you what actually happened.

Laughton's Mayflower Pictures was to make three films at Elstree. The next one was *St Martin's Lane.* I wasn't on that but I was on the screen tests for the female lead. One of the contenders was Sally Gray, a lovely young actress. I had a big crush on her. The part ultimately went to Vivien Leigh but Sally autographed a photo for me, which I still have.

One scene in *St Martin's Lane* remains particularly vivid. Charles Laughton, playing a busker, works the queue outside a theatre while beautiful Vivien Leigh sings and dances as an impoverished street performer, at the end going round the crowd with a cap and a winning smile. Her next role but one would be Scarlett O'Hara in *Gone with the Wind* for which she would win an Oscar, while the film itself would win 12 more Oscars and remain one of the greatest and best loved movies ever made.

As I was on the payroll at Elstree, whenever there was a gap between pictures and I wasn't being second assistant I was loaned out to different departments. Wherever another pair of hands was needed, that's where you would find me. It could be the cutting rooms or the sound department or camera maintenance. It didn't matter. I enjoyed anything and everything to do with the making of a film.

Back on the floor, as second assistant, I had a day when one of those departments would have been not just enjoyable but heaven. It wasn't a big picture, so there were only two of us in the way of assistants, the first and myself. The first, needing to leave the studio to work on the call sheet for the next day, put me in charge. This was not a big deal. I knew what to do. I had to call for the red light before a take, nothing more. I was in the middle of doing that when I heard a voice say, "Hold it!" A chippy was peering round the studio door. "Can we bring this ladder through?" he asked.

"Yes," I said, "but hurry up." In he came, behind him the ladder, which I was expecting to be a standard one, six foot, say. It wasn't. It was a 60 foot one. On and on it went, seemingly without end, and when the whole thing was in it jammed against the opposite wall and wouldn't move, try as everyone did to shift it. Paul Stein, the director, was usually quite nice. He wasn't now. He had a quick temper and he exploded.

"Look what you've done! You've stopped the filming, you incompetent! Go up to Clarence Elder and tell him you're sacked!"

Shattered but managing to say, "You fucking idiot," to the chippy, I made my way upstairs to see Clarence Elder. All he did was laugh. Lose Gilbert? It was out of the question. Was I not on the football team and the table tennis team too? No, all I had to do was go back downstairs. I did, rather slowly, and by the time I arrived, Paul Stein had forgotten all about it. Football had indeed stood me in good stead.

Painful in a different way was the evening I was asked to drop by the West End theatre where Michael Wilding was performing to give him his call for the next day's work. That, anyway, is what I thought I had to do. The first assistant called me into his office. "They've decided," he said, jerking his head upwards, "they want to replace him. So you can tell him not to bother coming in tomorrow." I was stunned but I couldn't question the order because I was only a teenager. I knew something was definitely wrong though. Surely a famous actor like Michael Wilding should be told by the producer, not me. Still, there was nothing for it and off to the theatre I had to go. Michael Wilding, an extremely good natured fellow, smiled as I entered his dressing room and held out his hand for the call sheet.

"I'm very sorry Mr Wilding," I said, "but they don't want you to come in tomorrow morning."

"Oh really? When then?" he asked.

"They don't want you to come in at all," I murmured, "They're finding another actor." When it comes to deciding who was more embarrassed by this moment, the famous actor or the squeaky voiced kid who was sacking him, I think you could say we were both level pegging.

Life at Elstree wasn't all work. At weekends, I generally went home to Charing Cross Road. From there, I could take my current girlfriend out to a show or a film. In those innocent days though, a girlfriend was literally that, a girl friend. A kiss and a cuddle was all you could expect, most frustrating for a lusty young man but, back then, that's the way it was.

At other times, my friend and room-mate Max Kemp would invite me down to his family home at Staines on the river Thames, not far from Windsor. There was quite a lot of family too, eccentric, jolly parents and four brothers, one of them, Max's identical twin. Some years before, the father had been rich but subsequently had lost his fortune, probably during the Depression. Nevertheless, a constant stream of friends and family turned up at the house expecting hospitality. What happened was that the cook fed them and the butler, her husband, served them. Having done that, both would then, as a matter of course, sit down to eat with the guests and family. They received no wage, but at least had their board and lodging. The family, when not at table, liked to make 8 mm films. These were shown in a mini-cinema out in the garden and were paid for by a dotty rich uncle on condition that he appeared in every film as the hunchback. It was a hilarious and bohemian family.

Back at my weekday job, the third of Charles Laughton's productions at Elstree was *Jamaica Inn*, taken from the novel by Daphne du Maurier. Alfred Hitchcock, well on his way to iconic status, was the director and the young female star was beautiful Maureen FitzSimons who, in a few months time, would become Maureen O'Hara.

Hitch had a quirky, almost schoolboyish sense of humour. He

loved to play tricks on people. Some of these were genuinely funny. Others could be quite disturbing. Canvas chairs are provided on set for the actors. They're the ones with names on the back. One day, Hitch snuck up behind an actress who was sitting down and held his cigarette lighter under the seat. The canvas was flameproof but it soon got very hot and the poor girl jumped up in alarm. Hitch clapped his hands in delight.

Another day, Hitch played a more serious trick. It nearly went awry. Up on the lot, which is the space next to the studio where exterior sets are built, a dramatic scene was about to be filmed on the deck of a ship. A storm would be raging. The ship would pitch and yaw and mountainous waves would be simulated by floods of water falling from massive tanks on either side of the deck. All this would be controlled by Hitch pressing a series of buttons on a panel next to his chair. Because it would show up the water more clearly, this scene would take place after dark. For the 20 stuntmen who were going to be drenched and sliding from one side of the deck to the other, it was going to be a cold, wet night.

Not long before it all started, a break was called and the crew went off for hot soup and coffee, leaving Hitch alone. At that moment, on to the empty set came the production manager Hugh Perceval, deeply unpopular owing to his self-importance and pomposity. He was forever strutting around, throwing his weight about, checking and criticising all that he saw. As usual, he had on a thick brown suit, which he wore whatever the weather. Hitch, with a gleam in his eye, allowed his fingers to wander casually over the buttons on the panel next to him. When his target was in the most vulnerable position, he accidentally on purpose pressed all the buttons at once. The powerful slabs of water knocked his victim over and soaked him to the skin, while the heaving deck threw him from one side to the other. It was payback time and Hugh Perceval deserved it but you couldn't help feeling sorry for the man. Hitch quickly turned the water off and abjectly apologised to Perceval for his clumsiness, all of which he managed to do without moving from his chair. There weren't a lot of laughs from the crew but an awful lot of appreciative grins.

By the time I came to *Jamaica Inn* I'd been watching directors at work for a while and I knew the procedure. They looked through the camera and said, "You stand over there. You go over there. Now, we'll rehearse … No, it's not playing properly. You go over there, dear," and, having said "Cut!" at the end, would jump up and perhaps whisper to an actor to take it down a bit. Hitchcock did none of that. He never got out of his chair. He never looked through the camera. What he did do was take a sheet of paper, divide it up into squares and draw each set-up how he wanted it, a big face in the foreground, say, and a full length figure in the middle distance. This, he would hand to the operator.

"Would you like to see it?" a new operator would sometimes ask.

"No," Hitchcock would answer, "you have the set-up. You do it." When shots were finished, operators crumpled up the drawings and threw them to the floor. It was Graham Greene's pages all over again, only worse.

With actors, Hitchcock had a wonderful way. There was no whispering. He would turn his direction into a funny line. Sometimes, having said "Print that," he would be faced with an actor asking for an extra take. "You may have an extra take," he would reply. "Whether I put any film in the camera is another matter." After that, the actor clammed up. None got the better of him. Laughton, being the co-producer, was slightly harder to handle as Hitchcock was, in effect, an employee. Nevertheless, he managed it. Laughton would be at take 17, begging, "Just one more, Hitch, just one more. I know I can do better, I know," with Hitch allowing him to do it, only to come back with, "It wasn't very good, was it? Print two and four," which he said in a loud voice for everyone to hear.

Sometimes Hitchcock could be kind. "Lewis, tell that extra to walk a bit slower, will you?" When he said that, I floated over the floor. It was the first time he had called me Lewis. Perhaps emboldened by this, I took a quiet moment, when a shot was being lit, as a chance to speak.

"Excuse me, sir. Do you mind if I ask you a question?"

"No, what is it?"

"How do you decide which lens to use for a particular shot?"

Next to one of his drawings, I had seen him scribble 'Use a 24.' "You shouldn't worry about things like that," he answered. "They're not important. What's important is the script. If that is right, it doesn't matter what lens you use. You simply have to be clear in your mind what you want to see on the screen at any point in the film."

"Thank you," I said and stepped back for the scene to be shot.

Hitchcock, however, had noticed the rest of the crew clocking our little conversation, so when the shot was over he called out, "That's it. We'll print takes three and five!" as you would expect, but then added, "How was it for you, Mr Gilbert?" I wanted the floor to open up.

Jamaica Inn was to be my last film before the war.

4
Aircraftman Gilbert

On 1st September 1939, we were all fired from Elstree Studios with two weeks' notice. Anyone who was eligible for call-up at that time will remember the utter chaos. My own experience must have been typical.

On 2nd September I rushed to the recruitment centre in Kingsway to volunteer. If you volunteered you could choose your service: army, navy or air force. Films about the misery of trench warfare in the First World War had put me off the army and I was keen to join the RAF. When I arrived, a queue was already winding round the block. We waited patiently until a sergeant came out and said, "That's all for today. Come back tomorrow."

On the morning of 3rd September I was up early. Two hours later, I was at a desk giving my particulars to a recruiting sergeant when I heard a BBC voice announce over the Tannoy, "The Prime Minister will now speak to the nation." In silence we listened to Neville Chamberlain's solemn words. "...this country is at war with Germany." Even as they were sinking in, the wail of air raid sirens could be heard and everyone was ordered to the cellars. We went in a most undisciplined rush. Hardly had we reached the cellars than we heard the mournful moan of the all clear. Trooping upstairs again, we learned that it had been a mistake. Our radar had picked up not a wave of Luftwaffe bombers but three of our Spitfires, scrambled into the air to defend London.

A worried-looking officer came up to our desk and whispered something about official numbers changing as from now, to distinguish between conscripts and volunteers. I immediately feared the worst. Did this mean I could be conscripted into the army instead of being able to choose the RAF? For a moment my heart sank. Then, to my huge relief, I saw the sergeant methodically completing my form as before. The last thing he asked was, "Occupation?"

"Assistant film director," I answered. 900106 AC2 Gilbert was handed a train warrant to RAF Uxbridge.

To a civilian like me, Uxbridge was a daunting place. Grim barrack blocks, named after famous First World War battles, surrounded the parade ground. New recruits were told to report to the quartermaster's store to collect their uniforms. Unfortunately no uniforms were available but we were issued with a forage cap. Our civilian gas masks were then collected from us, after which we were dispersed to different barrack blocks.

At 1.00 am the air raid siren went. There was a mad scramble out of beds, across the pitch dark square and into the shelter. "Adjust your gas masks," we heard the Sergeant say as we sat there. 'What gas masks?' we wondered. Our civilian ones had been taken away and no-one had issued us with service respirators. It couldn't have been worse.

One kid, only 18, started to cry, "But Sergeant, we haven't got any gas masks."

"Got a handkerchief?" said the sergeant.

"Yes."

"Piss on it and put it over your mouth. That's just as good."

The kid did as he was told but it was painfully embarrassing. Doing that in front of others was something he would never have dreamed of.

It was another false alarm. How ill prepared Britain was for war. It was just as well that there were no real air raids for months.

Next day we had our medical. Poor eyesight let me down which meant I had no chance of being air crew and soon it was apparent I wouldn't be any use for ground crew either. My mechanical skills were nil. I'd never had a clue how to even change a wheel or mend a puncture. I was posted to the RAF Cookery School at Halton.

At Halton railway station I arrived expecting some sort of transport – films, you see – but there was none and no-one seemed to know where the school was. So, rather enterprisingly I thought, I phoned the Halton duty sergeant to send a truck or something. It seemed logical enough. A short while later, a staff car arrived driven by a pretty young WAAF. I congratulated myself, slung in my duffel bag and settled into the comfortable leather of the Humber. As we arrived at the guardhouse, the guard sprang to attention and everyone saluted – God knows who they were expecting – but when AC2 Gilbert stepped out with his duffel bag, it was slap bang into a bollocking of quite some decibels.

The instructors at the cookery school tried their best to uncover a latent talent in me. They gave me the recipe and ingredients to make a batch of rock cakes. I puzzled a lot over the recipe and followed instructions to the letter, but when it said 'Add an egg' it didn't say anything about removing the shell first. Within a week I was back at Uxbridge, posted to Headquarters 11 Group, a grand old building in whose grounds the recruitment centre was also situated. It was 11 Group's task to defend London and the whole of the south of England from air attack. On my arrival, two officers interviewed me and, having come to the conclusion that I was useless, decided the best place for me was Intelligence. There, I would be safely out of the way.

The Intelligence department was in another part of the huge base and here, instead of a brick barrack block, we had a Nissen hut – curved corrugated iron – to live in with an upright cast iron stove for heating.

I went for my interview. Squadron Leader Nelson was the first bit of sanity I'd come across. I really appreciated his opening question. "What are you good at?"

"Football," I replied. "I'm quite good at that, sir."

He laughed, thinking I was joking. I wasn't. However, as football turned out to be an interest of his, he took me on as one of his assistants.

Those months of nothing happening, which had started with the false alarms, continued. The war seemed totally unreal and became known as the Phoney War. It was a time for playing a lot of football and I was chosen for the 11 Group team. One afternoon, that caused a problem.

I had been picked to play an important match against an army team but my boots had disintegrated with age. As my earnings were only two shillings a day, one of which had to go towards my mother's small pension, there was nothing I could do. The remaining shilling did not go far. I was gloomily surveying my old boots when Squadron Leader Nelson came by. "Are you playing this afternoon?" he asked.

"Yes, but my boots have had it." I answered.

"For heaven's sake, man," he said, "buy another pair."

"I'm sorry sir. I can't afford to." I said, rather shamefaced.

He reached into his pocket and produced seven shillings and sixpence. "Here, now you can." It was a fantastic thing to do. I was a nobody and he had made this kind gesture. To this day I have not forgotten it.

One night, before another football match, I was on guard when I saw a parachute descending with a man-sized something hanging beneath it. As it neared the ground, the canopy caught in a tall tree. I ran to tell the duty officer. He looked even younger than I did. Peering through his binoculars, he said, "Should I shoot it?"

"No!" I burst out in alarm, "It might be a bomb." A more senior officer took a look and confirmed that it was a land mine. The whole area was evacuated and the bomb disposal unit sent for. As it was dark, the unit took the land mine to a patch of waste ground nearby to deal with the next day.

The match, this time against the Metropolitan Police, was a ding-dong affair but half way through the second half there were still no goals. I had a new friend, Cardew Robinson, a comedian before the war and now almost as out of place as I was. He too was in the match, and at this point it was his job to take a corner. As he stepped back in preparation, most of the rest of us crowded into the goal area. Once he was ready, he ran forward, kicked and the ball was sailing over our heads when there was a colossal explosion. In a field about a mile away, someone had detonated the land mine. We froze. None of us made any contact with the ball but the explosion's shock wave blasted it into the net. "No goal!" yelled the police. The ref blew his whistle.

"An act of God," he ruled. "Goal!" It was immortalised in the local press as 'THE BOMB ASSISTED GOAL.' The Phoney War was over.

Germany's preparation for the invasion of England was well under way and the first priority of its High Command was to gain control of the sky. The Luftwaffe had to eliminate the British fighter squadrons and their airfields. Day after day, high in the summer skies, one of the most important battles was fought, later to be known as The Battle of Britain.

It was an interesting job being an assistant to Squadron Leader Nelson. With him, I could go anywhere. My favourite place was the bunker. Everyone who has seen a film about the Battle of Britain will be familiar with the command bunker where, deep underground, young WAAFs sit, with croupier style rakes, round a huge table map of southern England, plotting, by means of radar, the positions of incoming German aircraft and our fighters sent up to intercept them. The bunker had frequent VIP visitors, including Winston Churchill and the then Duke of Kent, chief welfare officer of Home Command. On his way to Iceland a while later, the Duke's Sunderland flying boat crashed into a Scottish mountain. He and all the crew were killed. Nine bodies were found, which was something of a mystery as only eight people had boarded the plane.

In the bunker I was merely a privileged spectator but, just by being there, I felt in the centre of things. Every day, I could see on the blackboard the growing tally of our victories and losses. Soon I was given the chance to get rather closer to the action.

One of the key 'hub' airfields was Tangmere, with six smaller satellites along the south coast. Squadron Leader Nelson was planning to fly there for a visit. Would I like to go along? Not having been up in an aircraft before, I jumped at the chance. As we walked across the airstrip I was surprised to see that we were closing in on a small, single-engine monoplane with an open cockpit and two seats, one behind the other. Even though I had been handed a leather helmet and goggles I hadn't put two and two together. Squadron Leader Nelson was going to be flying us himself. My childhood confusion between fact and fantasy hit me all over again. I was Biggles.

We were well on our way to Tangmere when the Squadron Leader raised a hand to point out, high above us to our right, six approaching aircraft with Luftwaffe markings. He dived steeply, then levelled out at treetop height. This was my first close sight of the enemy and I admit my heart was pounding. Luckily the planes ignored us. They were looking for more important prey.

In due course, the hard-pressed 11 Group was reinforced by the Spitfires and Hurricanes of 12 Group which, as it happens, was led by Douglas Bader, whom years later I would come to know quite well. Some days, every serviceable British fighter was in the air at the same time. During that long, hot summer, both sides suffered dreadful losses but the Luftwaffe couldn't replace their lost fighters as speedily as we could. This was thanks to Churchill's appointment of the dynamic Max Beaverbrook as Minister for Aircraft Production. By the end of September 1940, the Battle of Britain was won.

The Luftwaffe, forced to adopt different tactics, switched from daylight to night-time raids, starting with the Blitz of London, confident that this would break the will of the British people and achieve surrender.

Many stories emerged from those who lived in London during the Blitz, stories of courage and companionship, of families lost and homes destroyed. In the midst of all this horror and destruction, there was one small incident I was caught up in, a chance encounter.

I had been given a ticket for a concert at the Queen's Hall in central London. Although the place was packed, the seat next to mine was still unoccupied as the lights went down, so I moved my coat and cap from my lap on to the empty seat. Soon I was lost, gone, enraptured by Elgar's Enigma Variations.

The wailing of the air raid siren brought us back to reality. For a moment, the orchestra hesitated then, to the siren's harsh accompaniment, played on. At a pause in the music the concert hall manager came on stage, first for a word with the conductor, then with the audience. It would probably be safer to remain in the hall, he advised, but we were free to leave if we wished. The orchestra, in the meanwhile, would be continuing with the concert. This brought a ripple of applause. We could hear from outside the constant pounding of anti-aircraft guns, and while the distant sound of exploding bombs was gradually drawing closer no-one moved to leave. The conductor raised his baton and the orchestra played on. Only then did I realise that I had a new neighbour, a young girl in naval uniform with 'Netherlands' on her sleeve and, neatly folded in her lap, my coat and cap. I moved to take them from her but, with a gesture and a smile, she stopped me before turning her face back to the enchanting music. During the rest of the concert I found my head turning of its own volition to steal another lingering glance at that so expressive face. The air raid steadily grew in intensity, the bomb blasts louder and louder. It was clear that tonight's target was no longer the strategic dock area alone but the whole of London and its seven million inhabitants.

At the end of the concert, when the applause had died down, the conductor made a suggestion. As it didn't seem a good idea to leave while the bombs were still falling, the orchestra would play other pieces from its repertoire but, to make it more fun, the players would swap instruments. There was much appreciative laughter and no-one left the hall as the smiling players moved around the platform, choosing their new instruments. The results were less than perfect but we entered into the fun and enjoyed it hugely, despite the fact the hall was now shaking to its foundations with every near miss.

When the players had run out of pieces they all knew, the conductor made another suggestion. They would play popular dance tunes of the day. The music started and, moments later, the aisles were packed with dancing couples. My neighbour and I took one look at each other, grabbed hands and joined the throng, where we were pressed together as close as sardines in a tin, a most pleasant way to pass an air raid.

Eventually the exhausted players ran out of steam. The manager announced that, things being just the same outside, we were welcome to stay until the all clear went. We should, however, try and get some sleep if we could. As the players made their way backstage with their instruments my eye fell on the grand piano. Still holding her hand, I led my new friend past couples that were settling down in the aisles and climbed on to the stage, determined that the piano would be our shelter for the night. As we crawled underneath, I saw that it was a Bechstein and felt a frisson of poetic justice. While the Luftwaffe was trying to bomb London out of existence, our two lives could be saved by a German piano. I suggested to my friend that, as we were spending the night together, we should, for propriety's sake, introduce ourselves. She told me that her name was Ruth. "Ruth what?" I asked. She said that her family name was quite unpronounceable and that Ruth would have to do.

Dawn was breaking when, at last, we heard the steady drone of the all clear. Thirsting for a coffee, we left the Queen's Hall hoping to find an all night stall. We found ourselves in shattered streets, stepping through the smoking remains of what had once been homes but now were gaps, like broken teeth in the serried ranks of houses. We walked across St James's Park, passing an ack-ack battery tucked behind a sandbagged emplacement, its guns pointing skywards, ready for the next attack. Standing at the foot of a mountain of empty shell cases was the crew, wearily tossing them, one by one, on to trucks.

Unable to find a coffee stall, we walked to Ruth's small apartment in Dolphin Square which was a whole block of apartments on the Embankment. I was saying "Goodbye," when she said, "Why don't you come in? I can give you a cup of coffee."

Mugs in hand, we went out on to her small balcony to stare down river, thrilled and horrified by the sight of St Paul's Cathedral as it stood defiant above the still rising smoke and silhouetted against the red glow of blazing warehouses. What a night. The chance ticket, the girl in the next seat, the shuddering hall, the music, serious at first then popular, the intimacy under the piano, only the Second World War could have done that. Until then I had been an observer. Now I was in it and, being young, I wasn't really frightened. That raid, one of the first after the Battle of Britain, had been designed to shake our resolve. It had shaken us physically all right but the spirit of fun in the hall had told me something quite different about our resolve. We were in with a chance – that was its message. The effect of all this excitement on a boy and a girl is perhaps not hard to imagine. In a second, that extraordinary night's experience catapulted two shy virgins past all the usual peacetime procedure of chaste dates, flowers, chocolates and engagement rings, straight into each other's arms and into bed. It seemed entirely natural because, in the few hours we had been together, we had lived a lifetime. We knew each other completely.

A routine was established between us of meeting whenever we

could. Night after night, bombs falling all around, I would stand under the Admiralty Arch waiting for Ruth's spell of duty in the nearby admiralty building to finish. It could be six o'clock. It could be midnight. I didn't care. A kind of madness seized both of us. Oblivious of the bombs, we strolled along the Embankment, chatted happily over a cup of tea in a Lyons Corner House, if one was open, or visited a dance hall if we had enough money. Either way, as often as not, we ended up in bed.

Out of the blue, I was sent to Wales on a fortnight's course but, as soon as I arrived back, I phoned Ruth to arrange our next rendezvous. A man's voice answered. Startled, I checked the number with him and also the number of the flat. Yes, both were right but he'd never heard of Ruth. Might there be a forwarding address or number somewhere? No, there was nothing. I was incredulous. I told him that she was my girlfriend and that I had been to the flat many times. I pleaded with him, by now desperate, but I could hear the man growing impatient. "In wartime," he said, "you should never ask questions," and down went the receiver. My heart sank.

It took me very little time to realise that finding Ruth was going to be impossible. For a start, that's all I knew about her, Ruth, her first name. During our intense, living-only-in-the-moment relationship, we had not talked once about her family or, of course, work. A Dutch girl called Ruth was all I could inquire about and that wasn't going to get me anywhere. This torture of not knowing what to do lasted three weeks. It was then brought to an abrupt halt. I was posted abroad, never to see or hear from Ruth again. I can only be grateful that, during our short time together, we shared so much happiness.

All this while, my mother was still living in the Charing Cross Road and still going out to work as an extra. At night, however, she had a new job. As darkness fell, she and countless other Londoners used to seek refuge from the bombing by setting up home on the platforms of underground stations. Since a bit of order was needed, she was appointed Shelter Marshal with the task of allocating everyone a space. It quite went to her head. Added to that, passing by on a train each evening was a casting director who also required her services, this time as a senior member of the Film Artistes Association. He wanted her to rustle up extras for the next day. Boy, was she pleased with herself.

She would get into his carriage which would always be at the same position in the train and, by the time they were at the next stop, he would have told her what he wanted. When the doors opened, my mother only had to lean out and call across the platform because her fellow extras, knowing she'd be passing, were always in the same position. "Got a dinner jacket, Charlie?" she might yell and when she'd heard a "Yes!", would add, "Tomorrow, Gainsborough Studios, 7.30. Ready made up!" before going on to Hyde Park Corner where she knew Mrs Jones had a pretty daughter and a smart cocktail frock. It was the middle of the Blitz. Above her, ambulances and fire engines were racing across London to rescue people who may well have been dying, but down where she was a different kind of war was going on. People needed entertainment, mainly films, and films needed extras.

Things, however, were not always like that. One night, I was waiting on an underground platform to get back to Uxbridge when an explosion above me sent hundreds of people running down the stairs. This time, their chins were not up. They were not smiling as their hearts were breaking. They were panicking and screaming. I heard shouts of "People are dying up there!"

"My house has gone!" "I can't find my children!" "They've got to stop. We can't take it anymore!" Incidents like that were rarely broadcast, if at all. Preserving the image of the stoical Londoner was vital.

My posting abroad came at the end of 1940. It was to Greece and I was promoted to Leading Aircraftman. While I was thinking that it could have been worse, a young man leant across to say that he was ecstatic. His posting was Singapore, where there was no war at all. I have often thought of that boy. His chances of survival after the Japanese invasion would have been minimal. Chance was what it was all about too. He and I were just numbers on a list to be sent where troops were needed, never mind whether we were suitable or not.

A rail voucher was handed to me for St Athan which, I assumed in my innocence, was close to Liverpool where convoys collected. It turned out to be a vast assembly point on the South Wales coast, two hundred miles from our destination. I suppose that was a security measure but it meant another slow and tedious journey, this time on a train packed with a motley collection of navy, army and air force personnel. Thankfully they were a cheerful bunch, which was just as well as we would soon be at sea together, sleeping in hammocks and living in conditions reminiscent of Nelson's time.

Shortly before Christmas, the largest convoy ever assembled left the Mersey estuary escorted by one aircraft carrier, two stately battleships and a host of destroyers that swooped around us like excited swallows, impossible to count.

Two days before Christmas, it was foggy as we headed south in the Atlantic, our thoughts only of family, home fires and Christmas trees. Then we heard gunfire. A few moments later two of our destroyers swept past, guns blazing. Our convoy was under attack. For a while all we heard were rumours, but soon more reliable information trickled through. Concealed by the fog, the sprawling convoy had actually sailed right past the giant German battle cruiser *Scharnhorst*, while she was taking on fuel from a supply ship. During a momentary gap in the fog the *Scharnhorst*, seeing a ship all by itself, had opened fire, not suspecting that it was at the tail end of a well escorted convoy. Our destroyers managed to sink the supply ship but the *Scharnhorst* disappeared into the fog.

It's strange, isn't it, as one grows older, that so many events in one's past resonate further on in life. Years later, that chance encounter with the *Scharnhorst* contributed both insight and empathy to the making of my film, *Sink the Bismarck!*

We were heading for the straits of Gibraltar when our next surprise came. Greece, we were informed, had fallen, so our presence there was no longer required. The convoy was split up and our destination became Rhodesia, to be reached via Port Elizabeth on the coast of South Africa. After a week or so in a transit camp at Port Elizabeth, the different arms of the three services were sent wherever they could be most useful. I was put on a train and sent to a vast Rhodesian training camp miles from anywhere. There, I spent a year giving the occasional lecture to trainees for the new RAF regiment. My subject: the vital role played by 11 Group in the Battle of Britain. On most days, however, I played tennis in the morning and football in the afternoon. Many people would have envied me my cushy job in this beautiful country, safe and isolated from the war, but I felt thoroughly frustrated, stuck in a backwater, wasting my life.

How quickly things can change. I went before an Officer Selection Board and passed. Pilot Officer Gilbert was posted to 6 Group Intelligence at HQ Middle East in Cairo. As a very junior newcomer, my first job there was to censor letters home to ensure that no information leaked out, however inadvertently, which could be useful to the enemy. It was a sad and depressing task. I had to read every letter right through, but even after I'd learned to skim through the personal bits, domestic problems – separation from sick children, family losses from bombs, heartbreaks at disintegrating marriages – jumped out at me and haunted my brain. Separation, I learned, was the hardest thing to bear, separation from everyone and everything you love.

At this time I was sharing an apartment in Heliopolis, a suburb of Cairo, with three other young officers. One evening, I was returning home from HQ on the bus when I saw a pretty girl, a very pretty girl, sitting in the next row. I smiled at her and, as I bought my ticket in bad Egyptian, she smiled back. We started to talk. Egypt wasn't her home country either. Switzerland was. She was sweet. She was lovely and I asked her if she would come out with me. "Yes," she said, but first I had to meet her father. The next evening, with her address in my hand, I went to her apartment block. It had a concierge, but when I asked him for Apartment 9 he said nothing, just gave me an odd, questioning sort of look and jerked his head towards a lift. I went up and as I waited for someone to answer the door, beside it I noticed a plaque. It read, 'Dr Pierre Henri. Consultant in venereal disease.' Now I understood the concierge's odd look.

Her father was a charming man who spoke a delightfully Edwardian English. He welcomed me warmly and said that he hoped we would have a pleasant evening and would I be sure to escort his daughter home. We did have a pleasant evening and a very good meal. She was a delightful girl, unpretentious, unspoilt and innocent as a snowdrop. I delivered her safely home and never saw her again.

After Montgomery's triumph at El Alamein, the war in North Africa gradually turned in our favour. I was given a new task. It was to help arrange airlifts of the most seriously wounded from field dressing stations to hospitals all along the North African coast. I flew with the transport planes everywhere there was fighting, from Benghazi to Tripoli, to Tunis and to Algiers. This was a terrible eye-opener, a grim education in the bloody horror of war. I tried to close out the images of unspeakable wounds and shattered bodies but the smell and the heart-rending moans all came flooding back in nightmares.

One job at this time was to escort 250 servicemen, supposedly recovered from their wounds, back to their units. Physically recovered they may have been. Mentally, I doubt it. All were a bit crazy. In any case, they didn't want to be sent to the front again. They wanted to go home. Being the senior officer I was the one in charge, but in rank only. These men were mixed army and air force with their own chain of command. Lip service was all I got.

The journey was four or five days across the desert. We didn't have tents. I slept underneath a truck on a camp bed. Two gay boys, who used to bring me tea in the morning – queer they would have been called then – built themselves a little house out of tins. They were the sweetest couple. "How would you like to be on the upper reaches of the Thames, sir?" was their daily greeting.

Those two looked after me but they couldn't be of any use when, one night, a beautiful night, I needed a pee and wandered off. On turning round to go back, I didn't know where I was. Everything was silent. Everyone was asleep. It was only too easy to lose your bearings because everywhere looked the same. 'If I start wandering about,' I thought, 'I really will be in the shit,' so

I lay down on the spot. It wasn't until the morning that I saw people moving around in the distance and finally made my way back.

Horrific sights and bolshy soldiers both had a bad effect on me. As a result I was sent to a convalescent home in Algiers. They were all crackers there too. Every night we went out on the booze. Once, on my return, I found the biggest rat you have ever seen sitting on my bed. I jumped back and darted out of the room, bumping into a bloke who was passing. "What's the problem?" he asked.

"Look!" I said, pushing him in front of me. He took out his revolver and shot the bloody thing. All over the bed, it went. The racket brought Matron down. She was furious.

By now the war was drawing to an end and I had been abroad for three-and-a-half years. A lot of us in that convalescent home were hoping that we would be sent home, and indeed many of us were. I wasn't. A chap who had been there some weeks before and had gone on to a job at HQ in Algiers, dropped by. "What the hell are you doing here?" he asked, "You should have gone ages ago." He went off to make inquiries and discovered the reason.

The title 'Matron' makes a woman sound old. Ours wasn't. She was only seven years older than me and she was my girl-friend. At night I used to climb out of the window and meet her on the beach, where a vigorous exploration of carnal knowledge took place. She had been keeping me back. Every time my case had come up for review she had insisted that I wasn't well enough to go. My HQ friend quickly got me under way and I went straight back to England.

5
Hollywood Beckons?

On my return from North Africa I was given a month's leave which allowed me to go at once to my mother's flat in the Charing Cross Road. I had seen neither her nor my sister for three-and-a-half years and our reunion was wonderful. I was able to settle in, look up old friends and begin to pick up the threads of my pre-war life.

When the four weeks were over I was instructed to report to the RAF Film Unit at the Air Ministry. At long last I was going to be back in a world that I understood. Someone, somewhere had spotted that films was my job. That too felt like a homecoming. Better still, the commanding officer I had to report to was Wing Commander Derek Twist. Before the war he had been a film editor and I knew him. After a friendly chat, he told me that he had an interesting assignment for me. I was to go round to the Mayfair Hotel and ask for Colonel Keighley of the US Army Air Corps Film Unit. I thanked him profusely, bursting to get round to the Mayfair. On my way, I wondered if Colonel Keighley was also a film man.

He turned out to be a quiet, relaxed sort of fellow and, though considerably older than myself, a man I felt immediately at ease with. He wanted to know what films I'd worked on and, while I talked about Korda, Hitchcock, Laurence Olivier and Vivien

Leigh, he seemed genuinely interested. He never mentioned his own work and it wasn't until some weeks later that I found out he was the well respected Hollywood film director William Keighley, many of whose films I had seen, *The Fighting 69th*, *The Man who Came to Dinner*, *George Washington Slept Here* and, especially exciting, *G-Men*, one of James Cagney's best gangster films.

At the end of our chat he told me that he was about to start shooting a documentary for the US Air Corps called *Target for Today*. It was to be a story of American air crews and their bombers. Would I like to join him as his assistant? "Yes, please," I said, thrilled. There and then, he phoned Wing Commander Twist and asked if I could start with him as from the next day.

Everyone working in American films, coming to England at that time, passed through Keighley's office. Legendary directors like Frank Capra (*It Happened One Night*, *Mr Deeds Goes to Town*, *Lost Horizon*) and big stars like Clark Gable and Jimmy Stewart would wander in and, if they found Keighley busy on the phone, they'd pull up a chair and chat to me. What's more these stars, whose faces and films were familiar to millions all over the world, were treating me as an equal. That is what really excited me, but was that not the American way?

Once attached to the US Air Force I found many things different from the RAF. For instance, in the RAF each officer had his own batman or, in some cases, a batwoman. The Americans didn't, nor did they have comfortable officers' messes with waiters to serve. They had commissaries where all officers lined up together regardless of rank, tray in hand, to collect their food. It certainly opened my eyes to the way they did things over there. What interested me more personally, though, was getting a PX card. I applied for one and received it almost immediately. I was lucky. The nearest officers' PX to the Mayfair Hotel, my base, was the huge store in Oxford Street. There, in that vast emporium, everything that was rationed or unobtainable in Britain was available – silk stockings, chocolates, nylons, household cookers, sheets, anything you might want or dream of, anything you could have bought at Selfridges in peacetime, and all of it very cheap.

It was here that I arranged to meet my cousin, Jack Cantor, to whose home in Clapton I had cycled years before. I thought it would be fun for him to look round the PX and, while we were at it, I could buy some stuff for him.

Like me he was also in the RAF, a flight sergeant, and since I was an officer he clowned a salute on seeing me before giving me a big hug. He had just come from the latest in a series of medicals, all of them to do with his ears. Every time he took off he suffered excruciating pain and, as his job was rear gunner in a bomber, the firing of the guns only added to the agony. At this last medical he had been told that he should stop flying. "Take the medics' advice," I said. "Haven't you done enough?" Shaking his head, he explained that his crew and he had been together a long time, made dozens of raids and, so far, had been very lucky. To let them down now would be out of the question. I saw that arguing with him was pointless and changed tack. "Let's get down to the serious business," I said, opening the door of the PX. "We'll start with you. What do you fancy?"

"Chocolate," he answered.

"And what about your crew?"

"Chocolate."

A great smile spread over his face when I handed him a whole stack of bars. As we parted, I said that I hoped we would meet again soon. "With your PX card, it'll be very soon," said Jack before disappearing into the crowd on Oxford Street.

Two weeks later my mother, in tears, told me that she'd just heard from Aunt Bessie, Jack's mother. He had been killed in action. I was in total shock. As soon as I was able to, I rang Jack's station, knowing that my officer status would get me through. The station adjutant answered. Jack had been killed instantly, he told me, the only one on board to die. The plane had made it back. Everyone who knew Jack at the station was very sad. My cousin was a great chap, they said, and they all loved him.

I rang Jack's mother, at least able to reassure her that he hadn't suffered as his death had been instantaneous. After that, I repeated all the nice things the station adjutant had said.

Many years later, maybe 20 or 30, I went to visit his grave. The cemetery he was buried at was an ordinary one but he was in an area devoted to RAF personnel. I stared at the headstone:

Flight Sergeant J Cantor
RAF Bomber Command
13 September 1944
Aged 24

and as I stood there, recalling so many memories, my blurring eyes moved over to the next grave.

Sergeant Pilot R Ginsberg
RAF Fighter Command
7 August 1944
Aged 23

That was a vicious blow. Jack's death I'd sort of come to terms with but Reuby Ginsberg, no, this was new. He and I had been at school together. Aged 12 or 13, we had been the two boys to open the innings at cricket and I could see him just as he was then. Once, on a beautiful summer's day, we had, between us, scored 50 runs. He'd got 30, I'd got 20. A great moment in our lives, we had both thought. Then I remembered his five sisters who used to spoil their brother rotten because he was the only boy. Reuben had joined up early in the war but there he was, killed nearly at the end of it, lying forever next to my cousin. I hurried away, trying hopelessly to keep back my tears.

Colonel Keighley was anxious to make a start on *Target for Today* but a lack of equipment, some of it important, was holding him up. Having given me a list of what was needed and put a car plus driver at my disposal, he asked me to go round the studios and see what I could do.

In a style I was quite unaccustomed to, I was driven from studio to studio, all of them places I'd worked in before the war and where I had contacts, Gainsborough, Elstree, Denham and Pinewood. At Gainsborough, I walked on to the stage where I had acted in a Will Hay comedy to find Vic Oliver in a dinner jacket and Margaret Lockwood in a cocktail frock drinking champagne. It seemed unbelievably incongruous. To them, the war did not exist. The scene they were playing was everything. That was their life and it was fine. Audiences needed diverting and studios were obliging them with throwbacks to the idea of how the upper classes lived pre-war. For an hour or two, the horrors of the conflict could be forgotten.

At Denham, I saw the distinguished actor Robert Donat, playing a scene in a film called *Perfect Strangers*. A group of about 15 sailors were watching too. I found myself next to them. They had been torpedoed in the Pacific and, for three weeks, with the sun beating down on them, had floated around in an open boat, forced to pitch the dead amongst them over the side. Now they were recuperating at an English hospital and this day out was their treat. Lunch was going to be with some of the actors and they were thrilled. As I too was in uniform but also seemed to know what was going on, I was collared for information. One sailor asked if the man he could see being lit was Robert Donat. "Oh no," I said, "he's his stand-in."

"What's a stand-in?" asked the sailor. I explained that he stood in for the actor while the lights were being fixed. The cameraman would then get him to move around the set just like the actor had done in rehearsal so that lights could be positioned and adjusted to cover all those moves. "Why can't Robert Donat do that?" asked the sailor. I explained that these lights were very hot and that standing there, maybe for an hour or more, would make the actor tired and sweaty when he needed to be fresh and alert for the actual shot. The sailor, who was still not recovered from his three week ordeal, said bitterly, "Hot? Tired? Poor bastard." In print it's hard to capture the scorn in that remark. An actor unable to stand under the lights because he might get *tired.* It was sad and I've never forgotten it. The disparity between what was going on here in the studio and what that sailor had been through back in the Pacific, the two different realities were beyond his understanding.

The reunion with old studio friends and colleagues was great and, what's more, they loaned the necessary equipment, a gesture of immense generosity. Keighley was delighted. We could start filming.

One thing about England the colonel couldn't stand was the cold. Sometimes, on a really bitter day, he would say, "Oh, you go and film this bit." I jumped at the chance and went away to shoot lots of take-offs and landings. Even these simple shots could tell a story as it was clear to see that bombers had often been shot up after a raid. I too hated the cold but I knew this gritty reality stuff would stand me in good stead for the future.

Target for Today didn't use actors but a real bomber air crew. One day, Colonel Keighley handed me some pages of script and said, "Here you can do this." I read the pages with mounting excitement. It was a scene, just before take-off, where the air crew had to hand in all their valuables: photographs, letters, anything that could be useful to enemy intelligence if their planes were shot down. Up until now, the material I had been filming was all to do with aircraft. For the first time in my life I would be directing a scene with human beings, even if they were not actors and not speaking lines but using their own words.

At the back of my mind I knew that this ritual handover had a deeper meaning, one that the air crew was only too aware of. Those possessions of theirs would be handed to their next of kin should they not return. I could immediately see what a great scene this would make and that I would have to be really incompetent to muck it up. I suppose this tells you something about the ruthlessness of the director.

The next day I asked Colonel Keighley if I could accompany him to London to watch the rushes of the scenes I'd directed the day before. "I don't need to see the rushes," he said casually. "You go. I trust you." I tore up to London.

As I entered the viewing theatre I noticed a man with a beard sitting at the back. He explained politely that he had arrived early for his own screening and asked if he could stay to watch mine, if that was no bother. With a touch of panic, I agreed.

"Who shot this stuff?" asked the bearded man when the lights went up at the end.

"I did," I replied.

"Well done. It's very good," he said. When I had finished thanking him, he told me that his name was Arthur Elton and that he was in charge of films at the Ministry of Information. "If you ever come out of the air force," he said, "drop round." With that, he handed me his card which I put into my top pocket and promptly forgot.

Filming on *Target for Today* was almost complete when Colonel Keighley told me that he'd had enough of the British cold weather and was taking the film back to Hollywood for editing. "Maybe you'd like to come along for the ride?" he said.

"What do you mean?" I asked.

"If you came it would be a great help to me – that's if you would like to."

"If I would like to?"

For a moment, I saw it all – Hollywood, the mecca of film making, the kudos of going around with a famous director, meeting important people, making contacts, the stars I would chat to, Greta Garbo, Merle Oberon ... And then I came down to earth. "But the RAF," I said, "They'd never let me go, never."

"If we ask for you," said the Colonel calmly, "they'll let you go." I got up and walked to the door.

"Where are you off to?" he asked.

"To buy a pair of sunglasses," I replied and for days I thought about Hollywood and nothing else.

A call came from the Air Ministry. Since I had recently returned from the Middle East I had to go before a medical board. St Hugh's, Oxford, was the place to report to, a women's college that was being used as a hospital for the duration. It meant staying there overnight and that gave me the heebie-jeebies. All around me were terrible cases, patients with serious head injuries and mental illnesses. I slept fitfully, my nightmares from North Africa rushing back and mixing themselves with the groans and cries from nearby wards.

The most haunting memory of that place I have is of a long, long, corridor, down which a young soldier, blind, bandages over his eyes, totally alone, was pushing an ordinary kitchen chair for no obvious reason. I see it now and I still don't understand it.

The next morning I went before the medical board. Behind a big table sat an air commodore and various other types with my papers in front of them. Someone spoke:

"Four-and-a-half years you've been in the air force, I see."

"Yes, sir."

"And you volunteered on the very first day of the war. That was very patriotic of you."

"Thank you, sir," I said, not mentioning that the real reason for my joining up early was an aversion to the army.

"Four-and-a-half years is a long time," the medic went on.

"Three-and-a-half overseas," added another.

"And quite recently, you had to convalesce in North Africa, didn't you?" said the first medic.

"That's right, sir."

"The point is," said the air commodore, interrupting his colleague, "we think it's time that we let you go." For a moment I couldn't speak.

"But I don't want to go, sir," I burst out, "I'm going to Hollywood!" The members of the board exchanged glances but that was that. I was out and shattered.

I went back to London to say goodbye to everyone, Colonel Keighley in particular. He had been like a father to me.

The next two weeks were about the worst of my life. The RAF gave me demobilisation leave and a hundred pounds for buying clothes but, with no work forthcoming, they were of little comfort. I could think of nothing. A return to the job of assistant director was a possibility but it was not what I wanted. That taste of directing Colonel Keighley had given me had got me hooked and directing was, after all, what I had always wanted to do since childhood. Thoughts of Hollywood and the Colonel were made all the more wistful when his wife, Genevieve Tobin, quite a well-known actress, wrote from America. She said that she'd heard a lot about me from her husband and thanked me for looking after him while he was in England. With the Colonel thousands of miles away and no directing job in the offing, my ambition was in ashes.

To cheer myself up, one lunchtime I went to a Lyons Corner House and ordered sausage and chips and a cup of tea. "That'll be a shilling," said the waitress as she plonked the plate down. I reached into my top pocket – I was still in uniform – and pulled out a ten shilling note. With it, came something else which fell on to the sausages. A card. I picked it out. "Arthur Elton," I read aloud.

"I beg your pardon?" said the waitress.

"Ministry of Information," I went on, picking up my change and concentrating on the card at the same time. Then I remembered. So quickly was I out of that café, you would not have seen me go.

"Hey!" called the waitress, adding as she picked up the sausage and chips. "What a waste."

On entering Arthur Elton's office I was greeted with a smile that was pleasant enough but a bit blank. It was obvious that he didn't remember me. "Lewis Gilbert?" I said, "You saw my rushes?"

"Yes, yes, of course," he said, recognition coming into his

eyes. "They were excellent. What can I do for you?" I explained that I was out of the air force and looking for a job directing documentaries. I knew that this was the kind of film the Ministry of Information tended to put out. He thought for a moment, picked up the phone and asked for a Mr Bruce Woolfe. "Bruce," he said, "you remember the other day you were telling me you were short of a young director? Well I've got just the chap. He's standing right in front of me. I've seen his stuff and he's very good." Down went the receiver. "Get yourself over to Lime Grove Studios," said Arthur, "and ask for a Mr Bruce Woolfe. There's a job waiting for you. Good luck!"

Little did I know just how lucky that studio at Shepherd's Bush would be for me. H Bruce Woolfe, boss of Gaumont British Instructional, GBI, took me on as a director. That was the first piece of luck, though some may say I was lucky to be alive, never mind jobs. The second piece of luck was quite another matter.

6

Love and Cod Liver Oil

Suddenly that hundred pound cheque became what it always was, useful. Feeling like a millionaire, I paid it into Cox and King's, the RAF bank, the first account I ever had. That done, I went out to buy a new suit and some other necessities for civilian life. At the same time my sister Renée, knowing I needed somewhere to live, came up with the very thing – a flat in The White House on the corner of Regent's Park. As it was bang next to Great Portland Street tube station, Lime Grove Studios was only a short journey away.

The flat was small, very small, about 12 foot square including bathroom and minute kitchen, but as I had practically no possessions, size didn't matter. Sitting on the narrow bed, I gazed out across Regent's Park, alive with its early spring flowers and budding trees. I was 24. I had a job and a home. I was in heaven and I had survived.

GBI taking me on at once was a stroke of luck and I had been lucky too that a couple of coincidences had got me to that point, firstly sharing a viewing theatre with Arthur Elton, and secondly being released early from the air force. So, gratitude for getting this documentary work should have been uppermost in my mind and it was. Deep down, however, I was thinking that it might provide some stepping stones towards my lifelong ambition to become a director of feature films.

They didn't hang about at GBI. The very next day my chief called me in to describe a project he had for me. In cities all over the country the Blitz had caused an acute housing shortage. As a result, the government was developing a scheme to provide thousands of prefabricated bungalows as temporary homes, 'prefabs'. "They're putting up a prototype," the chief said, "and I want you to cover it." Once the insulated walls and roof had been made, the actual assembly on site with fully equipped kitchen and bathroom plus central heating only took two days.

At GBI the camera crews were rather inexperienced and could easily have been daunted by my requests. Fortunately I had already found out that cameramen who made newsreels were quick, competent and understood what you said right away. I booked two, went to the site and, over the two days, shot six thousand feet, an hour and three quarters if you sat and watched it from end to end.

Back in a cutting room at GBI I was working with the editor to bring this mass of material down to a manageable length and some coherence when I realised that the normal procedure in documentaries would simply not do. This project may have been important but it was also boring and the disembodied voice of a commentator telling you what you could perfectly well see for yourself was not going to help. I hit on an idea but it meant selling it to the chief. With plenty of enthusiasm and a little trepidation, I told him that the film needed a hook. "What do you have in mind?" he asked. I told him that it was more a question of who did have in mind. I wanted to make the film more human, give it a lighter touch. I had already sounded out an actor friend of mine, Charles Hawtrey, and now I mentioned him. Charles of the spindly legs and big glasses had played a somewhat overaged schoolboy in the Will Hay comedies I'd been in. Today, he's better known as one of the Carry On team. "And what's the story?" asked the chief. I explained that it was a film within a film. Charles would play the part of a writer who had to come up with a script on a subject he knew damn all about. Each day, to keep his producer sweet, he would have to report back to tell him what was happening on the site, how speedy, how efficient it all was. Coming from Charles Hawtrey's mouth this would be hilarious because it would sound like a monumental cock-up. Finding the inspiration for this character had not been hard. It was me. I can't say the idea was very original but, since the chief seemed pleased enough, I was given the go ahead.

As I had hoped, the film turned out to be entertaining as well as informative. Because of that it was released in cinemas right across the country and, fortunately, was liked by the public. It made money and was a great advertisement for the merits of the prefab, so the Iron and Steel Federation, who had commissioned it, were delighted. I wasn't too unhappy either. The film getting a release felt like a move in the right direction.

I think some of the more dedicated, serious documentary directors did not approve. Many were intellectuals, striving to emulate the achievements of great documentary directors like Flaherty and Grierson. Seemingly indifferent to money, most of them were from middle or upper class backgrounds, so very different from mine. The fact is, since the age of four I had been in the business of entertainment and I knew that entertainment was where I belonged.

As soon as the war ended, prefabs were indeed built by the thousand and, although intended to last only ten years (hence the title of the film, *Ten Year Plan*) some are still around today,

60 years later! Very British, that. But then prefabs were highly thought of. After the squalor of slums and the cold of outside lavatories, it was only to be expected that people would welcome all mod cons.

One morning I pressed the button for the lift at Lime Grove Studios, and when the doors opened I was faced with two girls, both very pretty, wearing 18th century dresses. Up we went in the huge, unglamorous lift that was used for taking personnel, props and scenery to the various floors. One of the girls, Sheila, I knew well as I'd been out with her quite often. It wasn't serious between us. We were simply good friends who shared the same sense of humour and went out together from time to time. We'd go to the Metropolitan Music Hall in the Edgware Road and have a good laugh at Max Miller, for instance. Sheila just had time to say, "This is my friend Hylda. Call me," before the lift stopped and I had to get out. Even so I had, in those seconds, been very struck by her friend, Hylda. She was not just pretty but beautiful.

That evening I was walking up the road, on my way home, when I spotted the same two girls ahead of me. Not one to let the grass grow under my feet, I ran forward to catch up with them. What film were they in, I asked. *The Wicked Lady* with Margaret Lockwood they told me. Sheila then introduced me properly to her friend. She was called Hylda Lawrence but she told me that her everyday name was Hylda Tafler. It was all I found out though, because she was in a hurry and had to catch a train to go and see her mother. We said goodbye, but as I watched her go I asked Sheila if she would give me Hylda's phone number. She hesitated. No, that wouldn't be right. Hylda would have to be asked first.

Next day, both the girls were on call and Sheila popped her

head round my office door. "It's OK," she said and gave me the number. That evening, I rang Hylda and we arranged to meet. Our first date was at a small café in the Lex Garage off Brewer Street, hardly a romantic spot for a rendezvous nor a likely place to find a café, but the war was still on and coffee houses were non-existent.

As we sat there, we asked each other questions about our lives so far and spoke about what we'd like to do. We weren't old – both 24 as it happened – but nor were we teenagers, so we weren't stuck for subjects. I gave Hylda a load of flannel about being a documentary film director who was absolutely, definitely, no question, going to direct features, and amazingly she didn't pooh-pooh me. She was amused but she was also genuinely interested. It may have been because her own interests were similar, she being an actress and her brother, Sydney, an actor.

When I let her get a word in edgeways she told me that she earned her living by modelling as well as acting. In fact she was rather successful at it, no bad thing because she already had responsibilities, or rather one special responsibility. This led her to tell me that, at 19, she had for a very short while been married and given birth to a boy. Before the child's birth, however, the husband, a man called Maitland Lawrence, had been whisked off by the war and, as so often happened with people's lives being completely changed, divorce followed. The boy, of whom she had custody, was now four. Since I too had mostly been brought up by my mother, I felt somehow involved and, as the conversation continued, I could feel that we were getting on very well. When it was time to go, I asked if we could meet on Sunday. Sunday, however, was no good for Hylda. On that day she had promised to visit a cousin, an hour away from London.

Then, out of the blue, she said, "Why don't you come with me? I'm sure my cousin would like to meet you." We arranged to rendezvous by the ticket office at Waterloo Station.

I was there before the agreed time. I have always been fanatical about time-keeping and would rather be half an hour early than a minute late. Working in theatre and film had taught me that. But then I waited and waited and waited, all the while keeping an eye on the station clock, as well as looking out for Hylda. An hour after we were supposed to have met she had still not shown up. 'Well, that's it,' I thought and went home, thoroughly put out, convinced that this was the classic brush-off. As the hours went by, gloom turned to annoyance. That evening, when I guessed that Hylda would be back, I rang. "And where were you this morning?" I asked accusingly.

"What do you mean where was I?" she answered sharply. "Where were *you*? I waited so long I had to run for my train." After some tight-lipped questioning back and forth, we realised that there were two ticket offices at Waterloo. It was a great relief to laugh about it and arrange our next meeting. Life is extraordinary. If that morning at Lime Grove Studios I had caught the lift two minutes earlier or left the studio two minutes later or stopped to talk to someone, we would never have met. That was my second piece of luck.

Our next meeting was an invitation from Hylda to go for tea. Walking towards her flat I was, for an instant, taken by surprise. She was coming towards me with a little boy. It was her son, of course, John. Despite his obvious shyness, he managed a smile, and before long was chatting away 19 to the dozen. By the end of the afternoon the two of us were hitting it off so well you might have taken us for old friends.

My next assignment was an appeal film for a naval charity

called *Sailors Do Care*. As I had seen people edging out of auditoriums or finding the floor very interesting when that sort of film came on, I didn't want it to be a straightforward hard sell. I wanted something different, something an audience could relate to and enjoy. Also, if it got a circuit release like *Ten Year Plan*, it would be another stepping stone across the river and into features. So, I came up with a little story. It was about a boy joining the Navy.

When it was finished, we learned to our amazement that Queen Mary, the widow of King George V, had heard about the film and wanted to see it. She was a patroness of the charity, so that must have been her reason. Anyway, she came. This was odd because we couldn't think why she would want to go all the way to Film House in Wardour Street when she could easily have had the film screened at the Palace. The visit caused a huge disruption in London's Soho. The entire street was closed off and everybody, except the six or so of us who had been involved in the film's making, was kept out of Film House. We who were left were lined up to be introduced. Outside, at the front of the onlookers, was my mother. Royalty was far more aloof in those days and coming face to face with an icon was quite disorientating. I was amazed at her heavily accented voice. If anything, it was German. Two weeks later we got another call. Queen Mary had enjoyed the film so much she would like to come and see it again. This time, when she turned up – my mother outside again – we weren't presented. We just stood there and she kind of nodded as she went past into the viewing theatre. Given that the film lasted only ten minutes, waiting for her to come out again was no hardship. In any case, it was pleasing to know that she had seen something in it the first time round that had made her want to see it again. It was a foretaste of what was to happen afterwards. As I had hoped, *Sailors Do Care* did get a circuit release and cinemas told us that audiences were enjoying it and that business was good.

Over the months after our first meeting, Hylda and I met up from time to time, usually to go to a picture or have a meal. As we had other friends it wasn't exactly serious. Still, we were getting on well and there came a time when Hylda thought it would be a good idea to invite me round for dinner with her parents. Out of consideration, she had warned me that they fought like cat and dog but nothing as bad as that happened while I was there. Maybe the presence of Hylda's brother, the actor Sydney Tafler, helped. Sydney was his mother's favourite. What's more he was accompanied by his wife, the actress Joy Shelton, who was doing rather well at the time. She had recently been fought over by John Mills and Stewart Granger in the film *Waterloo Road*. For all that, I could feel an atmosphere. Father was fine. His knowledge of music hall was encyclopaedic, and obviously that brought us together. We could share memories and sing songs. He had even seen my parents' variety act. That was the best bit. Hylda's mother, on the other hand, was obviously not seeing me as a future son-in-law. All she could see was a cash register that was not in good working order. I can say one nice thing about her – dinner was good.

By this time I had already started work on my next film, *Arctic Harvest*. The job had come just as the war in Europe was ending. It was to be a documentary about cod liver oil and Crawford's, the advertising agency, had commissioned it. Up until then all I had known about cod liver oil was that it came in bottles and, even if it did do you good, tasted disgusting. 'Another dull subject,' I thought. What was I going to do with it? And then I began to use my imagination. Cod livers come from cod and cod has to be caught and boats have to go out to sea to catch them. My story would be about a deep sea trawler and its crew – human beings, in other words. That was better and it was getting closer to a feature. As soon as I had roughed out a script I began to look around for a cameraman and was lucky enough to find a very good one, Leon Schouder, from South Africa. We were all set.

The night before I had to leave for Hull where my story was to begin, I went to Hylda's flat. She was giving her sister Sheila's 21st birthday party and it was a good opportunity to meet the Tafler clan. I enjoyed it but couldn't stay long as I had to be up at five the next morning. When I had made my excuses, Hylda walked me to the lift. As the doors opened I stepped in and looked at her. "Well, you won't be seeing me for a month," I said and we gazed at each other for a long time.

Suddenly, she said, "I shall miss you." I pressed the lift button and, before the doors could close, she leant forward and kissed me tenderly. The doors closed, leaving me with an image that was to take me through the whole of the following four weeks.

The next day, Leon Schouder, his assistant and I caught the train for Hull. There, I gained the confidence of the captain and his crew, who agreed that the three of us could accompany them on a trip to search the Arctic fishing grounds for cod. To reach the Arctic Circle would take a week, as would the actual fishing, and then it would be another week before we would be back in Hull. We would be at sea for three weeks in all.

We set sail and for four days I and my crew did nothing but throw up. Leon Schouder's assistant was in such a bad way that the captain seriously thought of radioing for a helicopter. After the fourth day the sea calmed down and we felt better. As we sped along in the sunshine I was able to take in the beauty of what I saw and listen to the captain – Dawlish was his name – telling me what to expect at our destination. It was then I realised that I could make a documentary quite different from the two I had made before. This time there was no need to dream up fictional devices to add entertainment value. This story could tell itself. It would be – odd for me to be saying this – a documentary in the classic style. Simply observing men pitted against the elements would give us all the drama we needed, and visually it would be very powerful. Striking images were already coming into my head along with the thought that a good, strong documentary could become a second feature and gain a national release.

Our destination was Bear Island. The great banks there hadn't been fished by anybody for five years because of the war in Europe, so we knew that the waters would be teeming with cod. Even amongst those experienced fishermen there was considerable excitement. However, 60 years ago there was no sophisticated sonar system to locate the shoals. Each boat had to rely on the skipper's past experience and guesswork. In this vast, featureless ocean, he had to decide where to lower his trawl nets. If he got it right, it could be just a few minutes before they were hauled up again, bulging, the size of houses. During this fishing period, the crew was prepared to work a 20-hour shift as every man had a share in the catch and big money could be earned.

The gutting of the fish took place right there and then on deck. It was hard and hazardous work, often in appalling conditions. Frequently whipped by icy winds on a boat that was pitching and yawing, with spray forming icicles on the rigging and rails, the crew stood at long tables, rhythmically cutting and throwing. The cod went into the hold and the livers into a tank to be boiled up to make the oil. The entrails went overboard to be feasted on by scavenging birds. As it was fiddly work, only mittens could be worn and the crew's fingers became very raw. Sometimes a man would become so exhausted he would fall asleep at the table and have to be woken by his mate. Over the days and nights I saw young men turn into old men.

The captain had two cabins, a day one and a night one. I was given the day cabin which was actually quite comfortable. The only trouble was, when I went there to sleep I couldn't. There was never any night-time. The sun would disappear over the horizon for only a few minutes and then come back up again. Our meals, I couldn't grumble about. They were fine – only fish, but what fish! Straight from the ocean and pretty much straight on to the plate, served with a few vegetables. They were the like of which I had never tasted before. Occasionally we would be served a salmon, which was an unexpected treat.

In leisure moments a fair amount of ribbing went on amongst the crew and the one who tended to be the butt of all this was the radio operator. Although his job was very important he didn't have anything to do with the fishing and, as his work was not physical, he was made an outsider.

After the week of fishing the boat was so low in the water the sea was practically over the Plimsoll Line. This is a circle with a horizontal line through it which you will find painted on either side of every British merchant vessel. Once the water reaches the line you have to stop loading. Samuel Plimsoll introduced it more than a century ago and we must thank him. Before the line, greedy merchants encouraged overloading and caused several ships to sink. Plimsoll stopped that and prevented many deaths at sea.

At the end of the seven days everyone was stretched to the limit. It was time to head for home. As we went, the skipper got on to his radio and told other boats where to find the best fish. I thought this a fine gesture, the cameraderie of the sea. On board the going got easier. The crew went back to normal watches and youth was restored to their faces.

We were only a day from home, and back in the North Sea when the radio operator ran out of his cabin, very excited. "What's going on?" asked the skipper.

"There's been a huge bomb," gabbled the operator, "Something's happened. I can't make it out at the moment but this bomb, it's wiped out an entire Japanese city and they don't think the war will go on much longer." That was the first any of us had heard about the atom bomb. They were wrong about the Japanese, though. They fought on.

So the war was still continuing when we arrived back in Hull. The cod, a record catch, was unloaded immediately to be auctioned on the quayside there and then. In the finished film, the triumphant swinging of the baskets from the boat to the quay became one of the best sequences. As each basket swung, a cry would go up of "C-o-o-o-d!" to help the shoremen in their sorting. The tank of cod livers was sent to Seven Seas, the company that still produces cod liver oil today, though now in capsules so you don't have the nasty taste. Because the catch was so magnificent the crew earned a lot of money. The skipper took about 40 or 50 per cent, while the crew shared the rest. On their five days off the first thing they did was get roaring drunk. Next, they treated to a drink any fisherman who, through age or injury, couldn't go to sea anymore, and then gave him a few shillings to keep him going. It was another example of cameraderie among fishermen. My job at sea was over. Theirs wasn't. After the five days off, they set sail again for the Arctic.

My immediate priority was a bath and some sleep. We were

booked into a rather nice hotel, and when I stepped into the lift I found myself next to four people who were very smartly dressed. As the doors closed they begin to move away from me. It was natural enough. I had been living amongst fish and not had a proper wash for three weeks. I must have stunk. Sliding into a bath, at long last, was a delicious feeling.

Before going to sleep, I rang Hylda to say I was back. Naturally, the conversation turned to the bomb. Both of us were aware that we, along with the rest of the world, had entered a new phase of neither peace nor war, a limbo but not a static one. It was active and full of promise. No equivalent has occurred between that time in 1945 and today. Five years of war had changed not only people's lives but people themselves. Many were doing what they would never have dreamed of in pre-war days. What was to happen next?

It was during this period of uncertainty that I finished shooting the film. I needed a few days to observe the fishermen as they returned to their shore lives in Hull. Around me I noticed that a fever had taken hold. If the war was going to end, and it looked as if it would, people's worlds would once more be turned upside down. Soldiers would return expecting to take up their old lives again but, in many cases, their old lives would be over. New lives had already been started, often enough with someone else.

Two days after my return from the sea a second atom bomb was dropped, this time on Nagasaki. The tension grew even greater. Surely that had to be an end to it all, but no, the Japanese were still talking tough. However many bombs were dropped, they insisted, they would fight on. If some arrangement was not arrived at, America, when it invaded, would lose a million men. America, however, was not interested in conditions and four more days went by with no outcome.

On the 14th of August, at midnight our time, the Deputy Prime Minister Clement Attlee broadcast to the nation that Japan had surrendered unconditionally. The nation, however, was sound asleep. I wasn't and, unaware of the time, rang Hylda. She evidently woke with a start, because for a moment I could hear both irritation and sleep in her voice. When she realised what I was saying, there was no scream. She said quite simply, "I feel strange."

"Of course, you do," I said. "So do I. We're starting a new life."

At that moment, I longed to be in London and Hylda, reading my mind, said, "Come down. Lots of friends will be over. It'll be fun."

The next day, most people went to work as usual. Like Hylda, they hadn't heard the broadcast. I caught the train. It was only during the course of the morning that the news spread and those at work stopped and went home for two days' holiday.

I had hardly arrived at Hylda's flat in Westbourne Terrace than she hurried me out into the street and into a friend's car. Eight or nine of us, trying to introduce ourselves, piled in. As the car moved off, Hylda's hand closed over mine. Knowing that she was pleased to see me after those four weeks apart was very reassuring.

When the crowds that were heading for Piccadilly Circus became too thick, the friend of Hylda's who was driving the car stopped and we got out. Everyone around us was going crazy. Girls were being carried on the shoulders of soldiers and sailors. Total strangers were kissing each other. Only by holding hands tightly were Hylda and I able to keep together. As for staying with her friends, it was hopeless. We shouted over to them but they couldn't hear in the din. While being swept along, they and we were being forced further and further apart. Eventually they disappeared completely. Hylda looked around at the increasingly boisterous crowd and laughed. "Oh, this is impossible." I nodded, seized the moment and shouted, "Come on! I'm taking you home!"

As we started to walk back I realised that this was not going to be so easy. Only after pushing through the crowd for quite some time did we find it thinning out. At that moment, a car full of people pulled up beside us. One of its passengers, over the cheering of his friends, yelled, "Where are you going?"

"Paddington!" I shouted back.

"Jump in!" he signalled. We did, only to realise that all in the car, including the driver, were completely drunk. We swerved from one side of the road to the other. No policeman was going to stop us because, in all that chaos, none was to be seen or, if one was, a girl would be on his shoulder wearing his helmet. That was the good bit. The rest was scary. Hylda and I clutched each other as we were thrown about.

When Paddington appeared in the distance it was with relief I shouted, "Please stop. We're all right now."

"Are you sure?" said the chap at the wheel.

"Yes, yes," I answered. "From here, it's quicker to walk." We climbed out. "Thanks," I said. "You've been wonderful."

Waving his hand, the driver shot off, calling out, "Have a good future!"

The rickety lift climbed to Hylda's flat. Alone for the first time that evening and, reminded of our parting four weeks earlier, we embraced, then kissed passionately. That was the night when we ceased to be very good friends and became lovers.

I arrived back at GBI, loaded down with cans of undeveloped

film. We had shot a huge amount of footage. The exposed film was then developed ready for me to see in the viewing theatre the next morning. To our surprise, as Leon Schouder and I went in we found other people already there, including the chief and Darrell Catling, another director who was a well established figure in the documentary world. Even before my departure for Hull they had sensed that the subject was interesting and were now curious to see the result.

After the screening, with the usual nods of approval and encouraging remarks, all the people dispersed except Darrell. "I think your rushes are great," he said, "and I'd love to help you edit the film." Can you imagine that on a feature film? It couldn't happen. That was the peculiar thing about documentary makers. They were a different race. They knew what they wanted and they knew what they enjoyed doing but, unlike me, they were not ambitious. They respected and admired each other's work and really they were a kind of brotherhood. It was being mostly university undergraduates and probably not very poor to begin with that accounted for their lack of interest in money. They certainly didn't make much.

Getting documentaries a proper showing in cinemas was quite rare but *Arctic Harvest* did. It gained a circuit release and a good one too. I had my wish and, for Seven Seas cod liver oil, it was an incredible coup. The head of the advertising agency Crawford's sent me an elegant silver cigarette case, which I think sums up that time. Nobody today would ever give anybody a cigarette case as a present. That was 60 years ago, and since then not one cigarette has been in it. Now it is a little tired, but inside it has a very nice inscription thanking me for *Arctic Harvest.*

If it were not for one piece of sad news, I could say that this was altogether a happy time because things were going well with

Hylda too. The sad piece of news was that Leon Schouder, whose camerawork for *Arctic Harvest* had been terrific and who had become a good friend, was killed in a flying accident back in South Africa. That hit me badly.

The relationship Hylda and I established was nice and easy-going. Her flat in Westbourne Terrace had three bedrooms, where from time to time I could spend the night but always be in the third bedroom when her son, John, woke in the morning. Very early, he would tiptoe into my room and climb into bed, impatient for me to tell him a story. When it wasn't convenient for me to be at Hylda's place I had my own flat to go back to. This was no longer the one in the White House but a bigger place in Eton Hall round Chalk Farm way. I shared it with Cardew Robinson, the chap I had made friends with at Uxbridge during the Phoney War. Somehow, over the years that had followed, we had never lost touch. When we met up again he was performing in Ralph Reader's Gang Show, mostly on tour, so I frequently had the flat to myself.

Sometimes Hylda had to work long hours, her job of the moment being Batchelors Peas. She was the face in all the advertisements. On those demanding days she was lucky enough to be able to leave John with a merry Irish woman called Mary McBurney who had a little girl, Moira. She and John became great playmates and, even today, Moira sends us a Christmas card. When evenings were free, friends used to come round because Hylda loved dinner parties. She also thought it would be a very good thing for me to meet and talk to new people, something I tend to struggle with. My favourite time, though, was the odd weekend when we had nothing to do. That's when we went to Rottingdean where, for two pounds a night, a Mrs Dear was happy to put us up and cook breakfast. I suppose

Hylda and I were living a bachelor cum married life, keeping at our jobs while at the same time bringing up John. For the first time in his life he had a father. Ahead seemed to lie a bright future.

7

Margot Fonteyn and *The Little Ballerina*

Along the corridor from me at Lime Grove Studios was the office of Mary Field. For GBI she made a series called *Secrets of Nature* but she also had another job. It was on J Arthur Rank's board for commissioning children's films, the Children's Entertainment Films Division. As well as being a film and flour magnate Rank was a Methodist who took a particular interest in promoting films with a religious or social slant that could be shown at his children's cinema clubs. These took place in his cinemas on Saturday mornings. News came through that Children's Entertainment Films had a slightly different idea for a film and I was sent along to see Mary Field as a potential director.

She explained to me that up until then their films had mostly been directed towards boys, but as girls made up an equal part of the audience it was time to do something for them, not forgetting, of course, to keep the interest of the boys. There had to be excitement and mischief in it. As I could see this opening up all sorts of possibilities I told her that I would love to direct a film like that. She was rather surprised. Was I not a maker of serious documentaries, like *Arctic Harvest*? "I was brought up in entertainment films," I said quickly, "and this is exactly what I want to do." That seemed to please her and must have convinced her that I was right for the job, because shortly afterwards she told me that the board had agreed to my being the director. I thanked her, overwhelmed at the confidence she had placed in me. At last, I was to direct an entertainment film that really was entertainment.

In due course I was summoned to a meeting with the committee in order to talk further about their new idea. The members told me that after making a number of two reelers (25-minute shorts) they had now decided to make a supporting feature of normal length with a budget of £30,000. This was very exciting. £30,000 was a lot in those days and many a supporting feature was made for far less. My mind went back to Quota Quickies that had cost only five or six thousand pounds.

I asked if they had a story in mind. Yes, they said, one set in and around a ballet school. While I was thinking that this could be very beautiful but might lack appeal for boys, they added that the ingredient necessary to make the story equally interesting for boys was not there yet. A writer they had in mind was going to work with me. I left the meeting walking on air. That evening, I had a date with Hylda. By then she and I were becoming quite serious. I couldn't wait to tell her my good news.

When she heard that I was going to direct my first feature she was as excited as I was. "What will it be about?" she asked. When I answered, "Ballet," her eyes sparkled. She was crazy about ballet. Immediately she started having ideas, the biggest being that there was only one person I simply had to have in the film – Margot Fonteyn.

As Hylda and I had already been to Sadler's Wells and Covent Garden I knew that Margot Fonteyn was the prima ballerina at both those theatres and that we were aiming high. I spoke to Mary Field about it the next day. While she thought Margot Fonteyn was an excellent idea, she was pretty sure that getting a star like her would be impossible. Nevertheless she promised to talk to Ninette de Valois, the founder of the Sadler's Wells Ballet School and Artistic Director of the Sadler's Wells Ballet Company, soon to become the Royal Ballet.

Mary was right. She got the brush-off. Well, more a flat refusal really. Margot was under contract. Her mornings were taken up with practice, her afternoons with rehearsals for the new season. It was out of the question. However, Mary could be very persuasive. Had it occurred to Ninette, she asked, that a film about ballet shown to children all over the country could be a good way to inspire young girls with the unique magic of the art? After all, in the film there would be an excerpt from a real ballet. Wouldn't she at least look at the script? Ninette de Valois finally gave in and must have seen something in our effort, because next thing Margot had read it and wanted to do it. She hadn't acted before but then she was only going to be playing herself. It looked like we could start filming.

Obviously, during this period of negotiation other things were going on at the same time. The writer the board had mentioned was Mary Cathcart Borer, a well respected professional of the time. Working with her was a new experience for me because I was used to developing my own scripts. However the two of us got on fine and we came up with the missing ingredients for the boys, excitement and mischief.

It was a simple story. At a ballet school there is one pupil who is obviously very gifted and her inspiration is Margot Fonteyn. Sometimes she is even allowed to watch Margot from the wings, dancing with her partner Michael Somes. And when Margot gives her a smile on leaving the stage, the girl is overwhelmed.

The school holds a competition to see who is the best. Naturally it's our young pupil but she has a rival who sees to it that on the big day our heroine is locked in the changing room at the school when the event is taking place the other side of town. What is to be done? A friend who loves roller skating comes to the rescue. She releases the trapped heroine and skates across town with her to make it just in time. When we were making the film we sometimes found it difficult to remember that it was for children and that it was no use getting too sophisticated.

The girl who played the part of the heroine had to be able to both act and dance. This made for a problem. We saw two girls. One could dance well but wasn't very good at acting. The other could act but was weak in the dance area. We chose the one who could act and decided that, if necessary, a double would be used if the dancing became too difficult. As it happened, young Yvonne Marsh who played the part worked so hard at the choreography that she was able to do all her own dancing. In those days Yvonne seemed set to do better than her sister, Jean, who was appearing as an extra in the film. But it's Jean who, with Eileen Atkins, went on to devise the TV series *Upstairs, Downstairs* and still works today.

Watching the ballet school students train for the film was a revelation. The work was so hard and the discipline so strict. I saw it all in Margot Fonteyn herself when she came to work at the studio. She was never late and remained on the set stitching ribbons to her ballet shoes whether or not she was required for the scene being shot. If she ever needed to leave the set she always asked my permission first and promised to be back in ten minutes, a promise she always kept, unlike many actors. She was a delight to work with.

Hylda and I became increasingly fascinated by the ballet world and Ninette de Valois, having at first been sceptical, was very encouraging. She allowed us to go anywhere backstage at Covent Garden. So during a performance of *Les Sylphides*, an excerpt of which was used in the film, Hylda watched from the wings and I watched from the flies. The unusual view I had gave me ideas for different camera angles, ones that might be intriguing for boys. Later, Margot talked to Hylda and Hylda, never easily impressed, was for once carried away.

Very soon after the making of the film, the Royal Ballet went to New York in a new production of *Sleeping Beauty* and conquered the town. That visit set the seal both on the company and Margot Fonteyn. From then on she was a star of international stature. However, there is a touch of irony in our little heroine looking so longingly at her, desperately wanting to be the same. After the phenomenal Indian summer of her career, dancing with Rudolf Nureyev, Margot was forced to work right into her fifties. She shouldn't have done but needed the money to pay her husband Roberto Arias' medical bills. At the time everybody thought that he had been shot for political reasons. In fact the gun had been fired by the jealous husband of one of his mistresses. Arias didn't love Margot at all but she stuck by him, her iron discipline still there. As for Margot, having for many years performed for the Royal Ballet only as a guest artiste she was not entitled to a pension and died in poverty. A TV documentary about her was made. It used a clip from our film, a moment where the little heroine watches Margot from the wings. Evidently someone thought it was documentary footage and so failed to give it a credit. It wasn't and I was rather peeved.

Back in 1947, the film opened at a children's cinema club showing. I took John. It seemed a good idea, he being seven by then. The manager of the cinema came on to the stage, as he always did on these occasions, and started off, "Today's birthday boy is Charlie Sedgwick. He's eleven." Accompanied by a polite round of applause, Charlie Sedgwick and whoever else's birthday it was that Saturday climbed on to the stage to receive a bar of chocolate. "Now, everybody," said the manager when Charlie had found his seat again, "today we have something rather unusual for you, a new film called *The Little Ballerina*." A groan went up from the boys in the audience. John sunk down in his seat. Things improved, thank goodness. The locking of the heroine in the changing room held everyone, while the roller skating through the town got cheers, and when the rival dancer was confronted by the heroine arriving on time she was roundly booed.

Even so, I was not as happy with *The Little Ballerina* as I might have been. The influence of J Arthur Rank's board had been too heavy handed. Its members were either middle-aged or old. Their schooldays were long over. Having no idea of what post-war children were like, they had insisted on a kind of behaviour that was archaic, not to say a little ridiculous. I thought I knew how children of the time talked and behaved and would have loved to have put that in the film but it wasn't possible. We had to have a moral message that was more fit for Sunday school. Still, the film did well enough at the Saturday morning clubs to earn a general release in cinemas across the country. It went out with a very intellectual film called *The Upturned Glass*, one of J Arthur's Pinewood films. So unpopular was this main feature that some cinema managers took matters into their own hands and switched it round with *The Little Ballerina*, despite that being only 75 minutes. So, once again I had made it to a circuit release and this time with a feature of sorts.

Between 1945 and 1947, once you had made a feature film and got yourself a reasonable release you could be taken seriously as an up-and-coming feature director by those at the top. This inclined me to be a bit cocky. I imagined so many offers pouring in that I would be turning them down. It was absolutely not the case.

By 1947, all the servicemen still in the forces after the war had been demobilised. It meant that senior film-makers established before 1939 were able to take up their old jobs. The charmed life I had led since leaving the RAF in 1944 was over.

8

Down But Not Out

At first I didn't notice anything wrong because I was full of an idea I was keen to develop. It was going to start in a marriage bureau and then divide as the various clients – four, say – went off on their adventures. This was known as an omnibus film, a popular structure in those days. Holding the whole thing together would be two eccentric women who ran the bureau. For those parts, I wanted Hermione Gingold and Hermione Baddeley. They were great favourites in the West End, intimate revue being their speciality. During and just after the war they had appeared in three: *Sweet and Low*, *Sweeter and Lower* and *Sweetest and Lowest*. Their material, or quite a lot of it, was written by Denis Waldock, a sharp, witty man and it was to him I turned when it came to working on the screenplay. He liked the idea, which was to be called *Marry Me*, and we arranged that I would meet him every day at his house on Primrose Hill.

When I rang the front door bell on the first day, his mother answered, saying as she led me in, "Denis is still in bed."

"But I've come to work." I said. That sent her upstairs, where I assume she woke her son because, shortly afterwards, bleary-eyed and still in his dressing gown, Denis appeared. How he looked was not so surprising when you knew that he took drugs and drank heavily.

"I've brought you a cup of coffee, Denis," his mother said returning with a tray.

"Hunh," he responded, and when she asked, "Will you be in for lunch?" yelled, "Get out! Get out!" which had her running out of the room and slamming the door.

"God, that fucking woman will be the death of me," Denis carried on. "I wish she'd get cancer of the liver and die."

"How can you talk to your mother like that?" I asked and that was my introduction to this crazy household.

Once the coast was clear, Denis extracted from his handkerchief two pills which he swallowed with a mouthful of coffee. He consumed this healthy breakfast every day. A few minutes later, artificially energetic, pacing up and down the room, he clapped his hands together and said, "Now let's get to work."

I was not advanced enough in my career to direct *Marry Me*. The best I could manage was to sell the script to the producers, Sydney and Muriel Box. After their success with the James Mason film *The Seventh Veil* they had been appointed head of all Rank films. Once they owned my script, however, it was only too easy for them to rejig it. This they tended to do very quickly, a period Denis referred to as 'The Box weekend'. You could give them any script, and in those two days they could ruin it.

When it came to casting, Gingold and Baddeley were out. They were not film stars. Two other actresses were brought in but no spark came from them and certainly no comic invention, which I had been counting on the two Hermiones to provide. The clients who came to the bureau, instead of being talented character actors were from the Rank Charm School, pretty but vapid. It negated the whole idea. Pretty people don't go to marriage bureaux. They don't have to. When the film came out it received poor reviews and quietly disappeared into oblivion.

That began a period of disappointments. Popular at the time was a series of films about a working class family called the Huggetts. Jack Warner and Kathleen Harrison were Dad and Mum. Petula Clark was their daughter. One in the series was offered to me and I was glad to accept. Offers are reassuring. We started work at Lime Grove Studios but they closed down. We moved to Islington Studios and they closed down. We moved to Denham Studios and when they, in turn, closed down so did the picture. I did, at least, receive my initial payment but when something apparently so solid evaporates it's alarming. The entire industry was in fact facing bankruptcy.

With that money and what was left over from the *Marry Me* script I thought I'd try my hand at setting up some projects on my own. The idea of being a producer/director had always appealed to me as that gives you more control over your own work. So, drawing on my childhood memories I came up with a plot about a young couple touring in variety with a double act. They have a baby who, while their backs are turned, is stolen. It seemed to me that ideal casting would be Petula Clark, whom I had nearly worked with, and Dickie Valentine, the up-and-coming pop star. There would, of course, be plenty of opportunity for them both to sing. It got as far as Denis and I writing a script, Eros Films wanting it and me testing Dickie Valentine. But at that point Sid and Phil Hyams, owners of Eros, sold their company to Warwick Films and Warwick had no wish to do our film. They had their own list and ours didn't fit in. As I was quite far down the line with my project and had spent a lot of money I was badly shaken. One of Warwick's bosses, by the way, was Albert 'Cubby' Broccoli. Years later, he became the co-producer of the James Bond films.

Once the rot sets in, it spreads quickly. I desperately cast about for ideas. Perhaps Denis and I could re-do an old film or use material out of copyright. *Lady Windermere's Fan*, for instance, or a Shaw play or a Lonsdale comedy? This quickly taught me a couple of lessons. For a classic, you needed actors like John Gielgud or Ralph Richardson and they were hardly likely to appear in a film directed by a young unknown. As for Shaw and Lonsdale, they were still in copyright and taking out an option on one of their plays was way beyond my means. In trying to produce pictures, I was learning that money runs out faster than the pictures themselves.

At the same time, Denis was becoming increasingly unreliable. Work that he said he would do he didn't, and the less he did the more pills he took. I reluctantly realised that I would have to pull away and look elsewhere. Years later Denis went to bed one night having taken his sleeping pills. His coverlet slipped on to the electric fire which he hadn't turned off and the bed went up in flames. He was burnt to death. This was both horrific and quite unsurprising. It was a terrible waste. When we worked together Denis was only 37. He'd been a good-looking man and a champion athlete at Cambridge. He may never have written a great full-length play, but of sharp retorts and quick witticisms he was the master.

By now, things were looking bad. I had failed as a producer. No offers to direct were coming in, either for documentaries or for features. For the first time in my life I was without work or money. To put it another way, 28 years of my life had passed with no experience of failure. Perhaps I should have known a little. It might have toughened me up. As I saw it then this faltering of my career was a total disaster, particularly as I had responsibilities. There was my mother to support and Hylda was a worry too. She had been so busy encouraging me in my work that she had let the modelling drift and she needed the money. Her mother had split from her father and he was refusing to pay out one penny.

When the day arrived that we couldn't pay the rent I thought we had hit rock bottom, or certainly that I had hit rock bottom. Trying to put a brave face on it, I went to Hylda. "It's not a disgrace," I said, totally unconvinced. "I'll simply borrow." And I did, but it left my confidence in tatters.

Failure obsessed me. 'All those rich admirers Hylda has,' I thought, allowing their aura of success to unnerve me even more, 'the ones who come to her dinner parties.' And the idea took hold that Hylda would be much better off if I weren't around. A beautiful, popular woman like that, what right had I to stand in her way? And what about John? Didn't he deserve a decent chance in life? A father with money could give him that. The best thing I could do was to go.

When I started to talk like that to Hylda, she wouldn't have it. "We'll manage," she said, "Haven't we up till now? All we must do is sit tight and see it through."

But the months of nothing coming to fruition had taken their toll. "Not this time," I said.

"Oh?" said Hylda, "and what happened to the young man I met at the Lex garage, the one who was so funny and full of himself? That's the chap I fell for. Money wasn't the point then. It isn't now. I believed in you and I still do."

"I don't." I said and told her that we had to part and not see each other again. It would be better for both of us. Was there also just the tiniest thought that I could concentrate harder on reviving my career if I were alone? But at that moment I was at a pitch where failure had skewed my thinking altogether.

Having made the decision, I left Hylda and went back to my flat in Eton Hall. A terrible time followed. The loss of Hylda was bad enough but not seeing the little boy was grim. I had got used to driving to his school and finding him waiting at the gate. It had reminded me of those weeks in Hove when, at the age of seven, I had waited for my mother who had never come. By turning up at John's school and collecting him, I had somehow made things right. Now it was all over and I was missing the little boy, rather as my mother had once missed me. This I had not foreseen. Was I not the ambitious film director, in my aims utterly single-minded? Didn't the making of a film come first and wasn't that a world where human relationships couldn't figure? The child was proving me wrong.

A few weeks later I was offered a job, just as Hylda had predicted. I wish it had restored my confidence more. The United Nations commissioned it and Michael Balcon, the boss of Ealing Studios, said I was the man to do it. But it left me cold. As far as I was concerned it was only another documentary and I had done enough of those. In any case, there was to be no circuit release and I was to be paid very little. I did accept the offer but I was convinced I was heading nowhere.

The premise of *Under One Roof* was that wherever you go in the world, if you only take the trouble to look you will see that we're all the same. My job was to travel to a couple of widely differing places and prove the point. First I went to Egypt. That was all right. I was familiar with it and seeing how it had changed was interesting. The contrasting country was Norway. That I did not like. In my wobbly frame of mind I could only find it bleak. In fact I was bloody miserable there. My heart wasn't in my work and I couldn't wait to get home.

Back in London and still uncertain about pretty much everything, I began to think of Hylda. Was she OK? Was she getting by? I had to find out because she would not leave my mind. However, a long time had elapsed since we had last seen each other. Making contact again would be difficult. I decided to ring her mother. "Then you didn't know?" she said. My heart stopped. "Hylda was married three days ago. She's just off on honeymoon. You won't interfere, will you?"

"No," I said and, without asking why she had married or who the husband was, I put the phone down. We all have low points in our lives. That was the lowest I have ever been.

A few days later a letter arrived out of the blue. It was from Hylda. The marriage was a disaster. It was the worst mistake of her life. What was she to do? How could we have ever parted? On and on it went for ten pages, and a few days later another one came, also ten pages.

Not so long afterwards, the phone rang one day and it was Hylda. We had to talk, she said. We had to meet. How could we meet? Hearing her voice again was heaven. I had been so down. Mixed into my happiness, though, was a touch of fear. Her situation was tricky and things could easily go wrong. "You want to divorce him then?" I asked.

"As soon as possible," answered Hylda. "I've been talking to Eric." Eric was her brother-in-law, a brilliant businessman and well up in legal matters.

"I think I'll talk to him too," I said, knowing that, as a wise and good friend, he would stop us from doing anything foolish. One mistake now and our whole future could be thrown into jeopardy.

The first thing Eric said was that on no account were we to see each other. Hylda had to stay with her husband for the time being. If she left, she would be giving him grounds for divorce and it would be a nasty and protracted one. Her position was weak enough as it was.

At first, Hylda's husband wanted nothing to do with any kind of divorce. He was aggrieved and understandably so, but that didn't alter the situation. Hylda rang me again. It always had to be that way round. Me ringing her was far too dangerous. She had thought of a way to meet without being spotted. While working on a Batchelors Peas advertisement she had stayed at a nice but out of the way hotel near Gatwick. We could go there separately.

On a misty November afternoon I got in my car and set off from my flat. Anyone who knows me will already be hearing alarm bells. I have a very bad sense of direction and there were no motorways then. All I had were second class roads and first class roads that didn't feel first class. They had a way of twisting and shooting off at right angles. As I got more and more lost the mist thickened and turned into fog. I stopped frequently and asked for directions but to little effect. It was getting later and later. "7.30," I had told Hylda, but by the time I finally arrived it was 10 o'clock. "Oh, Mr Lawrence," said the receptionist, "I'm so glad you're here." Lawrence? What was he on about? And then I remembered. I was to use Hylda's stage name. That was the plan. "Your wife has been so anxious," he continued. "I'll ring up to her room right away." That was another thing I had to remember. Hylda and I were supposed to be married.

She came downstairs looking wonderful. It really had been a long time since our parting and the moment could not have been more emotional. Or rather it should have been were it not for the need to act like a married couple. "There you are, darling," said Hylda as we pecked each other on the cheek. "What a bore. Never mind, you're here now. Don't forget to sign the book." With Hylda looking over my shoulder, her eyes dancing, I signed the name Louis Lawrence and upstairs we went. It was only when the bedroom door was shut behind us that we collapsed into each other's arms, crying and laughing. The room, which looked out on to a garden and trees, was beautiful. The night we spent there together was a very happy one, but the next day we had to go back to our usual lives of being apart.

Eric decided to make a move. By now he could see that Hylda loved me and that I, in turn, would not let her down. "Don't do anything," he said. "Let me go and talk to the husband. I've met him already and I know him quite well." He went and pleaded our cause. Could the husband not see that the situation was hopeless? Miserable he may be but was there any point in making Hylda miserable too? A mistake had been made and perhaps it was best to admit it. The husband, still aggrieved, insisted that Hylda would have to give him grounds for divorce. Eric didn't give up. Why make things so unpleasant? Wouldn't it be simpler to do it the traditional way with the man giving the woman grounds for divorce? In the end the husband agreed.

This did not mean that Hylda and I could be together again immediately. The law was stricter in those days and divorce took much longer. Between the decree nisi and the decree absolute we had to remain apart, or at least appear to. Make one mistake during those six months and you could find yourself back at square one. That meant more clandestine meetings and a lot of secrecy. In the meantime I had another job offer. As it was to direct a feature film, I jumped at it. I shouldn't have. It was made by a producer whom I had met while working at Nettlefold Studios on *The Little Ballerina*. John Argyle was his name and he was known for making very cheap films which were either shown as co-features or first features, mainly in the north of England where he seemed able to get them well booked.

Before television, the cinema-going public was resigned to seeing some very poor films. It must have been because there were a lot of them about. I optimistically thought that I could do better than that. How wrong can you be?

We seemed to get off to quite a good start. The film, *Once a Sinner*, was to have Pat Kirkwood as its star. She had been a wartime hit in the West End of London and was now one of theatre's top names. We were fortunate. Pat was sweet and hard working but, try as she might, the odds were against her. The script was feeble and one disastrous piece of casting didn't help. The actress in question was not really an actress. She was, however, putting up some money and that explained her presence in the film. Par for the course in those days, I'm afraid.

I had thought that I could improve the script as we went along but every time I made a suggestion John Argyle would say, "How much is that going to cost?" and there would be no more talk of it. Towards the end of the shoot we were on location when the husband of the woman who had agreed to let us film there suddenly appeared. He had known nothing about it and out we were, on our ear. The next day things did not improve. It was an exterior scene and the rain wouldn't stop. Two whole days had been lost.

"We'll have to extend the actors' contracts," I said.

"No," said Argyle, "we can do something much simpler." He grabbed the script and tore out the unshot pages. I stood there gaping.

"But the end won't make any sense," I argued.

"That's no big deal, we do it all the time," he said. "Now, don't you worry, the film will go out." But the film going out was why I was worried and, of course, it did go out – down and out. John Argyle could not have cared less. All he wanted was some footage to put in those cinemas up north. The quality of the film meant nothing to him. It was distributed by a company aptly named Butchers.

Apart from the actress who couldn't act, the rest of the cast was surprisingly strong. At least it was possible to get good actors in those days. One of them, Jack Watling, became a lifelong friend. He was a nice chap, a fine actor, and subsequently appeared in many of my films.

During the shoot Pat Kirkwood became intrigued by my apparent lack of a girlfriend. "Or do you prefer boys?" she asked. I explained that I did have a girlfriend but that she was currently trying to extricate herself from an unhappy marriage. Discretion was vital. If Pat wanted to know any more she would have to refer to my girlfriend as Madam X. She did and it became our code name.

Decades later, when Pat was in her 70s, she made a comeback at the Wimbledon Theatre. I took Hylda to a matinee, feeling rather nervous. What had time done to Pat? Nothing, as it turned out. On to the stage came this slim woman who appeared to be no more than 30 and brought the house down. When the lights came up at the interval I looked around at the packed auditorium. It was a typical matinee audience, all grey-haired, including me.

"You haven't changed," I said to Pat backstage after the show.

"Only my husband," she said before looking over at Hylda.

"Ah yes," I said. "At last you can meet Madam X."

By the time the fine print of *Once a Sinner* was ready, Hylda and I were back together again. I invited her to a showing. If anything was grounds for divorce that was, except we weren't married. If Hylda had said, "This is dreadful," and left me there and then I couldn't have blamed her. She hummed and ha-ed. "I don't know," she said. "Perhaps this will lead to more work. In fact I wouldn't be at all surprised if it does." And she was right. It did.

In 1949, unlike today, you could walk down London's Wardour Street with a very average script and find 20 distributors, one of whom would put up the finance. Such a distributor was Butchers, the company that had put out *Once a Sinner*. The name was a joke and so were many of their films, but they did provide employment and it was they who offered me another directing job on one of those very average scripts, *The Scarlet Thread*. The writers, AR Rawlinson and Moie Charles, had first written it as a play but had failed to get it produced. I was probably offered the job because Butchers were the distributing arm of Nettlefold Studios, where *The Little Ballerina* and *Once a Sinner* had been made. The name Nettlefold came from Guest, Kean and Nettlefold, a north country firm that made screws but later diversified into films where they carried on screwing, this time film crews and audiences. They owned Kays laboratory too, so in its very small way it was a film-making empire.

I gave the script to Hylda to read. She was already taking on the role she would keep for the next 55 years, that of another voice. Over the years I would rely on her when choosing scripts and actors, even if I was not always to agree with her. "I don't understand," she said when she had finished reading. "You're going to do this, aren't you? But anyone can see it's no good."

I explained, "The finance is there. The offer is there. I will get paid. That's all I need at the moment. If I am ever to make any money it will only be through directing films. There's nothing else for me. I must build up a list of credits simply to prove that

I can do the job, bring a film in on schedule and on budget. When I have done that, better scripts and bigger budgets will follow and that will be the time for art." I think Hylda understood. Anyway, I did *The Scarlet Thread* and it wasn't any good but Butchers offered me another film and that one was better.

First though, on *The Scarlet Thread* came Laurence Harvey. He had already been in four pictures and AR Rawlinson thought that he was an up-and-coming star. When I presented him to the others at Butchers they were happy to go along with that.

Laurence Harvey was a good-looking South African boy whose parents were Lithuanian. This accounted for his real name, Larry Skikne. He was charming, down to earth and soon came to be thought of as a member of the family. After Friday night dinners at Hylda's sister's place he was always the first to attack the washing up. What he was to go on to do – exploit the reputations of well-known actresses older than himself and live off the fortunes of women with rich husbands – we never could have predicted. At the time, my only thought was that in Laurence Harvey we had one of our leading men for the next film, *There is Another Sun.*

It was set in a fairground where a boxing booth fighter and a wall of death rider vie for the affections of the girl who takes the money at the gate. Laurence Harvey, with his height and physique, seemed a good idea for the boxer and Butchers thought he would be perfect. As soon as he knew he had the part Larry was off down the gym, learning to box. For everyone at the studio he was the image of a keen and hard working young actor.

The wall of death rider and the girl on the gate were to be played by two up-and-coming young stars, both at the time better known than Laurence Harvey. They were Maxwell Reed and Susan Shaw. Also in the cast was Hermione Baddeley. After not getting her into *Marry Me* I was glad to make amends.

Maxwell Reed was a limited actor but big and handsome and that was enough for our purposes. The young Joan Collins, with whom I was to work in later years, was then his wife. During the shoot it was he who gave us the first clue as to how Laurence Harvey would proceed in his career.

Things started with Hermione Baddeley explaining that as Larry was finding it hard to get to the studio on time, he had accepted her suggestion to stay with her. That way she could see he would always be punctual. I thanked her profusely if, on reflection, a little naively. The following Monday, Maxwell Reed came into work, bubbling over. At one o'clock on Saturday morning he had dropped round Hermione's knowing that, day or night, he could get a drink there. After he had rung the bell he had heard a window open and seen Larry Harvey drop down a key. But when he had got up to the flat he had found Larry in bed with Hermione, she wearing a white face pack and him smoking a cigar. Putting two and two together had not taken Maxwell long. Laurence Harvey, with a load of ambition but very little money, was learning how to put his good looks to use. Hermione was famous and 44.

Susan Shaw, playing the girl who took the money at the gate, was a very pretty, very competent young actress who seemed set for an excellent career. Having appeared in nine films during the previous year she was already the most in-demand young female star. To have crammed all that work in she must have sometimes filmed two pictures at once. Signs of trouble ahead, however, were already there. When I looked through the camera at her one day these signs were plain enough. "Good God, Sue," I said. "What have you been up to? You look terrible."

"I didn't go to bed last night," she answered. "I came straight here from a party."

"But you can't do that while you're working," I said, imagining all too easily the late night drinking sessions her husband, the American actor Bonar Colleano, liked to go in for. He and his friend, the actor Paul Carpenter, were well known for them.

Sue shrugged her shoulders. "It doesn't make any difference to me. I can carry on."

"You can carry on," I said, "but whether you can carry on in this picture looking like that is another matter." She did get through but it was a struggle and her career was not to last. If only she had had more discipline. Some years later she was spotted in a café working as a waitress and who knows what else. Ironically this was in Wardour Street. Maxwell Reed had something of a career but that too faded out. The one who went to Hollywood and became an international star was Laurence Harvey. He was unstoppable.

The main problem with *There is Another Sun* was its fairground setting. Building one was out of the question, far too expensive on a budget of £30,000. "We're dealing in ha'pennies, Lewis, ha'pennies," wailed our production manager, shaking his hands slightly away from his body as if he were trying to get blood to flow into his fingers. This was ES Laurie and that's what he always did before going away to solve a problem. This time, he simply contacted a real fair. "What do you do during the winter?" he asked the boss.

"Hole up and mend the attractions," came the answer.

"Ah, well, you could hole up at Nettlefold Studios," said Mr Laurie. "We have a big lot there where we build our exterior sets. It won't cost you much." In this way we not only got our fairground with no outlay, we also had money coming in. I thought that was very shrewd.

In the event *There is Another Sun*, with its real fairground, turned out to be remarkably spectacular and action-packed. Most effective were the wall of death sequences with motorbikes going round and round inside a huge drum, criss-crossing and mounting higher and higher up the sides, all the while making a noise that was absolutely terrifying. For a small picture made on a tiny budget, this was unique. The business it did was good too and that led to distribution in America. In other words it bumped me up a level.

Subjects for films don't come from just plays and novels. They can come at you from anywhere. One morning I was glancing through the paper when a story about a child needing a complete blood transfusion caught my eye. What made it fascinating was the child being in a blood group so rare that only four or five other people in the whole country could donate. I passed the article to Hylda. "Yes?" she said when she had finished, "and what are you going to do about it?" Since the day was sunny I went straight up on to the roof, taking with me a pencil and some sheets of paper. As with *Marry Me*, I could see different stories forming. Each would be a hunt for a donor. They could make a multi-story film.

The ten-page treatment I came up with I sent to Exclusive Films. Their boss was James Carreras, who was also the head of Exclusive's subsidiary Hammer Films. He had been dropping heavy hints about getting a film out of me. Reaction came almost immediately with a telephone call, most unusual. Exclusive liked the treatment very much, but as they already had something much too similar they could not proceed with my story or the other person's until some kind of arrangement had been arrived at.

I needed a lawyer who knew about film and turned to Edwin Davis, legal adviser to the Rank Organisation. He told me that it was most important that I did not look at the other script. If I did and then made my film I could end up being sued and losing the case. 'Very sensible,' I thought until a week had gone by and nothing had happened. By then I was thinking, 'This is silly. My picture isn't being made, nor is the other one. Where's the point in that?' It was then I decided to speak to the other writer. Perhaps I could buy his script or he could buy mine. I rang him. At first he didn't want to talk. He too had a lawyer and his advice had been exactly the same as mine. However he realised, like me, that we weren't getting anywhere.

"I think our only chance is to meet." he said, "Have a chat and see what happens." As he sounded pleasant and reasonable, I agreed. "I'm bringing my wife and daughter up to town tomorrow," he said. "We're going to have a look round the Festival of Britain. [The year was 1951.] Perhaps we could meet by the Skylon." This was a slender, cigar-shaped structure, 300 foot tall, situated on the South Bank. It had been made specially for the Festival and symbolised the new, modern Britain we were all supposed to be looking forward to.

"Fine, I'll be there," I said.

The next day I was beginning to wonder whether this was such a bright idea. I was at the Skylon but could see no-one who looked right. Only when I was about to go home did I catch sight of a man, a pregnant woman and a child hanging on to the woman's skirt. It could have been any little family on a day out but I was getting desperate. "Vernon Harris?" I asked.

"Lewis Gilbert?" the man replied, and from that moment I knew that we were going to be all right.

At first we talked about ourselves. Before the war Vernon had been an actor at Birmingham Rep, a classical company where many big names had begun their careers. Robert Donat, whom I had seen filming at Elstree, had shared a flat with him. Vernon had then toured in Shakespeare with the Frank Benson Company, where it was essential to be a cricketer. At every town the company came to, the actors played a match against a local team. So that's how Benson advertised. 'Wanted. Laertes for *Hamlet*. Should be able to double as wicket keeper,' or words to that effect. At some point Vernon had stopped being an actor and become a writer/producer at the BBC, where he was still on the staff. During the war he had written for *Bandwagon*, a popular radio show starring Arthur Askey and Richard 'Stinker' Murdoch. One of his best known characters had been called Nausea Bagwash. It was clear that, at the very least, Vernon could turn his hand to pretty much anything.

When I told him what I had done workwise and we had run out of general topics of conversation, I brought up the subject of the two treatments. "Do you want to carry on?" I asked.

"What have we got to lose?" said Vernon and so we agreed to meet again at the Aeolian Hall in Bond Street where he had his BBC office.

This time we both had our ten-page treatments. We swapped and read. Mine was called *Emergency Call* and had two stories. His, *Trail of Blood*, had just the one but it was clever. The only person in the country with the right blood type was a murderer on the run. "Well," I said when we had finished reading, "we really have got ourselves into a pickle. Everything we have been told not to do, we've gone and done." Maybe it was an indication of our future at work together because we both found that funny and it wasn't long before I saw a way out. We could do all the stories and Vernon's could be the climax. At last things were looking up. Over the next few weeks, with Vernon grabbing any spare time he had from the BBC, we wrote the script.

I thought about who to send it to. Exclusive or Butchers? I settled for Butchers because, though not great, they at least had given me some breaks and, for once, the deal they were offering was OK. It was either a percentage or a thousand pounds. For a little film in those days, a thousand was a lot to pay a director of a small film and I was happy to accept it.

Two encouraging things happened. Jimmy Lawrie, head of the film bank, rang. "I've read your script," he said. "Can we have a chat?"

Hylda, overhearing the conversation, said, "Invite him for dinner," and round he came.

"I think it's a shame you're only spending fifteen thousand on *Emergency Call*," he said. "If the film bank were to give you five thousand extra you could improve it, couldn't you?" I didn't argue.

The phone rang again. It was Earl St John, the manager of Pinewood Studios. "We want you to come with us," he said. This was really flattering. I would never have suspected that such a little film could be of any interest to a large organisation like Rank. Tempting though their resources were, capable as they were of making the film much bigger, it was out of the question. Contracts had been signed. We had to stick with Butchers.

As it happened we weren't doing that badly anyway. Two British stars had agreed to be in it, Jack Warner and Anthony Steel. Jack was going to be the senior policeman who did the actual hunting. Anthony was going to be the doctor back at the hospital. The supporting cast was strong too. Sidney James, Thora Hird, Graham Stark and Dandy Nichols popped up, while a very important character, a black sailor, was played by Earl Cameron, one of the first generation post-war Caribbean actors. He was donor number one. Number two was supposed to be a boxer. I decided to go for the genuine article – Freddie Mills, former light heavyweight champion of the world. He had no acting experience but there was a quality about him that the public loved.

Tension is built in the film when Freddie's character loses not only a fight but a lot of blood. Will there be enough for him to donate? Obviously the fight was choreographed for Freddie to lose, but when it came to shooting it the stunt man opposing him got cocky and tried it on. Instinctively Freddie went into the attack. "Very good, Freddie," I said, "but you're supposed to lose."

"Oh yes, sorry," he said before collapsing on to the canvas.

At the end of Freddie's part of the story, his trainer (Sidney James) suggests, "Perhaps it's time to quit," and Freddie had a response, his only line in the picture: "Who knows when to quit?" "All night, he's been up rehearsing it," said his wife, "*Who* knows when to quit? Who *knows* when to quit? Who knows *when* to quit?"

As usual, I showed the finished film to Hylda. This time, she didn't hum and ha. "You've made it," she said, "I can feel it. This film is going to do you a lot of good." Soon after that a stroke of luck came its way, when the Leicester Square cinema unexpectedly fell empty. This was a prestigious booking and it gave the film a good send-off. Released in the UK, it grossed something like £125,000, which meant it was a big success. This, in turn, impressed America and a producer over there bought it for distribution. The title became *Hundred Hour Hunt.*

The man to strike the deal was Abby Greshler, a cheapskate

producer really, but fun to watch at work. He would sit beside the pool at the Beverly Hills Hotel, where every ten minutes the tannoy would blare out, "Mr Abby Greshler to the phone please, Mr Abby Greshler!" This was only to make himself look important, of course. The caller was his own secretary, nobody else, and naturally she had absolutely nothing to say to him. I kept in touch with Abby and when I was in Hollywood a few years later I received an invitation from him to drop round for dinner. By then he was an agent representing what we would now call B list actors. He was very excited because he wanted to introduce me to his latest client, one he was particularly proud of – Rita Hayworth. That evening I found myself sitting opposite one of the loveliest, most famous stars of the 1940s, but by then her looks had gone and she was drinking too much. I should have stayed away and kept my illusion.

The relationship I made so casually with Vernon Harris turned into perhaps the strongest and longest of my career. For the next 30 years he worked on nearly all my films. It could be anything from adapting a whole play to adding some lines of dialogue when a new scene was needed. If he ever had a contract to sign, that never happened until long after the work was done and the film was made. It was a mere formality.

The success of *Emergency Call* led to something that had never happened to me before and was never to happen again. A letter arrived containing a cheque for £250. Little, schlocky Butchers had sent it out of appreciation. They hadn't been obliged to. They just had and I was most touched.

On the whole, the film received very good notices and I was proud of them. Even so, you can get a hundred good notices and one bad one, and all your life it'll be the bad one you remember. On the Friday after *Emergency Call* opened I hurried into the high street to buy the *Evening Standard* because on Friday you had the film page. Milton Shulman was the critic. He hadn't yet moved to theatre. My eyes travelled up and down the columns past the reviews of all the other films. Only when I reached the very bottom of the last column did I find the review for mine. It consisted of four words: '*Emergency Call.* Don't answer.'

9
White Hot Technology?

That first meeting with Vernon Harris reminds me of a job I keep trying to forget but can't quite.

The Festival was a huge success for the most part. It offered Great Britain the chance to put on a bit of a show which, after the greyness of war, was badly needed. A big amusement park was built on the South Bank, and among the attractions were film shows. I was asked to contribute with a film that would be shot in 3D. It would be the very first one in the country and way ahead of its time. The people behind it were International Realist, eminent makers of documentaries. John Grierson and Basil Wright were among their number. There was one snag, though. Nobody had a 3D camera or any knowledge of how to make one. Still, some chap came up with an idea and did some tests which seemed OK. He took two Newman Sinclairs, old square cameras, not a nut or bolt of which had changed in 40 years, lashed them to a bar and had them both pointing at the same object, slightly out of kilter like a pair of eyes. The idea was that if you put on those cellophane spectacles, red for one eye, green for the other, the two pictures would be pulled together and appear in three dimensions.

Actually it worked quite well and I began to get excited. As with all the other documentaries I had made, I could see a way of raising the game and obtaining a national release by making the film pure entertainment. We would invent a little story about a street where all the shops had different variety acts in the windows. Popular stars of the day like Max Bygraves and the Beverley Sisters could be in it. Only, to show off the 3D effect they would have to move around as well as sing. There was a juggler who could balance a ball on the end of a billiard cue. If he pointed his cue at the camera the cue would seem to come right out over the audience's heads with the ball at the very tip. A skater could be swung round by her partner so that the audience would duck, thinking it was going to get an unwanted haircut from the blades of her skates. As an idea, it was not bad at all.

We did some tests and showed them to the top people at International Realist, as well as to Gerald Barry, the President of the Festival of Britain. They were most enthusiastic. Only one person wasn't. That was Norman Hyams, the son of one of the Hyams brothers who had run Eros Films. "It's flat," he said.

"What do you mean?" we said. "It's nothing of the sort. It's fantastic. It comes right out over the audience."

"It does not," said Norman stubbornly. "It's absolutely flat." And for a moment we were all quite puzzled. "Mind you," said Norman, after thinking for a while, "I do have only one eye." That was it. For stereoscopic vision you must have the use of both eyes.

We called the film *Harmony Lane*, and what with the technicalities and the cost of the acts it was not cheap. The outlay for the Festival of Britain must have been considerable. Did we recoup our losses with a national release? No. It was never shown. The whole thing dribbled away because cinemas didn't have the right projectors and it was all too difficult. You have to remember that the first 3D feature film, *House of Wax*, was still a couple of years away. Even so, two years after that the craze for the 3D system with red and green specs faded away altogether.

Some years later I took John, who was now eleven years old, to the London Pavilion cinema in Piccadilly Circus. We were going to see Charlie Chaplin's comedy *Modern Times*. John hadn't seen a full length Chaplin film before and I thought it would be a good example. As we entered the cinema I glanced at the board to check the programme times and, to my horror, saw just above *Modern Times*, 'Four o'clock: *Harmony Lane*.' Why was I horrified? Because I knew what was going to happen. However there was no getting out of it. You can't disappoint a child, so in we went. Up came *Harmony Lane*, and sure enough it was flat. There was no sense to it at all. A juggler balancing a ball on the end of a billiard cue, what was so great about that? And why did it have to go on for so long? To achieve the maximum 3D sensation, that's why, only with no 3D it was just boring. Soon poor old *Harmony Lane* was getting the bird. The film was dying, and as John joined in the whistling I was dying too. The thought that it would end soon brought no relief at all as the final humiliation of the credits was still to come. How was I going to explain this to John? I didn't have to. Since the venture had always been something of an experiment I had asked to be credited with another name. 'Director: Byron Gill,' it said. I was off the hook but still badly shaken.

10

Real Life: A Christmas Story

After *Emergency Call*, one film pretty much came on top of another for a while. None were big. Their budgets, mostly in the tens of thousands, today sound quaint. My attitude was, 'As long as they keep coming, that's fine. I can earn a reasonable living.' I shan't talk about all of them or indeed about all of the ones that came after that, only those where certain memories stick in the mind.

Despite the hard work in the early fifties – no exceeding the tiny budgets, no running over schedule – the life I was leading with Hylda and John was perfectly ordinary. Problems blew up and had to be solved just as they had to be in any other family. One of the biggest wasn't mine, but the memory of it remains vivid. Perhaps that's because it was the kind of problem that any parent would dread.

During the early years of working with Vernon Harris, hammering out screenplays together, I noticed one day that he was unusually distracted and I asked him what was the matter. "It's my daughter, Jo," he said. "She's five now, and the other day she was walking across the room when she stumbled for no reason. It was as if she was suddenly giddy, and then a few moments later she stumbled again. I rang the doctor and he told me to bring her in immediately but he didn't do anything. He just made an appointment to see a specialist."

A few days later Vernon rang to tell me that he and his wife, Joan, had taken Jo to the specialist. The news was not good. The specialist, Mr Murray Faulkner, had looked at Jo and tapped her head. Then, smiling at the little girl, had asked her to wait outside with her mother. When the door was closed, he told Vernon that his daughter had a tumour on the brain. There was no doubt of it. She would have to come in immediately for proper tests. In a state of shock, Vernon asked what his daughter's chances were of pulling through. "I shan't know until I perform the operation," replied Mr Faulkner. "I can only tell you that if it's benign I'll be able to get it all out, in which case your daughter can look forward to a natural life span."

"And if it's not benign?" asked Vernon.

There was a long pause. "We patch her up and wait for the end."

Two days later Vernon came to my house as usual. I begged him to forget about work and do everything possible for Jo and Joan. "There's nothing I can do," he said and burst out crying. To see dear, phlegmatic old Vernon sobbing, with tears running down his face, was very distressing. It was so untypical. I put my arm round his shoulder and took him across the road to the pub. Again I told him not to worry about work but, shaking his head, he said, "Work's what I need. Anything to take my mind off what's going on." By then, Christmas was fast approaching.

The hospital rang. Mr Faulkner had decided he couldn't wait any longer. He wanted to operate the next day even though that would be Christmas Day. Vernon rang his local cab firm, the one he always used. After apologising for requesting a car on Christmas Day he explained the situation. The manager came on the line. He'd been listening to the story of the child and wanted to do the job himself. "You'll miss your Christmas," said Vernon.

"Don't worry," said the manager. "My family will understand."

"But you realise it could take all day," Vernon continued. "You'll have to charge extra."

"Not only will I not charge extra," said the manager, "I will not charge you at all." This, coming from a near stranger, gave Vernon a curious feeling of hope. When you're in trouble, the most unexpected of people can turn up trumps.

The next morning the driver took Vernon and Joan to the hospital. On arrival they were led to a private ward where they found Jo, her head already bandaged, sitting up in bed, smiling. They both hugged her before a nurse escorted them from the room. As they went, Jo waved goodbye. The operation would take at least five hours, the ward sister said. Was there anywhere Mr and Mrs Harris could go as waiting in the hospital would do them little good? "If it's all right," said the driver, who was standing by, "I'll take you out for a drive."

There followed a passage of time that Vernon and Joan knew they would never forget. It was midday. The car drove round the back streets of London. All were empty, but in the lit-up windows of every house families were having their Christmas lunch. Vernon and Joan gazed in at the eating, the laughter and the pulling of crackers. The whole of London seemed to be enjoying itself.

Eventually the car had to go back to the hospital. This time, Vernon and Joan were shown into a comfortable waiting room. The operation was likely to be over in half an hour, the sister told them. They would hear the result from Mr Faulkner, who would come and tell them himself. It was the longest half hour of Vernon's life, he told me later. Keeping still was impossible. He walked up and down, up and down, until he heard the sound of approaching feet. The door opened. It was the sister. She said that Mr Faulkner would see them in five minutes. Before Vernon and Joan could ask anything, she left the room and closed the door. The two sat down and held hands, both hoping to gain some strength from each other.

Once more, footsteps could be heard in the corridor and once more the door opened. In came Mr Faulkner, still in his scrubs. He was a bluff New Zealander who, before they could speak, said, "It's all right, it was benign. I got it all out, no problem at all. She'll be perfect. You'll be able see her in the morning. You can feel very pleased. Happy Christmas." And with that he was gone. Vernon and Joan looked at each other, burst into tears and fell into each other's arms.

Jo grew up and never had a day's serious illness again but every Christmas she sent Mr Faulkner a card and every Christmas she received one in return. It was something neither of them forgot.

11

Juveniles, Delinquent and Delightful

Like a circling plane, the relationship between Hylda and myself was ready to land and gradually it did, starting with John's education. Mine had been patchy at best. Hylda's had been cut off early because her father had considered further education pointless for girls. Both of us wanted something better for John. Basil Wright, the documentary director who'd looked at the 3D experiment, had told me about the liberal outlook and the love of theatre that could be found at a school called Bryanston. It sounded right, and when John was 13 we sent him to Port Regis, a prep school that was geared towards Bryanston. It was then, having talked it over with him, that I changed his surname from Lawrence to Gilbert, while Hylda, though not married to me, became known as Mrs Gilbert. This was the beginning of a proper family. Would there be an addition?

During our time apart Hylda had been obliged to have an operation, resulting in the loss of an ovary. Now a check-up was needed and we went to the specialist, Mr Ducer. Although he was pleased with her progress, he took the opportunity to have a word with me while she was getting dressed. "I think you ought to know what it means to lose an ovary," he said. "Conception is not impossible but the chances are slim. You may have to face the fact that there will be no more children."

"That's not so bad," I said. "I have a son. We're a family and I'm happy with that."

Very early in 1952, Hylda woke up one morning convinced she was pregnant. We hurried back to Mr Ducer to make sure. "Congratulations, Mrs Gilbert," he said. "You *are* pregnant but you're going to have to be very careful. In fact, you're going to have to go to bed for a month and take things very easy, stay absolutely calm. Have you anyone to help?" Fortunately, and amazingly, there was Hylda's mother. On hearing of the tricky situation, daughter immobilised, me at work all day, she actually came through. It seemed she'd hopped a generation and was taking an interest in the new one. On some evenings, not all, she cooked dinner for two and put it on trays, so when I came home from work I could climb into bed with Hylda and the two of us could have dinner together. The scene became even more cosy when I brought John home to recover from pneumonia. Suddenly, the place was full of invalids but rather merry ones as they, and I too, were looking forward to the new arrival. Would it be a boy or a girl?

After the month in bed, Hylda returned to Mr Ducer who told her that all was well and that she should go if not to full term then to nearly full term, barring any accident. It was then I made up my mind to ask Hylda to marry me. My career was going well and there was money in the bank. "Yes," said Hylda, "but I don't want a big wedding. We've been living together for too long. Let's just invite a few close friends and go to a register office." Which is what we did. The close friends were our lawyer, André Bozamini, and some cousins of Hylda, Mr and Mrs Philip Renton, who had helped me during difficult times in my career. They gathered at the registry office in Kensington from where, after the ceremony, we set off for lunch at Les

Ambassadeurs. It was all very enjoyable but that was it. There could be no honeymoon. Work meant that I had to return to Hammersmith where I was setting up a new film at Riverside Studios. I don't know why I chose that particular day for the wedding because, in all the happiness, there was a touch of sadness. It was February the 14th – Valentine's Day, but also the anniversary of my father's death.

Although Hylda's flat in Westbourne Terrace was a fine one and its rent was still at its pre-war figure of four pounds a week, it was becoming rather small. There was the new baby to think of. I found a house in Chelsea. It had four storeys. "No," said Hylda's mother, "when the baby comes and you've got cots and prams to manage, you won't want to be rushing up and down flights of stairs." She had a point. I found, instead, a little house in Cope Place off the Earl's Court Road. It was newly built and cost £5,100, which today sounds unbelievable. With an affordable mortgage bought, we moved in. Now, we really had become a family.

Seven months after Hylda's pregnancy had been confirmed, I was about to set off for work when I heard her cry out, "The baby's coming!"

"But it's my first day on the new film," I said.

"To hell with the film!" shouted Hylda, "I'm about to give birth! It's premature!"

I pictured the unit, standing in the street, waiting for me. What was I to do? "I'll phone your mother," I said. "She's always good when there's an emergency." Before we knew it she was round in a taxi. "Don't let it go!" I said. Having got Hylda up and dressed I, together with her mother and the taxi driver, helped her into the cab.

As it was the school holidays, John and his best friend Tim

Corrie, whom he had met at nursery school, were also in the house. They were now both 11 and uncertain what the fuss was about. All they could do was hover. At the last moment they came towards Hylda. "Have a good time, Mum," said John.

"Yes, have a good time," said Tim. Even Hylda had to laugh at that. The taxi sped away and I went to work.

The new film was *Cosh Boy*. In the early fifties young men, unsupervised as children during the war, ran wild, coshing old ladies over the head to steal their handbags. Woodwork class was where the coshes were invariably made. One of these cosh boys was the central character and he lived in a house where also lived a prostitute. She was played by Hermione Gingold. Again, I had not forgotten my dream cast for *Marry Me*. With my brain half at the hospital I set up the first shot. Roy, the cosh boy, goes up the steps to his house just as Queenie, the prostitute, comes out with a man who is obviously a client. "Oh, Roy," says Queenie, "I'd like you to meet a very dear friend of mine," adding, as she turns to the man, "What's your name, dear?" Hermione, in a garish costume and dyed red wig, played that very well.

At ten o'clock, while a shot was being lit, I popped into one of the houses on the street and asked if I could use the phone to ring the hospital. "You'd better come immediately," said the doctor. "I think your wife is going to have the child any time now."

"I can't come," I said. "I'm shooting in the streets."

"What?" said the doctor, picturing me roaming round the streets firing a gun.

"No, no, I'm shooting a film," I explained.

"Oh yes, of course," he said. "You're a film director. Well, get here as soon as you can."

"I think I can be there by lunchtime," I said.

"Good," he said, to which I distraughtly added. "Good luck," and that made him laugh. The rest of the morning was hard going for me. At 12.30 I called an early lunch, jumped into the production car and rushed off to St Mary's Hospital Paddington, about 15 minutes away. In those days there was much less traffic. Hylda's mother was waiting for me on the hospital steps.

"You've got a boy! You've got a boy!" she shouted. God knows what any passer-by must have been thinking.

Hylda was wan, but happy. She had been desperately wanting to give me a child. The baby itself was, of course, not there. Being premature he had to be kept in an incubator. Having glanced at the tiny four pound creature which looked like a little wrinkled walnut, I returned to the location where I sent out for a couple of boxes of cigars to hand round to the unit in celebration. For the rest of the day I was on a high.

At seven o'clock the next morning – shooting had gone right through the night – we finished, only to realise that Hermione Gingold's taxi hadn't turned up. The production manager asked if I could give her a lift. "Of course," I said and in she got, heavy make-up, dyed red wig, garish costume and all. As we drove along I was terrified that anyone who knew me might see us together. What would they think? "Lewis with a wife who's just given birth, about town with a prostitute. Outrageous!" I said this to Hermione.

"Is that a compliment?" she asked.

"It's a compliment to your art," I answered and left it there.

I didn't mention the time when I had been caught in a situation with her that was equally embarrassing. Before the war her son Leslie, who used to work with me at Elstree, had, after a night out, suggested I stay at her flat and sleep in his mother's bed, she being away. I did, but at two in the morning I was woken by a hand shaking me and Hermione's voice saying, "Normally, I would be quite happy to find an 18 year-old boy in my bed," much to the amusement of her boyfriend, the actor Anthony Eustrel. With that, however, I was unceremoniously dumped on to the streets of London.

Cosh Boy was the first English film to be given an X certificate. A third of the country banned it altogether which, of course, gave it notoriety. This, of course, made it very successful. Nowadays, the censor wouldn't think twice before giving it a U.

It was during those days at Riverside Studios that a call came through from my local paper, *The Kensington Post.* Their show-business columnist wanted to come and interview me. As I could see no harm in it I agreed, but was rather taken aback when into my room came a 15 year-old schoolboy. Hesitating for not one second he announced himself as Michael Winner of Michael Winner's Showbiz Gossip. If nothing else, this boy could sort out his own billing. For all that, something must have clicked, probably to do with his sheer nerve, because we have never lost touch and he is one of our oldest family friends. You can judge the nature of our relationship when I tell you that I have been known to invite him up to the Arsenal as a very special treat. He can't stand football.

Only a few weeks passed after our tiny baby's birth before he had gained enough weight to go home. We called him Stephen, but for a while he was our little Cosh Boy, quite inappropriate because he's a gentle soul. Over the years I've made a lot of films and had a lot of success, but none of it was like the feeling of having two sons.

12

The Good and the Not So Good Die Young

Cosh Boy was produced by Remus Films, the production arm of an organisation run by the brothers James and John Woolf. Their father, CM Woolf, had been the boss of General Film Distributors, which had been taken over by J Arthur Rank. So the film business was in their blood, and in 1949 they started producing and distributing films on their own. Their arm for distribution was, unsurprisingly, called Romulus. Remus was run by James. Romulus was run by John.

From the beginning their eye had been on America, hence Ava Gardner being their first star and Albert Lewin, also an American, being their first director. The film was *Pandora and the Flying Dutchman*. Next had come *The African Queen* and soon would come *Moulin Rouge*, both directed by John Huston. Years later they would also produce *Room at the Top* and *The Day of the Jackal*. James Woolf, Jimmy, saw *Cosh Boy* and, thinking I deserved something bigger and better, handed me the novel *The Good Die Young*.

When I looked at the title page I got quite a surprise. The author was Richard Macaulay. I knew him. Back when I had been with the US Air Corps, working on *Target for Today* with William Keighley, he had been the scriptwriter. One of my jobs had been to lock him in his bedroom at the Mayfair Hotel to make sure he produced his five pages a day. When he had done that I was allowed to let him out. He was an alcoholic. As all access to drink had to be cut off, even room service had strict instructions not to oblige. The fact that he had now written a novel was pleasing, if a little unexpected.

His subject, topical again today with the Iraq conflict, was the ill usage of ex-servicemen. Four soldiers, all in the same platoon, return from the Second World War to find they are unwanted and reunite for revenge. With one of them acting as mastermind, they agree on a plan to steal a tank or an armoured car and smash it into the walls of a bank.

It was a good story and I could immediately see an exciting shoot-out in the streets, except for one thing. The book was set in America. The film was set in England, and here we didn't have Chicago-style gangland shootings. We had unarmed bobbies showing old ladies across the road. The simple solution would have been to make the film in America but that would have been too simple, and anyway I wouldn't have been the director. So it was a question of taking the rough with the smooth. The rough hit us right away. No British bank would countenance a bank raid. It would encourage copycats. As a bank was financing the film, this attitude was perhaps understandable. It meant, however, making do with a post office. So started a gradual chipping away at the original idea.

Focussing on America as usual, the Woolfs wanted the platoon to include Americans. But having American and British soldiers in the same platoon was ridiculous. Not only had there been no such platoon but cinemagoers, many of whom had lived through the war, were perfectly aware of that. They would find it unbelievable.

The casting went all right, but once fixed there was no going back. Among the British were Stanley Baker, Margaret Leighton, Joan Collins and Robert Morley, while from America came Richard Basehart, John Ireland and Gloria Grahame. Gloria had recently won an Oscar for *The Bad and the Beautiful.* That was fine, but then you had Laurence Harvey. During the making of *There is Another Sun* his youth had made us forgive him for not being very good, but now he was supposed to be the mastermind, the one who dominates the rest of the platoon. Toughness was needed but it wasn't forthcoming. His acting had not improved. It was still camp and stagey where camp and stagey were not called for. His ability to exert power over a platoon containing the naturally tough Stanley Baker didn't seem credible. What's more, Laurence Harvey was the principal star. How had that come about? To find the answer, you don't have to *cherchez la femme* so much as *cherchez l'homme.*

One person impressed by Laurence Harvey in *There is Another Sun* had been Jimmy Woolf, who at the time had asked me for an introduction. Naively I had agreed, not realising what was to happen. Jimmy, who was homosexual, was to fall for Larry in a big way. Years before in Hollywood Jimmy had learned the business of casting – not so much appropriate casting as commercial casting. That was his speciality, and in Larry he saw a future star. As Larry's driving ambition was already getting him plenty of work it's easy to see that the two would make a strong team, particularly as Larry was keeping up his other pursuit of exploiting famous actresses older than himself. At this time he was having an affair with Margaret Leighton. This didn't seem to bother Jimmy. I, on the other hand, could foresee a certain awkwardness on the set.

Gloria Grahame gave me cause for concern too, but I'm happy to say I was wrong there. The night before shooting was to start, Hylda and I were dining at a restaurant when a flurry across the room revealed Gloria Grahame and her writer boyfriend sitting down at a table. They had just arrived in England. "Why don't you introduce yourself?" said Hylda.

So I did. I went over and said how pleased I was to meet her before meeting her more formally the next day on the set, I being her new director. She looked up from her menu and, quite knocking the wind out of my sails, said, "You're very young, aren't you?"

The next morning at the studio I went to her dressing room where she was changing for a camera test. In front of her was a large box divided into lots of little compartments. "Do you have psychiatrists in England?" she asked.

"Yes, we do," I said, my eyes on the box. "What have you got there?"

"All my pills," she answered.

"Judging by the amount of them," I said, "you don't need a psychiatrist. You need a chemist shop."

"They're my uppers and downers," she said. "They're good for me. I use them a lot." Actresses and drugs conjured up a scene from Tennessee Williams. I didn't need it. As it turned out, she completely won me over. She was utterly professional, a good actress and a good sport. She had to be a good sport as there was one scene that was not going to be easy for her.

Her screen husband, John Ireland, returns to his flat to hear the bath running and to see his wife in the bedroom, beautifully dressed, close to a strange man in a dinner jacket. Having taken in the situation he throws the man out, returns to his wife, picks her up and holds her in his arms. A steamy sex scene appears to be imminent and sexy it is, all the way to the bathroom, where he dumps her in the water. We rehearsed it a few times with John always stopping just before letting Gloria go. "One more rehearsal," I said, nodding at the camera operator and whispering to John. What I said was, "This time, do it." So Gloria was utterly relaxed in John's arms before he threw her into the water. Of course, then she was very shocked but that was the scene. As John slammed his way out, I knew it was going to be terrific. Gloria, I'm relieved to say, understood.

Before filming with Margaret Leighton I became worried about her. It wasn't the acting – that would be no problem. In fact, given that the scene was Laurence Harvey as her young lover asking for money, not much acting was required from either of them anyway. What bothered me about her was how thin she had become. At lunch I sat with her to see what she would order. It was little more than a lettuce leaf. "This isn't good, Maggie," I said. "Why aren't you eating?"

"I am," she insisted.

"But it's not enough," I said. "You want to look your best for the film, don't you?"

"Larry likes me like this," she said.

'Well,' I thought, 'if he can get all these women he must have something. I just wish he could save it for the screen.'

The best part of the film comes towards the end when the four men have the money but are rumbled. The police are on to them and their only hope of escape is a fast night-time getaway along train lines, not just above ground but also below. As we used real stations and real lines, real danger was always present. While we were shooting, trains were rattling past and most of the lines still had current flowing through them. Because Richard Basehart's character had to stumble, fall across a line and die, one was switched off but only over a distance of ten yards. It was while Richard was lying across this non-live line, waiting for the scene to be lit, that his old friend John Ireland came up. "Good God, Richard," he said. "What are you doing down there?"

"It's OK, the line's dead," said Richard.

"You'll be dead, never mind the line," said John. "Do you realise what can happen? Right now, a guy is coming into the control box and he's thinking, 'Who's the idiot who's left that line off?' and up goes the lever."

"Lewis! Lewis!" I heard a petrified Richard call out. "Did you hear what John just said?"

"Forget it. He's pulling your leg," I said. "You're quite safe." If anyone was in danger it was me. When I am working out the next shot I am unaware of anything else and simply walk wherever I want to go. Fortunately my first assistant, Denis Johnson, knew me well. He drove a stake into the ground, tied a twenty foot length of rope to it and looped the other end round my waist. In this way he ensured my safety but further stretched the nerves of poor Richard Basehart, still sprawled across the line.

The scenes in the underground were even more striking, but the most memorable image was unfortunately not in the film. It happened by accident while we were working in one of the underground tunnels late at night. This was an eerie place. The walls had dust on them a foot thick, as if they had never been cleaned since the underground was built. The lines were dead, of course, but so was the ordinary station lighting. Only film lights, positioned for maximum drama, lit the scene. Quite unexpectedly Margaret Leighton stepped into them, looking a million dollars in a mink coat and hat. Backlit, she walked towards us, picking her way in high heels along the line, a perfect silhouette. It was surreal. All she was there to do, as it turned out, was collect Larry Harvey. The curtain had fallen on the play she was appearing in and she had come straight from the theatre. As shots go, it was an Oscar winner. I only wish I could have got it into the film.

It has to be said Laurence Harvey didn't hold back when something difficult came up. For *There is Another Sun* he learned to box. For *The Good Die Young* he took part, without question, in the most frightening action sequence. His character, Miles, is running along a tunnel when he hears a train coming. He presses himself up against the wall but it's clear that there's going to be just inches between him and the train, if that. When the time came to film this scene we took our places behind the camera, right in the middle of the track, and Larry positioned himself against the wall. The train, which we couldn't yet see, was given the signal, and as it rumbled through the tunnel I could feel the tension mounting among the crew. By the time the train was actually there, hurtling towards us, it was really frightening. At that speed it could never stop. Then, just as it was about to reach us, it swerved away on to a branch line, the lights from its windows flickering across Larry Harvey's face. A very dramatic moment. Of course, that's how we planned it, but if, for some reason, the train had stayed on our track it would have ploughed through the lot of us. Laurence Harvey ever so slightly rose in my estimation.

That climactic sequence made a very good ending to the film. Too good really, and if I'm honest *The Good Die Young* did better on its release than it should have done. One of its first reviews was the reason. Beverley Baxter, film critic of the *Evening Standard*, wrote: "This film is the most important picture made in England since the war." It was a good send-off and the other reviews, though not as good, were OK. Even Larry Harvey did fairly well, though I noticed the critics tended to concentrate on the rest of the cast.

Three years later Larry married Margaret Leighton, but she was already fulfilling what he saw as her function. As a member of the British theatre elite, Maggie was introducing him to the others. That's Noël Coward, Terence Rattigan, John Gielgud, Ralph Richardson and Hugh 'Binkie' Beaumont, who was the most powerful theatre manager in the West End. It didn't do much good. Larry got work in the West End all right but his acting let him down. His notices were not good and when he went to Stratford-upon-Avon to play Shakespeare, Shakespeare lost. Oddly, Larry didn't seem to mind. Fame and fortune were what appeared to interest him most, and anyway there was always his Svengali, Jimmy Woolf. Not a move did Larry make without him and Jimmy was to remain very active on his part.

My son John, by then a young man, got a job in the cutting room of *Saturday Night and Sunday Morning*. He became friendly with the film's star, Albert Finney, and Jimmy asked if I could fix an introduction. I arranged the meeting, and Jimmy asked Albie if he could handle his career. If Albie had accepted that would have been the end of it. Jimmy was prepared to sign up anyone he thought was a threat to Larry. His aim was merely to see that Albie did not work. Fortunately Albie was too cute for that. He could handle his own career.

Through the late fifties and early sixties Larry worked non-stop, usually with disastrous results. However one film, *The Manchurian Candidate*, suited him perfectly. He played a soldier in the Korean War who, after being captured and brainwashed by the enemy, is programmed to kill. It meant he could walk through the film with his usual blank expression, while for once finding favour with the critics.

His marriage to Margaret Leighton only lasted three years. He was then free to pull off his greatest coup, the wooing and marrying of Joan Cohn. She was the widow of Harry Cohn, the owner of Columbia Pictures and the man of whom it was said, "People get in line to hate him." As most of his stock went to his wife, she became very wealthy. Marriage to Joan put Larry in a position that was strong, not only from a money point of view but also for getting more work. The discovery that she was his senior by 17 years came as no surprise.

Round about this time Larry returned to England for talks about a film and installed himself at the Savoy Hotel. As I hadn't spoken to him for a long time I rang to catch up. Although he answered the phone himself he was cold and distant, impatient to bring the conversation to an end. This was the man who had once been looked on as a member of our family and on whose behalf I had worked hard when he was starting out.

No sooner was Larry married to Joan Cohn than, unusually, he fell for a woman who was several years his junior and not rich. This was a model called Paulene Stone. She had been in one of his films. A year later a little girl was born, and a year after that Larry and Joan were divorced. By the time he married Paulene Stone work had been thinning out for some years and he was ill. Romulus Films invited us both to a function at which he and I were sat next to each other. My reason for being there was a film, *Conduct Unbecoming*, which I was going to direct and Romulus was going to produce. It was a period whodunnit set in the Raj and needed lots of officer types. "Perhaps I could be in your film," said Larry, quite forgetting that chilly phone call.

"Some bloody chance," was my first reaction but then I looked at him. He really did not look well. "That's a very interesting thought," I said and left it there. In the end I didn't direct

Conduct Unbecoming, but by then Larry had died.

I think all those bad notices had finally got to him. His drive and determination had far outstripped his talent and this had pulled him apart. On discovering he was ill he said, "I think I'm being punished for my wicked ways." When he died he was 45 years old.

At the height of Larry's fame I had gone to the offices of Romulus Films to talk over a new picture, probably another one I didn't make. The place was in turmoil. Office doors were open. Secretaries were running to and fro. Convinced something terrible had happened, I stopped the first secretary I recognised and asked her what was going on. "It's Laurence Harvey," she said. "He's just left for America and he's forgotten his gold swizzle stick. We absolutely have to find it!" To me that gold swizzle stick became Laurence Harvey's epitaph, a life spent in pursuit of the superficial.

13

Reaching for the Sky Without a Pilot

Nearly 15 years after leading the Hurricanes and Spitfires of 12 Group in the Battle of Britain, Douglas Bader came back into my life. The producer Daniel Angel, with whom I had made a couple of pictures, gave me Paul Brickhill's book *Reach for the Sky*. To Danny it was of particular interest. While serving in India, where he attained the rank of Major, he had contracted polio and lost the use of both his legs. From then onwards he was only able to get about on crutches. Douglas Bader who walked unaided on artificial legs was an inspiration not only to him but to many other disabled people. *Reach for the Sky* told his story.

Bader had joined the RAF as a young man, assuming it was going to be his career. He had always been driven by action and already had a reputation as a great sportsman, rugby being his forte. He had been gifted enough to be chosen for the English trials. No sooner had he learned to fly than he began showing off his aerobatic skills. "Be careful," said his boss, a wise old bird called Wing Commander Day. "Flying is a dangerous art and one day you'll kill yourself." Bader took absolutely no notice and soon after that, while showing off for a group of civilians at Denham airfield, crashed his plane straight into the ground. This should have meant instant death, but by a miracle he survived. His legs, however, were badly crushed and one of them had to be amputated immediately, just above the knee. For Bader, who had a will of iron and undimmable optimism, this did not seem the end of the world. Instead of rugby, he would play golf. A few days later, however, he was told by his surgeon that the other leg would have to go too, this time just below the knee. Even golf seemed a forlorn hope then and his career as a pilot was definitely at an end. His surgeon, casting about for a crumb of comfort, told him not to worry as artificial legs were much improved. "I'm not worried," said Bader. "I've always wanted to be taller."

That was just the beginning. In time, Bader not only learned how to walk again but how to walk without sticks, a very rare achievement. Golf, the forlorn hope, then turned out not to be forlorn. He learned how to play, but for him that wasn't enough. Absurd as it sounded to everyone else, he had to get back into the RAF. He had to fly again. Useless to the force after the crash, he had been kicked out to make his way in a civilian job and he hated it. For the man who had once been looked up to as a daredevil pilot this was torture. The only thing that cheered him up was getting married. While continuing his flying studies – it was vital to stay up to date – he took to knocking on RAF doors, the approach of war adding to his determination. But how could someone with no legs run, quickly climb into a cockpit and keep his balance? It wasn't possible. It had never been done. These were invariably the objections he came up against, whilst unspoken was also the thought, 'Stop wasting our time and, for that matter, your own.' It had no effect. He continued knocking on doors and was finally granted an interview with someone important enough to say yes or no. Even so, the Warrant Officer sitting outside this Wing Commander's office did his darndest to put Bader off. "I don't know why you're bothering," he said. "You haven't a chance."

Bader took no notice – he'd heard it all before – and once inside the office launched his attack. "I don't need legs to fly," he argued, "and I have far more experience than any chap you have now." This was actually true and the Wing Commander, realising it, began to cave in.

"You've made your point, Bader," he said, "but you'll have to take a test. If you pass, you're back in the RAF." It was all Bader needed. He burst out of the office, gave a V sign to the Warrant Officer and went on to pass the test easily. After that, promotion came rapidly, and by the time the Battle of Britain started he was already a Squadron Leader.

The south of England bore the brunt of the attacks and this part of the country was the responsibility of 11 Group. Often, though, it was overstretched, and at peak times had all its planes in the air. Bader, by then commanding 12 Group with the responsibility for the middle of England, nagged and nagged until he was posted south and so was able to help to turn the tide. Winning the Battle of Britain would be a decisive victory because Germany, without supremacy of the air, could then never mount an invasion.

Towards the end of the battle Bader, on one of his foolhardy sorties, was shot down by two Messerschmidts over occupied France. His plane caught fire, and on trying to bale out he discovered that one of his artificial legs had got jammed underneath his seat. As the plane went into a dive and headed directly towards the ground, bringing him closer and closer to death, he tugged helplessly until the leg suddenly gave way and detached itself, freeing him to parachute to the ground.

He landed in a field where a dozen Germans were waiting.

They ran over and, seeing that Bader had only one leg, assumed that the other had been severed in the fall. What they couldn't understand was the lack of blood. They took Bader to a hospital from which news of the missing leg eventually reached Churchill. On hearing it he ordered a new leg, with a note attached, to be parachuted into France. There must have been some co-operation from the Germans because Bader received it.

Now stuck in a prisoner-of-war camp and bored, Bader tried every way to escape and succeeded too, managing to reach a village. However some German soldiers coming down the road towards him made him dart into the first house he saw. There, a husband and wife took him in and hid him in their back yard under a pile of straw. He might have got away with that, had not a Nazi search party come prodding with bayonets, forcing him to jump up and show himself. The French husband and wife, now in deep trouble, were taken away. Only the wife survived. Bader had to live out the rest of the war in the escape-proof castle of Colditz.

For our screenplay we approached two writers, HE Bates and William Douglas Home. Both turned it down, saying that the book was too big, too unmanageable. The person who seemed to solve the problem was Bader himself. "Why are you messing about with all these other writers?" he said to me. "You've written scripts, haven't you? So, do it yourself." Danny Angel was quite happy with this idea and suggested I spend some time with Paul Brickhill.

Paul lived in Italy and that's where I went with Hylda for a few very useful, if not very industrious, days talking over the basics – what should be in, what should be out and what was the kernel of the whole thing in the first place. As he had been a pilot in the Royal Australian Air Force Paul proved to be a mine of information. It was good too having Hylda there, because this time she was not only behind the project but determined to keep me at it. Paul's wife then told us about the writing of the book. Her husband and Bader had worked on it over very long periods of time, during which Bader's frequent outbursts of "You're wrong! This isn't working! I don't want to do this book anymore!" had nearly driven Paul to a nervous breakdown.

Very early on, we had to think about who was to play Bader. When your hero actually exists, getting the casting right is even harder than usual. Laurence Olivier turned us down. He thought it was impossible to play Bader and even suggested Bader play the part himself. We didn't go for that and tried Richard Burton. He was interested enough but a big Hollywood picture, *Alexander the Great*, came up and off he went to do that. It was not a success.

At this point, Danny Angel started talking about an actor whose first break had been with Vivian Van Damm, Danny's father-in-law, the man who ran the Windmill Theatre. This was Kenneth More. Kenny had left the Navy with no idea of what to do with himself. All he knew was that he had enjoyed reading the news for his ship's radio station because he had been able to throw the odd joke in. The job he got as Van Damm's assistant was probably an attempt to get near the girls who posed nude on the stage. He would have been disappointed. Those girls were very closely guarded. The strictness of the Windmill's rules can best be understood when you realise that the nude girls, once on stage and in position, were not allowed to move. If they had moved the theatre would have lost its licence. Kenny's job was to supervise the comics who came on between the nude tableaux. When one of them went missing, he rushed to Van Damm in a panic. "What shall I do?" he said.

"Do?" said Van Damm, "What you do is go on yourself. Nobody's going to notice. As you well know, our audiences have no interest in the comic at all. When he comes on the newspapers go up." So Kenny did go on, surprising himself and everybody else by getting a laugh. It happened by accident, simply because he had to wear the comic's costume. His trousers were too short and his boots were too big but that moment changed his life. As soon as he heard the laughter he was hooked. He became an actor, and little did he know how far along his chosen path he would travel. He hadn't trained but he had a natural talent, and he quickly rose to become a leading man.

One day he was playing golf with his great friend, the actor Roland Culver, when Roland told him that he had just been sent a new piece by Terence Rattigan which had a part in it that Kenny was born to play. The only trouble was, Jimmy Hanley had the job. Weeks went by during which the play was rehearsed and then taken to Edinburgh for a tryout. Only at that point was it seen that Jimmy Hanley wasn't making it. Roland Culver at once recommended Kenny and that is how he came to play the boyish ex-RAF lover Freddie Page in *The Deep Blue Sea*. He scored such a success in the part that he was asked to star in the film version opposite Vivien Leigh. It was round about then that Danny Angel started to talk about him. I asked Kenny to come and see us, and as soon as he walked through the door I knew he was Douglas Bader.

To help him find the character and learn Bader's distinctive walk, he and I and Bader went up to Gleneagles so that the two of them could play golf. Despite Kenny being a good player, Bader beat him. After an exhausting 18 holes we headed for the bar where Bader leant up against the fireplace with his pint and his pipe. "Now then, More," he said, "shall we make it another 18 this afternoon?"

"I don't think I could," said Kenny, "I'm absolutely pooped."

"In that case," said Bader, "I'd better get ready for lunch," and upstairs he went.

Kenny turned to Thelma, his wife. "That was the most amazing game I have ever played in my life," he said. "How does Douglas do it? His balance is phenomenal. But he wouldn't have played another round this afternoon, would he?"

"If you had said 'Yes' he would have, without a doubt, all 18 holes," said Thelma, "Right now, though, he'll be up in his room taking off his legs and the stumps will be raw and bleeding." This was the character we had to deal with.

When the script was finished we sent it to Bader. The next thing Douglas burst in, saying,"Gilbert, you've made a terrible hash of this. It's hopeless. You've left out half my friends."

"If I put all the friends that are in the book into the film," I said, "the script will run to a thousand pages and the film will last ten hours. We have to reduce the whole thing to a couple of hours."

"That's *your* problem," said Bader. "All I can say is that if you don't put my friends in, I won't co-operate and then you won't be able to make the film. In any case, how are you going to make a film about a man who's missing both his legs?"

"Douglas," I said, "this is film. If an ape can climb up the Empire State Building, we can solve the problem of the legs."

"Impossible," said Bader. All this was beginning to get on my nerves, particularly as Danny was also in the room and both men were walking up and down, crossing each other, Danny on crutches, Bader on his tin legs, both arguing at the tops of their voices. The only person there with a fully functioning set of real legs was me but I was sitting down, wishing I could get out of the room so that I could start sorting out the problem.

I went to the hospital at Roehampton where Bader's artificial legs had been fitted. Did they know of someone who had a similar disability? "Yes," said one of the doctors, "I've got just the man for you." We interviewed him, and indeed we could see that his disability was exactly the same as Bader's, and when I stood behind him I could see that he was remarkably similar to Kenny. We could shoot him from the back and, if we kept the camera far enough away, even from the front. We engaged him at once. At the same time, the doctor at Roehampton came up with a set of special clamps to keep Kenny's real legs rigid and force him to kick them outwards when he walked, just like Bader did. To a loud fanfare of publicity the shooting of the film went ahead.

The first few days were taken up with Kenny apparently walking on his artificial legs. I thought we'd better show these scenes to Bader, partly to make him feel included and partly to make sure we were on the right track. He was horrified. "This is terrible," he said. "It's nothing like me at all. We can't go on."

To calm him down, I suggested that we show the material to his friends in the RAF, famous pilots from the Battle of Britain like AC Deere and Peter Cadbury, great fellows. "If they agree with you that it's not the way you walk," I said, "we'll reshoot the scenes so they are happy and you are happy." About six of them came down to the studio, grinning away because they knew that Douglas had a short fuse and they were looking forward to teasing him, pulling his leg, so to speak.

"Well, what do you think?" asked Douglas when they'd seen the footage.

"It's not really like you – " said one.

"I told you so!" said Douglas jumping up. "I told you it was nothing like me – "

"Hang on Douglas, we haven't finished," said his colleague. "All we mean is that it isn't like you because Kenneth More is walking better than you." During the entire shoot, we never heard from Douglas again. He refused to visit the studio.

The film included a parade ground scene and this was shot on the very ground at Uxbridge I had marched across when I had joined up. It brought back the memory of a famous incident I had seen with my own eyes all those years ago. To walk across the parade ground then was absolutely forbidden, but doing just that was a character called Harry Tracy. He was an airman who toured the camps with an RAF variety production called *The Gang Show*, which meant he wore a uniform and had a rank but, apart from that, was pure showbusiness. In his case this meant long hair, an unbuttoned jacket and a cap set at a rakish angle on the back of his head. A sergeant, at first only seeing a man in the wrong place, yelled, "Airman!" but when Harry stopped and looked around this sergeant couldn't believe his eyes. "Get off the fucking parade ground!" he ordered. "And fucking get over here!" Harry adopted a charming smile and minced slowly over to him. Flabbergasted, the sergeant looked him up and down and said, "What the hell are you doing in this air force?"

"Well," said Harry, "since you ask, I'm a character lady."

Utterly bewildered by now, the sergeant screamed, "At least, get your fucking hair cut!"

"What?" said Harry sweetly, "And ruin my performance?"

Shortly after I had finished making the film a phone call came from Earl St John at the Rank Organisation. He said that 'JD' wanted a meeting with me. JD was John Davis, the top man at Rank and a monster whose employees lived in fear and trembling of him. "What time?" I asked.

"Eight o'clock," said Earl.

"Dinner, you mean?" I said.

"No," said Earl, "eight in the morning."

"That's a bit early for me," I said. "I may have to sleep with him."

"Please Lewis," said Earl, "don't make jokes like that."

When I arrived at the office there was Earl St John, standing discreetly behind John Davis. "Earl!" barked Davis. "Move yourself. Get Mr Gilbert a chair." This was terribly embarrassing. Earl St John was a very senior figure at Pinewood and old enough to be my father. He was also a very charming man. It turned out that all Davis wanted to discuss was the premiere. The actual film, he was delighted with.

"What about Douglas?" I asked. We had, after all, heard nothing from him since that showing of the early rushes.

"Don't worry about him," said Davis. "We'll invite him and his wife to a special showing just for them, and afterwards give them a really good lunch at the Dorchester."

Douglas and Thelma came, saw the film and sat down for lunch in one of the Dorchester's private rooms. A sumptuous meal was laid on, with champagne, cigars, the lot. Throughout the meal not one word about *Reach for the Sky* was spoken. Every other subject under the sun was touched on but not the film. As coffee was being poured, John Davis spoke up. "Douglas," he said, "we all think this is a great film and you should be very proud."

"I'm glad you think so because I don't." said Douglas. Davis's face began to redden. He too had a short temper and he was not used to being spoken to like that. However, he was now facing a man who was his equal. I could see it was a struggle for him.

The Four Kemptons. George, my father, at the top, Renée, my mother, just underneath.

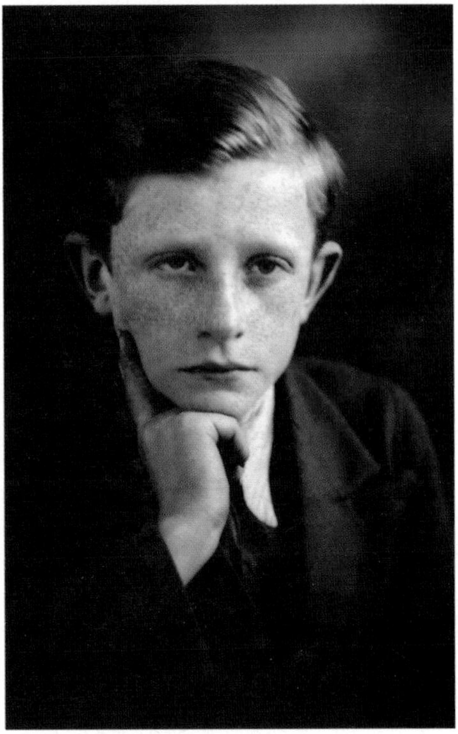

Lewis, the budding actor.

Good Morning, Boys! Will Hay in the middle, Graham Moffatt to the left of him, looking skywards, and me second from the right.

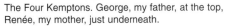

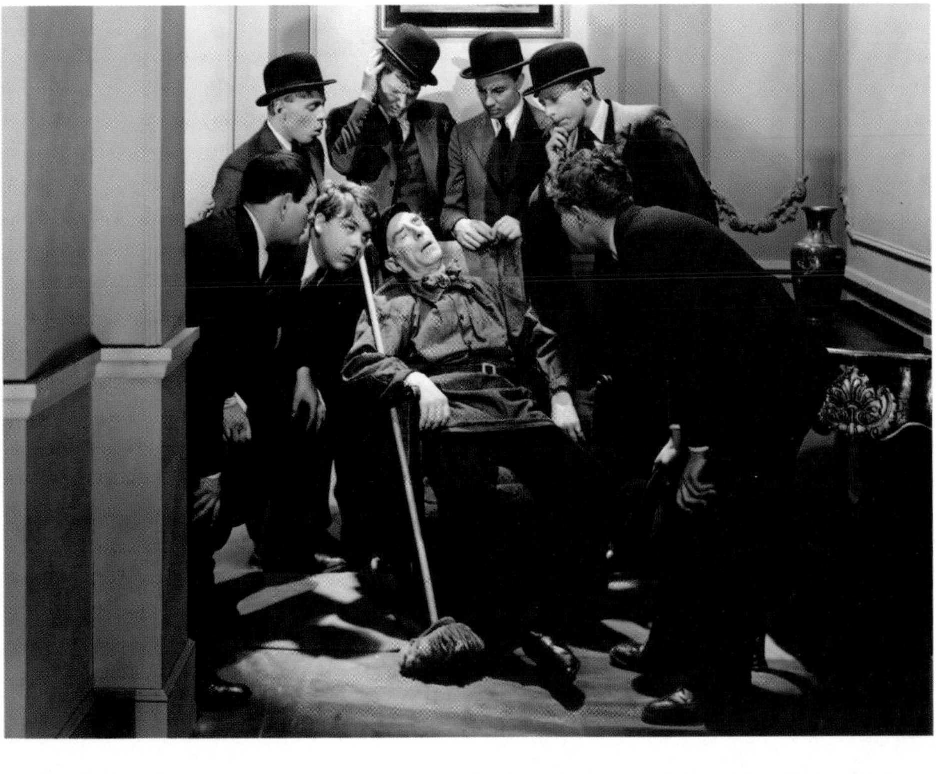

Laurence Olivier gives me an acting lesson in *The Divorce of Lady X*.

Flying Officer Gilbert in the unusual cold of Cairo.

Hylda, my wife, modelling for Batchelors Peas.

Kenneth More gave Douglas Bader a charm he didn't have.

On location in Bermuda for *The Admirable Crichton*. Me, Hylda, Kenneth More and Jack Watling.

Virginia McKenna gave a great performance as the true-life heroine, Violette Szabo.

With Hylda, two of my wartime friends from Johannesburg, Virginia McKenna and Bill Travers on the set of *Carve Her Name With Pride*.

On location with Curt Jürgens, making *Ferry to Hong Kong*.

Directing Susan Burnet and Tommy Steele in *Light Up The Sky*.

Hylda and myself with Kenneth More drafted in as clapper boy on *The Greengage Summer*.

The opening night of the smash hit *Alfie*.

My son, John, associate producer on *Alfie*, with cast member Jane Asher.

Michael Caine spread across Vivien Merchant, Jane Asher, Julia Foster and Shelley Winters at a photocall in London.

In discussion with Sean Connery during the making of *You Only Live Twice*.

Tetsuro Tamba, Mie Hama, myself, and Sean Connery on the volcano set at Pinewood.

My son, Stephen, in front of the real volcano in Japan.

Sean dedicated this picture to Hylda. I'm in the background, wearing a baseball cap.

On location in Japan with Tetsuro Tamba and Akiko Wakabayashi.

"No, it won't do," Douglas went on. "You'll get no co-operation from me. I mean, that scene when I've been a prisoner of war for three years and I come home and greet my wife, I never said stuff like that." John Davis was now bright red.

"Douglas," I said quickly, "are you telling us that after 15 years you can remember, word for word, what you said to Thelma? If you can, I think you should write the scene." Naturally he couldn't remember and that made him huff and puff all the more until finally he said that he would not be coming to the premiere.

John Davis, fighting hard to remain civil, said, "That's up to you but you'll miss a great evening."

A few weeks later the premiere took place at the Odeon Leicester Square and it really was a great evening. Half the British film industry turned up plus the bigwigs from the war and all those famous Battle of Britain pilots. It was marvellous. At midnight Hylda and I, and Hylda's brother Sydney (who was in the film) along with Kenny More and his wife, Billie, drove to Fleet Street to look at the very first review. In those days, newspapers were actually printed in Fleet Street, the most influential paper being *The Daily Express*. It had the biggest circulation and a very powerful film critic, Leonard Moseley. "Is the first edition up yet?" I asked the man at the door.

"Not just yet," he answered. "Why do you want to know?"

I pointed back at the others in the car. "We've just made a film and we wanted to see the review."

"Ah, well then," he said good-naturedly, "I happen to have a copy right here. It's mine but you can keep it." And, from behind his desk he produced the paper. I took it with trembling hands and, without reading it, went back to the car. Very nervously we turned the pages and there it was, a huge headline: 'Squadron

Leader Bader, you were wrong. You missed a great evening.' Underneath, the notice Moseley gave was excellent. We were cock-a-hoop. After all our worries with Bader, someone was at last taking our side.

A couple of days later I was walking across Leicester Square when I looked up at the Odeon Cinema and stopped dead in my tracks. Underneath the title *Reach for the Sky*, in lights it said: 'Directed by Lewis Gilbert.' I thought back to my grandmother, Louisa, who had said when I was a child, "You are the one who will have his name up in lights," and felt a little catch in my throat. How proud she would have been. For all her dodgy past and her blarney, she had started something and the job she had given me was to see it through.

As *Reach for the Sky* was my first big hit, one Sunday afternoon I took Hylda and my younger son, Stephen, out for a drive round the suburbs to see how the film was doing in the various cinemas. Hylda and I commented excitedly on all the queues we saw, and we saw many. Stephen, though very little, was taking this in. We knew, because as we approached yet another cinema he popped his head up and asked, "Any queues?" He was learning fast.

In due course, the film went on release countrywide where it made quite a stir, not to mention rather a lot of money. It was then that the Rank Organisation received a telephone call from the manager of the Odeon Southampton. The night before he had seen Douglas Bader come in with eight friends. Not only had they stayed all the way through, but they had come over to him afterwards to tell him how much they had enjoyed it. Gratifying as this was, I assumed that it would be the last I would hear of Bader. It wasn't quite. Many years later I was watching television when on came *This Is Your Life*. You never know who it's going to be, so I waited to see. To my great surprise it was Douglas Bader, now much older and by then, running Shell's fleet of aircraft. "How do you feel about the film, *Reach for the Sky*?" asked the presenter Eamonn Andrews. "I understand you weren't very impressed."

"At the time I think I was too close to it," said Bader, "but now, on looking back, I realise events have proved me wrong and I don't think it's so bad." At that I jumped out of my chair and practically ran round the room. At last, *at last*, I had got something out of him. He didn't think the picture was all that bad.

Years after that, John Davis's secretary rang inviting me for lunch with JD. By then he was retired but still had an office. I didn't know whether to be flattered or whether to think he was merely having difficulty finding lunch partners in his retirement. I went. What a transformation. The man who for decades had terrorised the Rank Organisation and been loathed by all was now just a kindly, white-haired old gentleman reminiscing about a golden past.

14
The Master and the Monster

When the playwright JM Barrie wrote *The Admirable Crichton* in 1902 he could have had little idea how, over the best part of a century, his play would inspire so many different versions in different media.

The success of *Reach for the Sky* had made Kenneth More and myself keen to do another film together and so, late in 1956, both of us were on the lookout for subjects. Kenny was under contract to Sir Alexander Korda, still the most famous producer in British films, and told him of our hunt. Without hesitation Korda said, "I've got the very subject, *The Admirable Crichton.* It's the perfect film for you both. Paramount used to own the rights but I did them a favour and now I have them in return. Actually I've been wanting to do it myself for years but I'd love you two to do it because you're young and I'm a bit too old, I'm afraid."

"What do you think?" said Kenny when we next met up, "Do you know the play?"

"Of course I do," I said. "I saw it not so long ago." And then I told him how Paramount had first made it in 1919 as a silent film and then again as a musical called *We're not Dressing* in the thirties with Bing Crosby and Carole Lombard.

"Could we do it?" said Kenny. At first I thought there might be a danger of staginess, but then I recalled what I remembered of the plot – Lord Loam and his three daughters are shipwrecked on a tropical island with their butler, Crichton, and the resourcefulness of the butler upends the status quo. It was simple. It was charming, and at that time in the fifties seemed like a colourful contrast to all the war films we were making.

So, in answer to Kenny's question, I said, "Perhaps we can but I ought to talk to Sir Alex first to make sure we're on the same wavelength."

The next day the phone rang. It was Sir Alex's secretary. Would I care to come round for dinner that evening at 7.30? Care? If anything I was overwhelmed. The man had meant so much both to the British film industry and, of course, to me. I went and was utterly charmed.

He started by recounting his own early struggles. First, he had been a journalist in Budapest. There he had got into silent films and then moved on to Paris and London. "And would you be interested in doing this film with Kenneth?" he finally asked.

"Please, give me a couple of days," I replied, "just to read the play and have a think. By then I'll be able to give you a definite answer."

As he was happy with that, he changed the subject. "Tell me," he asked, "when I meet young directors or actors I'm always curious to know how they got started."

'Ah, he doesn't remember me.' I thought. "You gave me my first break," I said.

"Did I?" said Korda, looking amused. "You'll have to tell me how." And so I told him of being a 17 year-old child actor who had acted in his film, *The Divorce of Lady X*, and how he had asked me if I wanted to go to drama school and I had said that I wanted to become a film director and he had given me a job as a third assistant. "Good God, you were that child actor. I remember now. Though I have to say, after I sent you to see Mr Cunynghame I probably forgot all about it. Still, it's nice to know I helped someone along in their career."

"Well?" said Kenny two days later after I had read the play. "Are you thinking of that tropical island and all that sunshine?"

"I am, I am," I said. "We'll do it."

"Come on," he said, "Let's ring Sir Alex now," and he handed me the receiver. I dialled Korda's office and explained to the secretary that he would be expecting my call. There was a long pause.

"I'm so sorry, Mr Gilbert," she said. "I was just about to ring you. Sir Alex died early this morning." For a moment I was in shock. Obviously Kenny could see this but couldn't imagine what had happened. When I was able to tell him he was, if anything, in a worse state than I. Not only was Korda handling his career, the two were the greatest of friends. I had one consolation. In the nick of time I had been able to thank Korda for setting me on the road to my career. *The Admiral Crichton*, on the other hand, looked like it was going nowhere.

Within a very short time Columbia Pictures not only took over Korda's backlist but also his current projects. A call came through. Would I still be interested in making the film? "If Kenny More is still the star, very much so," I said.

The location for our tropical island was Bermuda, which was a shame because it wasn't tropical. Someone who had discovered the same thing and who was shortly to move from there to Jamaica, where I wish we had gone, was Noël Coward. He had made his home in Bermuda for tax reasons, and one day the cast and I received an invitation to drop by for drinks. Home was actually two houses, one where he liked to be alone to work, the other where his two constant companions lived. The Loved Ones, he called them. These were his secretary Cole Lesley, and the actor Graham Payn, for whom he had written one of his most poignant songs, 'Matelot'. It was a memorable evening because Coward was such a good raconteur. His stories of working in the theatre were so funny that the next day I woke up with a pain in my side from laughing.

Although we had never met, Coward seemed to be aware of what I had done because, while describing his early career, he looked over at me and said, "You'd know something about this. I was a child actor out of work at Christmas, just the time of year you would expect to be employed. *Peter Pan*, *Where the Rainbow Ends*, pantomimes, I was in none of them. Nothing worse can happen to you, nothing." So that, for him, was the one moment in his entire life when he had hit rock bottom. As I had experienced this myself, it was something we shared.

Coward told us his latest passion was cooking. He loved it. The Loved Ones told us they loved it too and couldn't wait for his next creation. "The Master's amazing," they said, "an absolute natural, and the cooking is so inventive." At that moment the telephone rang and Coward left the room. Hardly was the door shut than the Loved Ones clutched our arms and said, "He's killing us. He's killing us with his bloody cooking. Whatever you do, don't encourage him." We, the guests, fell about, barely having time to compose ourselves before Coward returned and the Loved Ones could resume their flattery as if nothing had happened.

Hylda had not been with us that evening as she had flown to New York to see her old friend Sheila Huntingdon, the one who had introduced me to her in 1944. When I phoned New York that night to tell Hylda about the party she sounded rather cool.

She was heartbroken – Coward was one of her idols and she would so liked to have been there.

In 1969 a celebration of Noël Coward's 70th birthday was held at the Phoenix Theatre in London before an invited audience. The place was packed, and after colleagues had told stories and sung songs Coward's old friend Lord Mountbatten made a speech. It began, "I suppose there have been better actors than Noël Coward," which startled me a bit but then it went on, "and I suppose there have been better playwrights than Noël Coward and better novelists and better short story writers and better revue sketch writers and better poets and better diarists and better composers and better lyricists and better theatre directors and better film directors and better ballet librettists and better cabaret performers and better painters than Noël Coward, but never in the history of the world has one man contributed so much to so many different fields in art and entertainment." It was true too. There was nothing Coward hadn't attempted and excelled at.

The Admirable Crichton was not only an enjoyable film to make and one I remember with pleasure, it also provoked an unexpected reaction from an unexpected quarter. I was finishing my next film *A Cry from the Streets*, a story about some cockney children in an orphanage, while simultaneously working on the screenplay of *Carve Her Name With Pride*, the film that was to come afterwards, when I received a phone call from Mike Frankovich, head of Columbia in the UK. He told me that an advance print of *The Admirable Crichton* had been sent to Columbia Pictures in America. "And Harry Cohn's fallen in love with it," he went on excitedly. "You've got to get over to New York tomorrow morning. Be on the first plane, so get there early."

Mike was talking about Harry Cohn, the head of Columbia Pictures and the monster whose widow, Joan, would one day marry Laurence Harvey. "I know when a picture's no good," Cohn would say. "It's when I start to shift about in my seat." This pronouncement gave rise to Orson Welles's remark, "So the whole of Columbia is plugged into Harry Cohn's ass." Which made Welles another enemy. The character of Cohn was taken by the writer Clifford Odets and put into a play *The Big Knife*. Odets changed the name but nobody was in any doubt who he was talking about. In real life Cohn had a mistress, Kim Novak, with whom Sammy Davis Jr had an affair. He paid for it with a beating and a lost eye, said to have been organised by Cohn. Later, Davis changed his religion to Judaism and, on being asked over a game of golf for his handicap, answered, "I'm a one-eyed Jewish black man and you have to ask what my handicap is?"

As Mike Frankovich talked, these were the thoughts that were running through my head. "Just a minute, Mike," I said. "This is all very exciting and flattering but I haven't any money. There's a restriction on dollars here. How would I get a ticket? Where would I get it from?"

"Don't be naive," said Mike. "We're talking about Harry Cohn. You go to the airport and you collect your ticket at the desk."

"But I'll be landing in New York without a penny," I said.

"Yes," said Mike, "and somebody will meet you at the airport and look after you. Don't worry. Get on the plane and go. Remember, nobody disappoints Harry Cohn."

The thought of meeting the most hated of Hollywood studio bosses was not one I relished but ambition got the better of me. I went to the airport and, just as Mike had said, there at the desk was a ticket for me. A first class ticket. Even so, on the plane and walking across the tarmac at the airport in New York, I was still convinced that nobody would meet me and that I would have no money and that extricating myself from such a fix would be near impossible.

"Mr Gilbert?" It was a man from Columbia Pictures. "Come this way," and past customs the two of us sailed, out to the longest limousine I had ever seen. At the Waldorf Astoria Hotel we sailed past reception too, straight to the lift, in which I was informed that we were going up to a suite that Columbia owned. They kept it for special guests. When the door slid back I could see this with my own eyes. It was one of the biggest suites I have ever set foot in. I wasn't comfortable though. I still had no money. A tap at the door interrupted my fretting. Outside in the corridor I found an envelope containing a great wad of dollar bills and a note. 'Enjoy yourself. Harry,' it said. Nice words but to me they sounded like the voice of doom.

The next morning I rang Harry Cohn's New York office and was put through to his secretary. After I had told her who I was and had requested her to thank Mr Cohn for all he had done, I asked if I should come in that day. "Hold on one moment, Mr Gilbert," she answered and a silence followed. "Mr Cohn says it's impossible today," was the next thing I heard, "but he wants me to look after you. Is there anything you would particularly like to do?" This could have meant anything but I settled for theatre tickets and went to see Frank Loesser's latest show, *The Most Happy Fella*, a very good musical based on Sidney Howard's play *They Knew What they Wanted*.

The next day it was the same thing. "Mr Cohn wants to know if you're enjoying yourself."

"Yes," I said. "I am enjoying myself but I would like to see Mr

Cohn because I have to get back to England soon."

"That reminds me," said the secretary, ignoring my request, "Can you let us have your passport? We need it for immigration."

'Uh-oh,' I thought. 'This could be very difficult.' However, having no reason to refuse her I was soon handing the passport over to a messenger boy.

Four days went by during which I was treated like royalty. I ate huge meals and each night saw a show. On my way down Broadway to see one of them I bumped into Sid Hyams, one of the two brothers who had owned Eros Films, and with whom I had practically started out. I told him of my recent experience which he found very funny, even if I didn't. "Are you doing anything tonight?" I asked.

"Nothing special," he answered and, as I had two tickets for the show, off we trotted to the theatre. On the way, Sid, the pessimistic one – his brother, Phil, was outgoing – went on at me for having given up my passport to Harry Cohn. "You'll never get back now," he said. "You'll be stuck here forever."

At last, after four days came the telephone call I had been waiting for. Would I please come to Mr Cohn's office at ten o'clock the next morning? I couldn't help but wonder why I had been forced to hurry across the Atlantic for an urgent meeting, only to be kept waiting four days. I suppose that was Harry Cohn's way of demonstrating his powers. Still, when the next morning came I rushed to his office like a lunatic. Once there I was ushered into a huge room in which Harry Cohn sat at a desk, surrounded by five or six other men dotted around the desk, standing. These were Noddy men, because whenever Harry Cohn spoke they nodded vigorously like puppets on strings. "It's very good to see you," said Cohn whose chair, I noticed, was perched on a dais. "We thought your picture was terrific. We could never make a picture like that here."

'So far, so good,' I thought. 'Perhaps he'll give me another picture.' Certainly the Noddy men's heads were nodding so hard I was worried they might come off.

"Let me tell you why I've asked you here," Cohn went on, as I spotted the reason for the dais. His head was huge like a lion's but his body was small. "I've thought about it and I have the perfect picture for you. Right now what I want is for you to come back to Hollywood with me and I will put not just the picture but the whole studio in your hands." And with that, he clapped his hands together. This was going a bit far but I thought I'd better stick with it, for the time being at least.

"What's the picture you actually want me to do?" I asked.

"*The Solid Gold Cadillac*," he answered, "with Judy Holliday. You know Judy Holliday?"

"Of course I know Judy Holliday," I said. "I love Judy Holliday. I think she's the most wonderful actress."

"That's settled then," said Cohn, "You'll come back with me – "

"Excuse me," I said. "I have one slight problem. I'm already making a film with the Rank Organisation – "

"Don't worry about that," said Cohn. "John Davis is a great friend of mine. He'll cancel it. There's no problem."

"Yes, but I don't want to cancel it," I said. "I've been working on it for six months."

"What's the film?" asked Cohn. "*Carve Her Name With Pride*," I answered. "It's about a British secret agent during the war."

"You mean you're turning down a Judy Holliday comedy with Columbia for some crap war film?" said Harry.

"I have no choice," I answered. "I'm under contract. In any

case, it's a film I want to do and I must do it."

"I'll tell you what," said Harry, "go and see Judy tonight. She's in *Bells are Ringing* on Broadway. She'd love to meet you, I know." By now I was getting a bit worried, but as I thought it would be nice to meet Judy Holliday I agreed to go. "Fine," said Harry Cohn. "We'll talk tomorrow morning."

The show *Bells are Ringing* was very good and Judy Holliday was excellent in it. She sang the song 'The Party's Over', which includes the line, 'It's time to call it a day.' This made me feel sad because it seemed to be telling me something. After the show I went backstage. "I'm so glad you're here," said Judy. "Harry thinks you'd be wonderful for the film. I just wish I could see *The Admirable Crichton*."

"I'm sure Harry'll arrange it for you," I said, "but I must tell you I can only do this film if Harry puts it back. I'm contracted to do a picture in England and it starts in six weeks."

The next morning I rang Harry Cohn and hardly had time to say, "Judy's delightful," before he interrupted me with, "So you'll do the picture?"

"I would love to," I said, "but would you be prepared, in some way, to put it back until I've finished my film in England?"

The line went dead. 'Uh-oh,' I thought and, sure enough, I couldn't get through again. Then I remembered that I didn't have my passport. I also remembered Sid Hyams's pessimistic warnings. So how was I going to get it back? A sinister feeling that I was trapped in New York, never to go home, crept over me. The Sammy Davis Jr story lurking at the back of my mind didn't help either. How would I look with one eye, I wondered. Harry Cohn gave everyone, not just me, the feeling that he was capable of anything.

After that things got a bit more prosaic. The passport was

returned and I flew back to England where I told the whole story to John Davis. He looked at me and said, "Bloody cheek," nothing else. He had no idea what my loyalty to him had cost me. I imagined the conversation Harry Cohn would have had with him if I'd said yes to *The Solid Gold Cadillac*. "Listen John, don't you worry about a thing. I'll make it up to you." All that kind of stuff. Merely contemplating it was awful.

Funnily enough I went on to make quite a few films for Columbia, but by then Harry Cohn was dead. At his funeral someone expressed amazement because so many people had turned up. "Give the public what they want," said a spectator, "and they'll come." I like to imagine JM Barrie in Harry Cohn's office. What would those two have said to each other? And what would Barrie have made of the Noddy men?

Back in London around this time, Hylda and I badly needed someone to keep our affairs in order. A friend knew of a friend who could type. A few days later Tessa Hodgson, barely out of her teens, came to the house and was casually asked by us if she would like some work. She said yes, but that she had a holiday booked and would be away for a month. I explained that I needed to start work with her right away. "Let me think about it," she said, but in no time she had cancelled the holiday and was ready for work. None of us could predict that she was to become indispensable. Years passed. Decades passed. Tessa Hodgson became Tessa Bloy, had children and took on all the responsibilities which that entails. She also found herself with lots of other jobs. Even so, she still kept coming to our house to sort us out and keep us in order. One day this would take on an even greater importance.

15
Violette and Virginia

Carve Her Name With Pride turned out to be one of my favourite films. It started with a dinner organised by Hylda in 1957. Among the guests was RJ Minney, an old friend who had produced *The Wicked Lady* in the 1940s. This was the film that Hylda was acting in when I first met her. Later, in the early 1950s, he had written the screenplay of *Time, Gentlemen, Please!*, a comedy about almshouses that I had directed. He had also been the editor of a well respected newspaper, *The Sunday Referee*.

Our conversation that evening turned to what each of us was doing and this led Minney to tell the true story of Violette Szabo, a woman spy in the Second World War. She had been born Violette Bushell in South London, of a French mother and an English father, and had been married to a French man, Etienne Szabo, for only a few months when he was killed at the Battle of El Alamein in 1942. A few months later their daughter, Tania, was born. Instead of settling down to her job at the Bon Marché store in Brixton, Violette found that her grief at losing Etienne had turned into restlessness. She told her parents that she wanted to join the army and serve in the Auxiliary Territorial Service. As both mother and father had lived and fought through the First World War, they agreed and took on the child almost as their own.

Work in the ATS was at first pretty ordinary, but one day Violette read in Orders, 'Interesting jobs for women fluent in French.' With a French mother, a French husband and holidays spent in France with French relatives, she was completely fluent in the language and decided to apply. At the interview her knowledge proved so impressive that one of the jobs was offered to her. It would be dangerous, she was told, but it would be one she could do well. She accepted and next found herself at a school she realised was for training spies. Its task was to teach trainees not only parachute jumps, unarmed combat and the use of firearms, but also to test mental strength. What could an operative stand up to, if he or she were caught?

In a way, Violette's first test was having to say goodbye to her parents and daughter when she was told there was a mission she was needed for. The family could know nothing of it. Only the amount of emotion that was appropriate for someone travelling to a humdrum posting in the north of England could be shown. The rest had to be held back. "If you don't hear from me for a while, don't worry," had to be said quite casually.

The job was in occupied France, and was to liaise with a highly regarded British spy who had been working undercover there for some time. He had the code name Excalibur. The information he had collected needed passing on. Violette's task was to memorise it and bring it back. The danger of this particular mission came from her good looks. However it turned out that coping with the unwanted attention of German soldiers was something she was good at and she met Excalibur as planned. He gave her the information, checked that she had memorised it, and then told her that she would soon be contacted with details of her return journey. In the meantime he was going to give her some foreign currency to keep her going during the time left to her in France. With that, he handed her a large sum of French francs. Although this meeting had been formal and brief, it had been long enough for Violette to find herself attracted to him.

During the period of waiting Violette, being in some ways a typical girl, went shopping in Paris. Even at such an extraordinary and dangerous time, nothing was going to stop her from doing that. At the Dior fashion house in the Avenue Montaigne she saw an evening dress of such beauty that she had to have it. The French francs were supposed to be for an emergency, but in Violette's eyes this *was* an emergency. She would never find a dress like that in England. When she later met the French Resistance officer who was to help her out of the country, she had the dress under her arm, all wrapped up. At an improvised airfield, a little plane landed but only for a few seconds. Nevertheless, it was the package containing the dress that was on the plane first. Violette threw it ahead of herself and only then, with the plane's engine still running, did she herself jump aboard.

After she had been congratulated on the success of her mission, Violette was told that she could settle back into her old ATS life for the time being. At least this enabled her to see her family again.

A period of comparative flatness seemed all she could look forward to, but one day into the office walked the British officer whom she knew as Excalibur. Violette, in a manner quite un-military, gave him a big hug and went out with him to celebrate at a Knightsbridge nightclub. For the first time she could see him in his officer's uniform and he was able to see the dress. When she told him how she had come by it he was most amused and his reprimand for the misuse of official funds completely lacked conviction. He was not the only one to notice the dress. As Violette passed a table where two women were sitting, one of them was heard to say to the other, "Black market, I'll be bound. Some people don't know there's a war on."

Only a little time went by before Violette had to say goodbye to her new friend Excalibur. He was needed in France again. Worse still, when she was asked to go on another mission she was told it could not be with him. That would be too dangerous. Nevertheless, she accepted the job and, back at her family's house in Brixton, it was goodbyes all over again, this time even more painful. One mission you might get away with because you were unknown but a second mission was really dangerous. By then, you could well be on someone's list.

Once more in France, Violette teamed up with a group of Resistance fighters. Her task and theirs was to blow up a train. They succeeded but the getaway went wrong. The plan was to confuse pursuers by splitting up and running in different directions but Violette, in racing through a wood with her French contact, tripped and sprained her ankle. As she could no longer move, she begged the contact to go on without her. He argued, of course, but with the Germans gaining on them he reluctantly realised that he would have to do as she said. The only chance to pass on news of the operation's success was to swim across a nearby lake. As he swam, Violette gave him covering fire with a Sten gun. She even managed to wound a few Germans before her ammunition ran out and she was forced to limp forward to give herself up. The French contact had at least made it to freedom but Violette was taken to Ravensbrück, a concentration camp north of Berlin. Here she was to be tortured and executed. On the way, the train transporting her was bombed by the British and everyone aboard had to climb off. Only then did she discover that her British officer friend, Excalibur, was also on the train and also under arrest. For a brief moment they were able to hold hands and say goodbye, knowing that they probably would never meet again. Seconds later, the order came to march off in different directions.

The story did not quite end there. In 1946 Violette's parents took their granddaughter, Tania, to Buckingham Palace where King George VI gave the little girl the George Cross. It was Violette's posthumous award. "Never forget your mother," said the King as he pinned the medal to Tania's dress. "She was a very brave lady who loved you very much."

When Minney finished his tale, he explained that he had just written a book on the subject, hence the story being on his mind. The book was to be published very shortly, and the rights were available. I made up my mind to see John Davis as soon as possible. At our meeting I told him that Minney's book, *Carve Her Name With Pride*, was the next film I wanted to make. Davis went ahead and bought the rights on behalf of the Rank Organisation.

Virginia McKenna played Violette Szabo. She was gentler than Violette but that very gentleness gave the character a certain vulnerability. Nice English girls and machine guns didn't go together. This was borne out in real life only too well. Virginia hated firing the Sten gun. Like most of us, she screwed her face up and closed her eyes. When she taught herself to do it properly, the result was usefully shocking. Like Kenneth More bringing charm to Douglas Bader, Virginia brought a quality to Violette Szabo that Violette probably didn't have. Violette, with her directness and south London accent, was probably tougher, but Virginia's vulnerability added something to the film.

I chose Paul Scofield to play Violette's wartime colleague, Excalibur. In the late 1950s Paul was the white hope of British theatre. On screen he had a quirky, gentle quality. A standard beefy hero he was not, but then neither were many heroes in the war and that is what made him interesting.

During the shooting of the picture, the gap between Virginia McKenna and Violette Szabo was made even harder for Virginia to cross because of a testing time in her private life. As it was, the work itself demanded enough of her. Every day she was being recounted details of an undercover agent's life by Odette Churchill who, like Violette, had been a spy but had survived. Odette was our technical adviser and what she said was stressful just to listen to. Then there was the weight of the responsibility towards Violette. Virginia didn't want to let her down but simply re-enacting the emotions of what she must have gone through was sometimes overwhelming and, perhaps, more frightening for her than for Violette because Violette by nature was better able to cope. Virginia's actor's imagination was running wild, and she found it a struggle.

On top of all this she was waiting to hear whether her boyfriend Bill Travers' divorce was going to come through as the two were desperate to get married. They had met and fallen in love while rehearsing a play, but Bill had not only been married at the time but had fathered a child. Not wishing to upset anyone, particularly the child, Virginia and Bill had decided to part and Virginia had married the actor Denholm Elliott on the rebound. This was a mistake. Virginia and Bill, no longer able to deny their feelings for each other, had reunited and Bill had asked his wife for a divorce. At the time of filming he and Virginia were living together. The wait to hear whether the divorce would come through was unbearable, so it wasn't surprising if the whole experience, the tough filming and the tense waiting, caused Virginia to break down in tears from time to time.

Matters were not helped by our associate producer Hugh Perceval, he of the thorough dousing at Hitchcock's hands on *Jamaica Inn*. You couldn't question his competence but he was hopeless at understanding actors. It wouldn't occur to him that playing an emotional part could be stressful for a sensitive actor, so when he found Virginia crying in her dressing room he ticked her off for being unprofessional. This, together with her other problems, really hit hard. I found that proposing a rest and some cold water for her eyes worked much better. Once on the set, Virginia's feelings never interfered with her performance. She was completely professional.

Thank heavens for the day, though, when Bill Travers sneaked on to the back of the set and gave her the thumbs up. He was signalling that the divorce had come through, which was a great relief. At last they could get married and have children. Virginia asked me for some time off. I gave her two days and she and Bill went to Paris on their honeymoon. Hugh Perceval wasn't very pleased about that either.

When *Carve Her Name With Pride* came out Alfred Hitchcock saw it and, not remembering that I already knew him, gave me a call. Casting for his latest thriller was in full swing and he was looking for a leading lady or, to be precise, a new Hitchcock blonde as Grace Kelly had retired to marry Prince Rainier of Monaco. Virginia had been contacted but she had turned the part down. Could I change her mind?

I rang Virginia, who very calmly said that she had a good marriage, a pretty home and a young family. Why jeopardise that? If she were to make the film with Hitchcock she would have to uproot herself, move to Hollywood, go round the studios, be seen at the right parties and that sort of thing. How would Bill and the children react to that? It was a risk she was not prepared to take. "If the film offers here run out," she told me, "Bill and I can always get a job at the local repertory theatre in Guildford. We'll get by."

When I relayed this to Hitchcock, he said, "She sounds very intelligent." And there the conversation ended. I couldn't go on. By then I was a well established director, but I was still so much in awe of Hitchcock. I couldn't pluck up the courage to say that, as a lowly 19 year-old third assistant director, I had once worked with him.

At the time of filming *Carve Her Name With Pride* I was visited by the writer Leo Marks, who had worked in the Code Section of the Special Operations Executive. He brought me the poem he had written for Violette to use as her signature code in 1943. It included the lines:

The love that I have
Of the life that I have
Is yours and yours and yours.

These lines of verse became an important feature of the film and people often remember those words first. Some time after the film was completed, they were set to music and Virginia McKenna sang them on a record. They echo the life of Violette Zsabo and act as her epitaph.

16

Real Life: On the Home Front

While Hylda was looking after our two sons, helping me in my career and being someone I was totally dependent on, she was also following her own private inclination – that of taking an interest in other people. These would not necessarily be people she knew well. In fact, the more unfamilar a person was the more her curiosity was aroused, and if she spotted a problem she didn't just make sympathetic noises. She tried to help out. It was on one of these occasions that a certain relationship with the family began which has lasted over 60 years.

Shortly after the war, we were friendly with a young couple called the Corries. We came to know them through John being at the same infants' school as their son, Tim. The two boys were exactly the same age, and it was they who waved Hylda off to hospital when she was about to have our son, Stephen.

Tim's father was an actor who had served in the RAF and lost an arm. In the immediate post-war period he fell on hard times. Together with his wife he would often come round to borrow five shillings, quite a sum in those days, to buy food. One day he walked into the sea and drowned. The mother fell apart. Whenever things got particularly bad, Hylda made a point of inviting Tim round to the house, maybe for an afternoon, maybe to spend the night. At this time, his mother came to see her. "If anything happens to me," she said, "please keep an eye out for Tim." This was not merely puzzling but alarming. The mother was neither old nor ill.

Shortly afterwards, the mother sent Tim to live with a man she had met but knew only a little. It was an extraordinary thing for her to do. He was a bachelor and lived alone. He was also horrible. Sexual abuse was not the problem. It was still abuse, though. He made the boy think that he could never do anything right. This reached such a pitch that Tim, aged six, ran out into the street and asked the first person he saw to direct him to the nearest police station. Whenever I think about this I'm amazed at the presence of mind in one so young. The stranger Tim spoke to didn't hesitate. He walked the little boy to the police station himself.

When the police heard the story they were appalled. They took Tim back to his mother and severely reprimanded her. If anything like that were to happen again, they said, she would be in serious trouble. It was not long afterwards that she died. How exactly I don't know, and we never really found out. Tim went to live with his grandmother. That was fine, but when he reached 12 the question of his secondary education arose. Hylda sprang into action. She knew, from my being in the RAF, that there was a fund for relatives of servicemen. She applied to it, and as a result Tim was sent to Reeds, a well-known public school. At holiday time he would either return to his grandmother or come to us, and that is how things continued for some years. During that time, Tim and John formed a friendship that lasts until today. He became one of the family. On leaving school he went to university, and among his first jobs was one with me in films. He married and became a fond father to three children. Now he is a well-known TV and film agent. I often ring him for advice.

17

Genius Sinks Ferry

In 1958 I made a film called *Ferry to Hong Kong*, a clash of personalities story with plenty of action and a colourful faraway location. It was unusual for the Rank Organisation to travel long distances at the time, so making the film in Hong Kong meant that we had to be the Picture of the Year.

The basic conflict in the story was between a sea captain and a tramp. The sea captain, a stickler for order and smartness, is a self-deluding martinet. He thinks his boat is a glamorous transatlantic liner. It isn't. It's nothing more than a ferry shuttling backwards and forwards between Hong Kong and Macao, a trip of four or five hours at the most.

The tramp is a decent man who, unable to face life, hides his true nature at the bottom of a bottle. His real problems, though, start when the local police, determined to be rid of a tiresome drunk, throw him on to the ferry without any papers. The scruffiness of his appearance is an immediate threat to the captain's order and smartness. Worse, when the ferry reaches Macao he can't be offloaded because that's Portuguese territory and he doesn't have a passport. He has to stay on the ferry, apparently forever, his unshaven face and dirty clothes driving the captain mad with frustration. The situation is exacerbated when a pretty schoolteacher and her 15 pupils meet the tramp and think he's really attractive and friendly. The captain is filled with a mixture of disgust and jealousy.

The German film star Curt Jürgens was to play this part. The tramp was to be an actor who had recently made his name in British films, having arrived here from Australia. His name was Peter Finch. Curt's strength was sternness with a hint of repression, while Peter's was a lazy, sexy charm. In other words they were well matched for the ensuing conflict, or would have been were it not for an unfortunate incident at Pinewood Studios. It occurred at a banquet held in honour of some Canadian sales executives the Rank Organisation was keen to impress. All the top brass had to be there and of course all the stars, including Peter Finch. In fact it was his job to make the official speech of welcome. Something I already knew about Peter was that, like his character in the film, he drank heavily. In his case this could lead to a souring of his mood. It happened at the banquet. What we got from him was a drunken tirade aimed directly at John Davis. The man was ruining the British film industry. He had no understanding of film, only money, and as long as he remained boss the Rank Organisation would never make a good film. That was the gist of it and the point was fair but it was not the time to make it, with John Davis sitting right there in front of us. The Canadians hadn't a clue what to think. They were merely shocked.

John Davis called me the next day. "You can forget Finch," he said. "That man does not come near this studio again." Which was all very well. The casting pool in those days was tiny. For your male lead you could have either Kenneth More or Dirk Bogarde and that was it. Peter Finch was a much-needed addition. As for John Mills, he was invariably hard at work on other films.

A few days later John Davis went to a premiere and saw *The Long, Hot Summer*, a film based on stories by William Faulkner. In it was Orson Welles playing a Deep South patriarch. "He was very good," said John. "Why don't we have him in the film?"

"If you pay him enough I'm sure you'll be able to," I said, "but what could he play?"

"The sea captain," said John.

"We've got a sea captain," I said, "Curt Jürgens. He's signed his contract."

"Maybe Curt could play the tramp," said John.

"But that's not so good," I said. "Curt as the captain is perfect." However it would have left Orson Welles playing the tramp which was really out of the question. He was far too old and unromantic. In the end Curt Jürgens decided that he wouldn't mind playing the tramp, because it would be something different. It certainly was but that's all it was. However, with him plumping for that part Orson Welles could only play the captain.

The two principal characters were supposed to dislike each other. The two actors playing them definitely did. Orson and Curt could not stand each other. An inkling of how this started came to me when Orson's Italian wife told Hylda that she hated Germans. During the Second World War her father had been persecuted by them. Evidently Orson had taken her side. I don't know whether he realised that Curt, himself ill at ease with his nationality, had become an Austrian. It didn't look like it, but anyway that wasn't all. Once upon a time, Orson had been a fine-looking man, and of course had directed the film that for years had topped many lists of best-ever films, *Citizen Kane*. Curt was a handsome matinee idol. Each wanted to be the other. Orson, fat and middle-aged, wanted to be young and handsome.

Curt wanted to be the genius of film and a great actor and that is also why neither could bear each other. Getting both of them to appear in the same shot was near impossible. In many scenes, each talked to the other from different shots. As for their close-ups, both refused to feed each other dialogue. That was left to the continuity girl who, as all continuity girls do, read the lines very flatly.

That was only one problem. Orson didn't have to be with Curt to be impossible. He could do that all by himself. I suppose his ship arriving at the wrong port in Hong Kong didn't help. Nobody was there to meet him and even though it was made clear that somebody was waiting at another port, it got us off to a bad start.

When I met him, I said that we would begin with a test which we would shoot the next day. "A test? What for?" said Orson. "I don't do tests."

"A make-up test," I said, "that's all. Just so the make-up man can settle on what he's going to do."

"No, that's not for me," said Orson. "I have one problem with my face – my nose. It's too small and I always fix that myself."

"How?" I asked.

"It's all arranged," said Orson, "I had a parcel sent ahead specially. Everything for making a false nose is in it."

"So it's here then?" I said.

"Yes," answered Orson, "it's here."

"But where?" I said, "We've heard nothing about it."

That night 20 people scoured every post office in Hong Kong. On this big picture with all its huge logistical problems, top of the agenda was the search for Orson's nose. Only after a very long time did someone find the missing parcel in one of the post offices. It was brought to us early the next morning.

Curiously, Orson didn't seem that pleased. "Now all we have to do," I said, "is hand this to the make-up man and we can get on with the test."

"But I shall be putting the nose on myself," said Orson, "Every day I'll be doing it. There's no need for a test." And that is what happened. He put the nose on himself every day. Only when scenes were cut together did we find out what we had let ourselves in for. Some shots had the nose tilting upwards. Others had it tilting downwards. Occasionally it went sideways, and in one shot it was suddenly big and hooked.

Directing his own films had made Orson wily. Because he knew all the answers, you couldn't challenge him. If you did argue, he'd call in sick. However, he would make sure it would only be for one day. Film insurance didn't cover one day and he knew that. It meant we would lose the day and have to tighten the schedule to make up for it, convenient for him but not for anyone else. Our production manager, the merrily bumptious John Dark, found his usual good humour melting away.

In the middle of all these shenanigans Orson came to me and said, "You're not using this set anymore, may I use it?"

"What do you mean 'Use it'?" I asked.

"I'm making my own film," he said, "and this set is just what I need. I could film on it at night." I was a little taken aback but at least I was familiar with the history of Orson and his own films. For many years he had received no directing offers because he had earned himself a reputation for being difficult. He tended to create major problems for other people to sort out and run miles over budget. If he wanted to direct he had to finance the picture himself and, because he frequently ran out of money, he often had to stop. One of his films, *Don Quixote*, was taking so long that some of his key players would die during the shooting, rendering it impossible to complete. 'But what harm can come from letting Orson shoot on a set we don't need anymore?' I thought, and told him that it would be all right, adding, "It's not as if your film will be coming out for ages, if ever." Orson laughed and reassured me that it was coming along very well.

It was only that evening, just before we broke, that I began to wonder how Orson was actually going to do these shots. Where was his cast and where was his crew? The answer to the first question was simple. Only he was going to do any acting – it was a scene where he smashed a room up by himself – but his crew was another matter. It was mine. He persuaded all the electricians, carpenters, prop men and lighting technicians on our film to work for him. They shot this scene over the course of one night, and only finished at five o'clock the next morning. When they reported for work on our film a few hours later they were so tired they were hanging over the ferry's handrails. "And what did he pay you?" I asked one of the boys.

"He gave us each a pewter mug," he answered. "They're engraved. They say 'Thank you very much' and they're signed, 'Orson'." It was a typical Orson gesture. The crew did all that work and received not one penny.

In the meantime, on our set Orson was still finding ways to play up. He decided that having applied the false nose he would now stuff his cheeks with cotton wool. As a result he was unable to talk properly and produced the most extraordinary sound. "Nobody will understand you," I said, but that didn't bother him. He would post-synch the whole part, or so he promised. Post-synching is where you re-record your dialogue in a sound studio, synchronising your voice with your lip movements on the screen. Where he was going to do this and how, I didn't yet know. We had enough trouble on our plate. 'Help, we're dying here,' was what most of our telegrams back home were saying by then. In response, Rank sent out a man called Roy Goddard, but what the hell was he able he do? He was out of his depth. The best thing would have been to sack Orson and start again, but that was simply not possible.

"I'm getting too fat," said Orson over a location lunch. "Tomorrow, I start a very strict diet."

"Splendid idea," we all said, or anyway thought. The next day I was walking through the lobby of the hotel when I spotted Orson sitting at a table. Since his back was to me it wasn't until I had nearly reached him that I realised what he was doing. He was digging into an ice cream the size of a head. The second he became aware of my presence, he quickly pushed the bowl away like a naughty boy who had been caught out.

"Just tasting it to see what it was like," he explained.

As the shoot limped to its end it was time to think of getting the crew home. Apart from some Chinese wardrobe assistants, most of it was British. They were Pinewood technicians who had been brought to Hong Kong by air. In 1958, long distance flights were still something of an adventure so unions insisted that members fly first class. This was not so easy to achieve when there weren't that many planes in the first place. We tried for a regular scheduled flight but none were available. Instead, we chartered an Argonaut, but that was a really old plane. The unit was not at all happy. Its union kicked up a fuss and John Dark had to send a telegram to Pinewood saying, 'Unit refuses to fly Argonaut.' Which was all very well but there was no alternative. It was the Argonaut or nothing. Eventually the unit gave in, probably persuaded by some extra money. John Dark and I stayed behind to wrap up, no small job as the entire picture had been shot on location. We went down to the airport to wave goodbye. The Argonaut trundled along the runway with the crew aboard. And it kept trundling. "Bloody hell! It's not going to take off!" we yelled, at which point the plane went ur-ur-ur and subsided on to the tarmac. The under carriage simply went. While all available vehicles rushed to the rescue, John Dark sent another telegram. It said, 'Argonaut refuses to fly unit.' In the end, lots of different planes took the unit home.

That was the good thing about John Dark. However difficult the problem, however black the mood, he could lift us out of it with just one mischievous remark. And his patience with Orson's absurd demands seemed to be limitless. Even when he had to crack the whip, John would always make up for it, either with a treat for his crew or something extra in their pay packet. I have worked with many good production managers but none who approached difficult tasks with such good humour. John went on to work with me on several films and remains a personal friend of mine.

Another good friend who came from that time was the actress playing the schoolmistress, the one on the ferry with the fifteen children. That was Sylvia Syms. In the 1950s Sylvia was the white hope of the British screen. Since then, instead of fading into genteel obscurity she has developed and adapted to become an excellent player of character parts.

"It's no problem," Orson said when we were back from location and I tackled the subject of post-synching his dialogue. "You can come to Rome and I'll re-do the whole part there." The reason for Rome was that he had a radio job there.

"That sounds nice," I said, "but do you know how we post-synch in England? We do one small bit at a time. We put it on a loop and you watch as it goes round and round. Then we cut out the sound, run the picture and you say the line."

"Fine, fine," said Orson. "I'm sure we can do all that in Rome. You bring your loops, I'll book the sound studio." And so came the time to re-record Orson's dialogue. Our sound editor made up the loops and both of us set out for Rome. "This is the only place I could get," said Orson as we walked into a studio that had no playback facility.

"But then how are we going to do it?" I asked.

"I have an idea," said Orson. "We'll channel the original soundtrack through some headphones. I'll wear them, listen to the soundtrack and record the dialogue over that."

"And how will I know it fits?" I asked.

"You can have a pair of headphones too," said Orson. This was all very well. With two Orson voices coming at me, one on top of the other, it was impossible to tell what was really going on. "Don't worry," said Orson, "I'll know."

At that moment, the crap game in *Guys and Dolls* came into my head. "But these dice ain't got no spots on'em. They're blank," says Nathan Detroit. "I had the spots removed for luck," says Big Jule, "but I remember where the spots formerly were."

Back in London, the sound editor stepped into a nightmare. Not only did the level of Orson's voice go up and down alarmingly, he was never in synch. Sometimes it was a case of pulling words, one at a time, backwards and forwards until the speech matched Orson's lips on the screen. It took hours and hours. So that was the Picture of the Year and probably the worst experience of my life.

When the film was finished John Davis said, "The best thing we can do is give it a good send off." And it did at least get that – the biggest, most spectacular premiere I have ever been part of. All along the Thames, where the Festival of Britain had taken place, Rank built a glittering, brightly-coloured Chinese market with real food stalls from which the guests at the premiere could be served. While eating, they could watch Chinese dragons and acrobats and jugglers accompanied by a Chinese orchestra. It couldn't be faulted. The film itself provoked a more muted reaction. "What lovely music," I heard a few people say. When you hear that kind of talk you know you're doomed. It was then, as I tried to force down a few grains of fried rice, that I was handed a telegram from Rome. It was from Orson Welles. 'Good luck for tonight,' it said, 'and thank you for being such a wonderful director and such a good friend.' It felt like my epitaph.

Decades later I was invited to Australia for a retrospective of my films. The organisers sent me two round-the-world plane tickets and I took Hylda. When the event was over we came back via Hong Kong, not having been there since the making of the film. When the plane touched down an announcement came over the loudspeaker: "Ladies and gentlemen, we are sorry to tell you that we have just heard that Orson Welles died today."

My immediate reaction was, "*Ferry to Hong Kong* died first."

18
The Queen Drops By

One of the most intriguing naval actions of the Second World War began with the search for the German battleship *Bismarck*. Launched in 1939, she was a new type of warship, faster and better-armed than the outdated British dreadnoughts. With Germany already causing severe damage to British merchant shipping, this formidable addition to its fleet had to be stopped. The ideal would have been to prevent her escaping from home waters in the first place. Once out in the North Atlantic she would be much harder to find. But on the 18th of May 1941 she set sail and did reach open seas.

What happened next was turned into a novel by CS Forester. The film producer John Brabourne bought it and, having commissioned a script from the writer Edmund North, found backing from 20th Century-Fox. John and I had often bumped into each other while walking down the main corridor at Pinewood Studios, so the next time this happened it was nothing unusual until John started to talk about the new book he had acquired. "I've read it," I told him. "It would make an exciting film."

"Good," he said, "because there's a script and I'd like you to have a look at it." Given that I had directed four quite large Second World War films by then, John's proposal was probably not as casual as it sounded.

I read the script. Ed North had done a good job. What made the subject gripping was the hunt. Searching for the *Bismarck* was like looking for a needle in a haystack. It was a detective story set at sea. The combination of this interesting idea and John Brabourne, whom I regarded as a thoroughly decent human being, made my answer a simple one when he asked me to direct the film. I said, "Certainly."

By 1959, when the film was made, there were already many people around who knew little of the war, so John had an idea to bring them up to speed: Ed Murrow appeared at the beginning to read a specially written radio broadcast. Murrow was the distinguished American journalist famous for broadcasting from London night after night during the Blitz. In 2005 George Clooney directed a film about Murrow, using his signing off phrase, "Good night, and good luck," as its title.

John Brabourne invited Ed and me to lunch. I was fascinated to meet him because it seemed there was no-one important in mid 20th century history that he didn't know. He agreed to do the film, in which he is seen making his broadcast over documentary footage of the damage Germany was inflicting in the North Atlantic during the early years of the war. The climax to this sequence was real footage of the building and launching of the *Bismarck*, and Ed's last line was, "The lights will be burning late tonight in the Admiralty." Our story centred on the man who was brought in to tackle the North Atlantic problem, and at that point it took over.

This man was Captain Shepherd, a stickler for discipline and apparently as cold as ice. To play this upright Englishman it was natural to choose Kenneth More. It was less natural for Kenny to play someone so stiff and buttoned up.

As Captain Shepherd arrives in the nerve centre of the operation, a bunker underneath the Admiralty, intelligence comes through that the *Bismarck* has been sighted off the coast of occupied Norway. He gives orders for two ships, the *Prince of Wales* and the *Hood*, to hunt her down. It is not a popular order as neither ship is ready to set sail. However, these two ships intercept a carelessly uncoded message sent by the *Bismarck*. The message reveals the *Bismarck*'s position, and as a result the ships achieve their aim only too well. Suddenly they find themselves alongside their very large and imposing target. The result of this encounter gives Winston Churchill a nasty shock. The *Bismarck* has sunk the *Hood*. He rings through to the Admiralty bunker and gives the order, "We must sink the *Bismarck*."

Shepherd's only option is to summon three ships that are already busy in the Mediterranean – the *Ark Royal*, the *King George V* and the *Rodney* – and send them up into the North Atlantic. Finding the *Bismarck* takes them three days, and when they do they exchange fire. The most important damage is caused, however, when a Swordfish biplane from the *Ark Royal* drops its single torpedo and wrecks the *Bismarck*'s steering. It is now forced to limp round in a circle. The three British ships move in. All well and good from a storytelling point of view, but how were we going to film it?

John Brabourne's wife was Patricia Mountbatten, daughter to Earl Mountbatten of Burma, who at the time of filming was First Sea Lord. For us this was very useful. If we were to film on real ships, explode old ones even, we would need the co-operation of the Admiralty. With Mountbatten putting a word in, we got it. Given that the film was a big project, without that word I doubt whether the picture would have been made.

Out at sea, the present and the past came together as we set up the shot where the Swordfish takes off from the *Ark Royal.* Pilots from a modern day aircraft carrier came to us asking us if they could fly the Swordfish. It was most touching. Here were these young men, trained to fly jets, wanting to fly a tiny biplane made of little more than wood and canvas. Three seats were all they had, one for the pilot, one for the observer and one for the gunner, each behind the other. The single torpedo was only just below. You were almost sitting on it. Speeds mounted to 138 miles an hour at most, and when the plane dived to aim and fire dropped to much less. This is what these boys wanted to experience, perhaps to understand the immense risks their predecessors had faced. Sadly, we had to tell them that we already had our own pilots.

Blowing up ships, or bits of ships, turned out to be not so hard. In Portsmouth's naval shipyards were old vessels whose fighting days were over. They were viewed as scrap metal, so before the main shooting started we were allowed to go down to Portsmouth and blow parts of them up. Because it was all real, these explosions gave the film extra conviction.

For long shots we had no alternative but to use models. Pinewood Studios, with its tank the size of a football pitch, was the right place to film them. For the models themselves, we imported an American by the name of Howard Lydecker, one of the top special effects men in the world. Unfortunately, he knew it. Never have I met anyone more boastful or arrogant. Whatever anyone had achieved, he had achieved it but better. When a technician said, "John Mills got a hole in one on the golf course yesterday," Lydecker said, "I'm the only man in America who got two holes in one on the same day," and this boasting would go on and on. He was caught out, though, when it came to the launching of his *Bismarck* model. This was admittedly a superb piece of craftsmanship, and the 20-foot model was impressive in its own right. As with a real ship, the launching took place from a ramp. The model slid down correctly enough, but instead of floating out into the water went gurgle, gurgle and sank to the bottom. Most of the crew held back their reaction, but not the clapperboy. "Oh dear," he said, turning to Lydecker, "Pearl Harbor all over again." Lydecker didn't see the funny side.

Once the model had been raised and, some days later, was happily floating on its pretend sea, a rigger working on the film suffered a stroke and collapsed in the water, dead. Those nearest jumped in and carried him to the most convenient dry spot, the *Bismarck*'s deck. Lydecker waded across, shouting, "Stand back everybody!" On reaching the body he said, "Yes, he's dead but I'll see what I can do." Despite the sadness of the scene the crew struggled to stifle their laughter.

As a little girl, Patricia Brabourne had been one of the Queen's playmates and then gone on to become one of her lifelong friends, so it was not totally unexpected when John told me the Queen would be dropping by for a visit. Her ten-year-old son, Charles, was starting term at his prep school in Cheam and she wanted to give him a treat first. "Still, we must make sure the press doesn't get to hear of it," said John. "We'll be inundated otherwise. This is absolutely unofficial." Indeed, when the Queen and Prince Charles did arrive they were alone, or appeared to be.

Of course, the little boy was fascinated by the models. I explained to him how it was a help to us that the weather during the real battle had been foul. Our model ships could emerge from fog which was much more realistic than being seen against a studio cyclorama. It was also much closer to life. Rarely in battle does one get a clear picture of all that's going on and this is what I had remembered from my own wartime experience at sea. We sailed past the *Scharnhorst* in a huge convoy but, because of fog, only one of our ships was visible to her. As for us, when the *Scharnhorst* opened fire we knew it from what we heard and felt, not from what we saw.

The camera operator, Austin Dempster, noticing the Prince's interest, asked if he would care to hop up and look through the lens. In so doing so, the Prince spotted a bar of chocolate perched on a ledge of the camera. It mesmerised him. "Would you like a piece?" asked Austin. The Prince turned round. It was all right. The Queen was talking to John Brabourne. "Yes, please," he said, "but don't tell my mother." He was rather chubby and had obviously been put on some kind of diet.

When the Queen had been introduced to most of the technicians on the set she turned to John Brabourne and said, "What about Mr Lydecker? I haven't met him yet." In her eyes was a look that was not entirely innocent.

"Oh, yes," said John and off he went to find him.

"Sure, of course, she wants to talk to me, I knew that," said Lydecker when John tracked him down, and on to the set he swaggered.

"Ah, Mr Lydecker," said the Queen, "I've been hearing so much about you." John had already shared stories of his boastfulness. Lydecker, failing to see the look in her eye, said that it was only natural that she would have heard of him, he being the best known special effects man in the world. "I made – " he continued and was about to list every film he had ever worked on when John murmured something about Her Majesty having to meet more studio staff.

"Are there any other films being made here?" asked the Queen.

"There is one, ma'am," I said, "*Conspiracy of Hearts*. It's about a group of nuns who hide children in their convent during the war."

"I'd like to see that," said the Queen.

"In that case," I said, "if you don't mind, ma'am, I'd better tell them you're coming." And with that off I went next door to speak to Betty Box, the other film's producer. "Would it bother you if I brought a friend in?" I asked.

"No, that's fine," said Betty. "Who is it? Anyone we know?"

"Yes, the Queen." I said.

"Oh, fuck off," said Betty and then, "Oh, bring anyone you like."

I went back to fetch the Queen, and as she and I walked down the corridor we saw a studio carpenter coming towards us. He was carrying some short wooden planks in both arms. "Afternoon, guv," said the chippy as he saw me. "Everything all right?" and then he stopped dead in his tracks. His brain began to whir. 'Is this the Queen?' he was thinking, 'Or is it an actress made up to look like the Queen? Oh no, it's the Queen.' By then he wasn't sure whether to salute or stand to attention. Slowly, his hands dropped to his sides, letting every last plank crash to the floor. The Queen, much amused, gave him the most charming smile, which I've no doubt he described in great detail to his friends in the pub that evening.

When we walked on to the *Conspiracy of Hearts* set the cast and crew, knowing nothing of our coming, were quite surprised but not nearly as surprised as Betty. Seeing the look on her face was one of the great moments of my life. Of course she recovered herself and introduced her stars, Lilli Palmer and

Yvonne Mitchell.

The time had now come for the young Prince to leave for his boarding school, a gloomy prospect for most boys, but at least this boy had something to tell his fellow pupils in the dormitory that night. The Queen later sent a message saying that he had thoroughly enjoyed his time with us.

Attention to authenticity was not only given to the models used in the film, it was also given to the sets. The bridge of the *Prince of Wales* was reproduced down to the last detail. Unlike the *Hood*, the *Prince of Wales* survived the first encounter with the *Bismarck*. She did not, however, escape unharmed. The *Bismarck* inflicted considerable damage and one of the officers wounded in the action was the actor Esmond Knight. He had virtually lost his sight. Esmond was in the film, playing himself. "It must be very strange for you standing here," I said to him as he took his position on the copy of the bridge he had actually stood on.

"It is," he said, "because I'm not totally sightless. I can see blobs and I can tell from them how correct this bridge is. Yes…" he touched the wheels, "it's a perfect replica."

Shepherd has an aide, a naval Wren specially appointed to look after him. She is the only person in the bunker who does not totally dislike him. He may be hard to understand, she thinks, but she wants to keep an open mind. This sympathetic aide was played by Dana Wynter. I had seen her on film but not worked with her before, and when she arrived for the first day's work she gave me quite a shock. "Of course, you know I'm pregnant," she said. The look on my face made her add hurriedly, "Don't worry, I won't show. The shoot'll be over before that happens." A potential nightmare faded away and I was able to relax and discover that our leading lady was not only charming but well cast. When she returned to Hollywood with her lawyer husband, Greg Bautzer, she and her family kept in touch with me and my family.

Sink the Bismarck! was a very successful picture and because, as war films go, it was slightly unusual – the Germans were not shown as villainous monsters, for instance – it played in many places that previously had not taken to British war films.

19

Yes, We Have No Greengages But We Do Have a Mutiny

By the time I had finished *Light up the Sky*, a little comedy set in a searchlight battery, starring tried and trusted types like Ian Carmichael, Tommy Steele and Benny Hill, I had notched up six Second World War films. Would I ever get to direct anything else, I was beginning to wonder. With perfect timing, I was lucky enough to be presented with two subjects, neither of which were like the war films and both of which contrasted with each other. The first was *The Greengage Summer*, which tells the story of four children who are taken to northern France to visit the war graves but find themselves alone when their mother falls ill.

Susannah York, in her first starring role, was to play Jos, the eldest child. The hard part to cast, however, was Jos's 14 year-old sister, a girl wise beyond her years who can see trouble where Jos can't. We needed a girl who, to use the language of the time, was nicely spoken. Most children who acted professionally were from stage schools and came from working class families. Their parents needed the income. Middle class parents, preferring their children to be properly educated, discouraged them from going to stage schools as the education they offered was, at best, patchy. As a result I spent an entire day sitting in a rehearsal room listening to a lot of girls who all spoke cockney. Despair was beginning to set in. We would never cast the part, I thought, and so began packing up to go home. The phone rang. It was an agent. "I've got a girl in my office I think you should see. I know what you're looking for and she's perfect."

"I don't think I can see anyone else," I said, "I'm exhausted."

"This girl you have to see," said the agent. "You'll give her the part, I promise you."

"How long will it take for her to get here?" I asked.

"Half an hour, 40 minutes. Please, just stay there. She's on her way." He was certainly very insistent, which was all very well but it left me with 40 minutes to fill. A piano in the corner of the room caught my eye. I wandered over and started to pick out tunes with one finger. Suddenly, I was aware of someone standing behind me. I turned round and there was this pretty 14 year-old with long red hair. Her name was Jane Asher, and I did indeed give her the part. This was all before Paul McCartney, West End leads, Gerald Scarfe and the cakes. Jane was one of those rare child actors who was to carry their career successfully on into adulthood.

Another piece of casting didn't go nearly as well but had the kind of sequel that teaches us lessons about how things turn out in life. In *The Greengage Summer* there's a young French gardener. Casting a real Frenchman seemed a good idea and we found a lad with dark, curly hair who looked just right. He couldn't speak English but there were three months to go before the shoot, plenty of time for him to familiarise himself with the dialogue. The three months went by and there he was again but now his curly hair was hidden under a bandage. He'd fallen off his motorbike. When he saw our faces he smiled and whipped the bandage off. That was not the end of our problems. I lined him up in front of the camera for a rehearsal and away he went. He was unintelligible. There was no sense to what he was saying at all. I took him to one side and told him that the situation was hopeless and that I would have to replace him. A British actor called David Saire took over. On the quiet, I thought that someone so chaotic as that curly-haired young Frenchman would never amount to anything. His name was Claude Berri and he went on to be one of France's best loved producers. He also directed *Jean de Florette* and *Manon des Sources*, two of the most successful French films ever made. They even did well in America and that's not so easy for a foreign language film.

Mishaps occur during film-making, sometimes small, often very big. *The Greengage Summer* suffered quite a big one but, all the same, it amused me. When we turned up for the first day's filming in the greengage orchard we expected lots of luscious fruit. There wasn't any. There were no greengages at all. A blight had withered them on the stalk and it wasn't just where we were. Right across France there was not one single greengage. Nothing, however, stops film-makers. The film's art director, John Stoll, whose job was to design the sets and prepare the locations, told me not to worry. He would get his prop buyer in London to buy hundreds and hundreds of greengages from Harrods. Did they have them, I wondered. They did. Greengages arrived by the sackful and, all that night, a little team of three sewed them on to the trees. The next morning, when the crew and I arrived at the location, it was like a miracle. Wherever we looked, we saw greengages.

There's a scene in the film where Jos gets drunk. The day before we shot it Susannah York, who was only at the start of her career, came to me and said, "This scene tomorrow, wouldn't it be a good idea if I really had a couple of drinks?"

"No, it would not," I said and explained that the scene wasn't going to be shot in five minutes. She would be acting drunk all day and, if, during that time, she kept topping up, there would be trouble.

"No, I'll be fine," said Susannah, young and keen on authenticity. The next day came and she wasn't fine. She got absolutely plastered and was unable to continue working. So it was off to bed with her and a fresh start the next day. Of course she turned up with one helluva hangover but a good thing came from the previous day. She had the memory of how she felt and this she could draw on.

The second film, yet another contrast, was *HMS Defiant*. It was a naval piece set during the Napoleonic wars with a ship's captain who was decent and a second in command who wasn't. Elements of other famous naval dramas were in it, *Mutiny on the Bounty*, for instance, while more specifically our captain was rather like Captain Vere in *Billy Budd*. Alec Guinness played him and, being a film star of international standing, wanted to make him as nuanced and magnetic as any of the other characters he had played on screen. In particular, he was good at playing tortured souls because he, himself, was a tortured soul. When he was already well known and playing at the Old Vic he was sometimes afraid to leave the theatre because his mother – he didn't have a father, not one that he knew anyway – would often be at the stage door, waiting to hurl abuse. The trouble was, all this high quality angst wasn't needed in our film. The captain was only there to be a feed to the sadistic second in command played by Dirk Bogarde and, strictly speaking, Alec shouldn't have accepted the part in the first place. Trying to talk him round was, in the end, a waste of time. He was too used to being centre screen.

The scenes on the ship were shot in the Mediterranean off the coast of Spain. I was reunited with John Brabourne who was, once again, producer. Once again his father-in-law, Lord Mountbatten of Burma, took an interest, a closer one than he had taken on *Sink the Bismarck!* as it turned out. When Mountbatten joined us on board the camera boat we were in the middle of lining up a very difficult shot, where one sailing ship had to stay in the same relationship to another sailing ship and the sun had to stay in the same relationship to both. The camera boat had to stay in the same relationship to all three. What was Mountbatten doing here in the first place, we asked ourselves.

The answer was quite sinister. It was the middle of the Cuban Missile Crisis and Britain, attempting to play it down, had sent him away on holiday. By then he had been promoted from First Sea Lord to Chief of the Defence Staff, so the idea was that if somebody that senior could be away on holiday then things couldn't be that bad. In fact they *were* that bad, if not worse. However, this was not what was concerning us at that very moment. We carried on struggling with the sailing ships and the sun and the direction of the wind as Mountbatten looked on. After a while, he spoke up. "You're making a right cock-up of that, Gilbert. Let me have a go."

"What a good idea," I said. "It'll be the first time I've had a Chief of the Defence Staff as my assistant."

I then watched him gradually realise what our problem was. When he had got himself into a complete tangle, shouting orders nobody understood, he handed the problem back to me saying, "Perhaps I'd better stick to the Navy."

A terrific battle was *HMS Defiant*'s climax. A mist wreathed its way between two ships. Sailors from one swung to the other, fought on the decks, fought in the rigging, used cutlasses, used pistols and, all the while, cannons did lots of damage amidships and gave off lots of smoke. This was a question of good choreography, patience and rhythmical editing. It was definitely the highlight of the film.

The title *HMS Defiant* was changed to *Damn the Defiant!* for its release in America, where it was mildly successful.

20

At Long Last Hollywood

The telephone rang. It was the Hollywood producer Charlie Feldman. He'd seen a film of mine and wanted to know if I would like to do one with him. What he had in mind was a novel called *The Durian Tree* which his co-producer, Karl Tunberg, and the novel's author, Michael Keon, had turned into a screenplay. Its stars were to be William Holden and Audrey Hepburn. I was such an admirer of those two artistes that I practically said "Yes," right there on the phone. Nevertheless, I thought it better to wait until the script came.

I was excited because Charlie Feldman was one of the legendary figures of Hollywood history. He arrived there in the 1930s, became an agent and rose rapidly to become the top man in his field. Clark Gable, Greta Garbo and pretty much every other major star were his clients. As he was also a lawyer, to him went the task of striking Darryl F Zanuck's deal with 20th Century-Fox when Zanuck formed the company. He was that big. Wanting to become a producer, though, and knowing that it was not possible to wear two hats (which was the law) he decided to leave Famous Artists, the firm he had so successfully built up. Some of the films he went on to make count amongst the best known of all-time, one of them being *A Streetcar Named Desire.* This was the man who was offering me a film.

The script was not the greatest but I thought I could make something of it, particularly with the addition of those two star personalities. They would help enormously. I rang Charlie and told him that I would do the picture. He, in turn, began negotiations with my lawyer. A deal was struck and all the contracts were signed. It was then that Charlie rang again. "Sad news, Lewis, Audrey Hepburn can't do the picture. There's some other movie she's been wanting to do for a long time and I don't have her under contract. There's nothing I can do. Never mind, we still have Bill Holden." And it was true. William Holden was, at the time, a very big name, so I didn't worry too much, especially as there was no great rush to find another female star.

William Holden and his wife were in Singapore just then and, as the film was set in Malaya, I thought I would do two things at once – get a feeling of the place and meet Bill. Hylda couldn't come with me on that occasion but she wasn't too worried. She knew that I would only be away for a fortnight and that most of that time would be taken up with talking to Bill.

The man I met in Singapore was very charming, not only when accompanied by his wife, but also alone with me. It was at one of these quiet meetings on our own – we usually went to his suite – that he talked about something that was worrying him. He had a good idea that Charlie Feldman would be angling to cast French model turned actress Capucine. "Whatever you do, Lewis," Bill said, "you must resist having her in the picture."

Knowing that Capucine, though very beautiful, didn't give out much, I replied, "I agree, but you've got to back me up. I haven't reached the stage yet where I can negotiate. If Charlie wants Capucine in the picture, it's going to be difficult to fight him. The character's a mixed race girl and Capucine has the looks for it. I would have to make the point that she's not a strong enough actress."

"Yes," said Bill, "I've just made a movie with her in Africa, *The Lion*, and she was not very good. I think, really, the picture suffered for it, and so if I make my next movie with her I'm going to look pretty stupid." That seemed conclusive. With Bill and his strong feelings behind me, I would be able to argue with Charlie. Bill, after all, had the clout of a major star. What I didn't yet understand was his relationship with Charlie. When Bill was 19 he had been discovered by him when Charlie gave him the star role in a film called *Golden Boy*. With Charlie's guidance he had risen swiftly to major stardom. In other words, he was rather in awe of Charlie.

We got on to the subject of the script. "I'm not too happy about it." I said.

"Neither am I," said Bill.

"My plan is to have a go at it," I went on, "to see if we can improve things." Again, it was good that Bill and I were agreed on this because the script was also a delicate matter. One of the co-writers, Karl Tunberg, was also Charlie's co-producer and therefore my producer. As I've often done the job myself I haven't worked with many producers, but I can safely say this one was hopeless. As the weeks went by I could see that he knew nothing, was lazy, stupid and went out of his way to prove it, everything you dread in a producer. When it came to the preparation stage in Malaya, his inertia provoked my production manager, Bill Kirby, to resign.

It was then, when I was in the middle of these preparations and still working on the script that I received a phone call from Charlie in Los Angeles. "We're taking the producer off the picture," he said. "We know your track record. You don't need one."

First of all, I thought, 'Thank God,' and then, 'But we've lost Bill Kirby and we needn't have.' Finally, I said out loud, "Thank you very much," at which point Charlie said, "But I think you ought to come to Los Angeles."

"Whatever for?" I asked. "Things are going to be much better, Charlie, but in some ways, they're going to be worse. I now have all this extra work to do on top of the script. There are permissions to get, small parts to cast, all that sort of thing and there are no real production people here. I've sent for John Dark now that Bill Kirby's gone. He was terrific on *Ferry to Hong Kong* and he'll be wonderful for us now because he's used to tough locations. The point is, though, he isn't actually here yet. So I really ought to stay. In fact, it's impossible for me to leave."

"Oh dear," said Charlie, "that's a shame. By the way, you know your wife's on the way and your son, Stephen."

"Wha-at? To Los Angeles?" I said.

"Yes," said Charlie, "I've brought them over and I've booked them into the best bungalow at the Beverly Hills Hotel, the one where Marilyn Monroe stays. I thought you'd be pleased. What do you say to that then?"

"I'll take the next plane!" I said. That is how clever Charlie Feldman was. He was very astute. You never could win with him. There was nobody he couldn't handle.

Charlie's own story, and the story of his childhood in particular, was extraordinary. He was orphaned when he was seven. Whether his parents died or got divorced, I don't know. He didn't tell me. He had a brother, though, two years older than him and both were placed in an orphanage. From it, couples who wanted children but not babies would adopt. If you were a child there, it was your last chance. Grow any older and you were no longer of any interest. Charlie desperately wanted a couple to adopt him. He couldn't wait to get away from the orphanage and have a mother and father just like he'd read about in books.

One day a couple appeared and word went round that they were looking for a boy. As they had never had any children of their own they weren't interested in adopting a baby. They wanted a son, ready made as it were, which is typical of Hollywood, where people prefer to buy everything ready made. After interviewing the boys to see which one would fit best into the family, the wife said, "Gee, I don't know what to do. They're all so cute and charming, I could adopt every one of them."

"We've got to do something," said the husband and, having thought, said, "I know. It's very simple and it'll give us the feeling we're getting the best. Why don't we make them race?"

"What a wonderful idea," said the wife and a race was arranged. There would be no heats, no whittling down, just the one race and every boy of whatever age would take part.

The night before the event, Charlie couldn't sleep. What could he do to win? He knew that his brother, being two years older, could beat him. Perhaps, if he tried very, very hard, he might just be able to do it. The next morning all the boys were lined up against a wall. The father-to-be waved his handkerchief and off they set at a great lick over the course which was about 80 to 100 yards long. The brother won. It broke Charlie's heart. He was so longing to be adopted. What his brother had done was unforgivable, Charlie thought, while watching him being taken away by his new parents.

As with all things in life, however, you never know what is going to happen to you. Shortly afterwards, Charlie was adopted by a nice Jewish couple. He was happy, had a wonderful life, changed his name to that of his new parents, Feldman, and went to university. He never really saw his brother again. By the time he did he was already a Hollywood legend while his brother, who had not had a nice time at all, was working as a clerk in a factory. In losing that race, Charlie had won by miles and miles and miles.

Sometimes he felt guilty though. After he left home he didn't really keep in touch with his adoptive family. Occasionally he phoned. Mostly he wrote, and in his letters he always talked about how well he was doing and enclosed some money. To a certain extent this was a salving of his conscience but it also allowed him to get on with his career unhindered, and have lots of affairs with glamorous women. His attitude was that he could always see his adoptive parents tomorrow.

The mother survived the father, and when she died Charlie's guilt came back to hit him hard. She left him a letter, in which she said that she and her husband had not believed one word of what he had written to them. They knew he had failed, and was too ashamed to come and see them. Consequently, she had kept all the money he had sent with those letters and now, because she knew that he would be needing it, she was returning every penny. It was a pretty sad story, and the way Charlie told me I could tell it was something he was never going to get over.

When I arrived in Los Angeles I went straight to the Beverly Hills Hotel where I found Hylda in the bungalow, beaming all over her face. She was living the life of riley and Stephen, in the second bedroom, wasn't doing too badly either. Even during the short time I had been in the air between Singapore and Los Angeles, Hylda had found a relative. In fact, wherever Hylda went in the world she found a relative. This time it was an aunt. She was not Jewish and her marriage, several years earlier to the brother of Hylda's mother, had caused a rift in the family. For decades, none of them had spoken to him. He had left England, settled in Los Angeles and done well but, only after 40 years, had returned to England, where there had been a joyful reunion with his sister. A couple of months later, back in Los Angeles, he had died. When Hylda met the wife she found her charming and so did Stephen. She, the aunt, loved children and so Stephen, who was now ten, was able to spend a lot of time with her while we were in Hollywood. Her son invited us for dinner. He was a teacher in a state-run primary school. The difference between his way of life and that of his equivalent back in England took my breath away. He had four sons between eight and 16 years old. He had a house, a car and a swimming pool. If his job had been in London, his home would have been a two room flat in a council block outside London.

"I'm so pleased you're here," said Charlie when I met him the morning after I had arrived in Beverly Hills. "Ben Hecht's rewritten the script and you're just in time for the reading."

"What do you mean, Ben Hecht's rewritten the script?" I said. "I thought we had a script, maybe not a very good one but we were working on it."

"Yes but Ben has such a famous name," said Charlie, "and he's so quick. He can knock out a script in three days and he makes them so terrific, I had to hire him. We're having the reading for Bill Graf and his guys at United Artists. It'll be at my place. Bill Holden's coming too and Ben'll be doing the reading."

"Look, Charlie, may I have this script beforehand," I said. "You know I can read and it's much easier for me than having someone read it to me. I like to stop and think."

"But Ben's used to this. He's very good at these presentation readings."

"OK, I'll be there," I said.

We gathered at Charlie's house. I had never met Ben Hecht before. I knew him by reputation, of course. With Charles MacArthur he had written the classic 1930s play *The Front Page*. He settled down to read the new script. The basic plot was similar, but apart from that it wasn't like the old script at all. Bill Holden's part kept shrinking, while the part of the mixed race girl kept getting bigger. I'd always wondered about Audrey Hepburn being interested in that part in the first place. It was a relatively minor role and had never seemed enough for her. Actually, I had also wondered whether she had ever seen the script and whether Charlie had ever talked to her. Still, that was irrelevant now because she wasn't doing it. But then who would be playing this new, improved part?

As I continued to listen, I seethed. This new script was really no good. I was on to a loser. Still, I thought it best to keep quiet until the end because I wanted to see what happened. What happened was the guys from United Artists got up, said, "Yeah, great," and left. So afraid were they of Charlie, they were out of the room before you could blink. That left Ben Hecht, Bill Holden, Bill Graf and, of course, Charlie. 'I'm still not going to say anything,' I thought, 'because any second now, Bill Holden is going to go nuts.' Charlie, having shown Ben Hecht and Bill Graf out, returned. "What did you think, Bill?" he asked and Bill Holden said nothing. He walked out of the room. Evidently he was putty in Charlie's hands. That, however, left me quite on my own. 'This is a no-no,' I thought and, when Charlie, in turn asked, "What did you think, Lewis?" I replied, "I think I'm at the end of the road, Charlie. I think I must take my wife and child, go back to England and do something I believe in, rather than this, because it's going to be a disaster."

"Oh, Lewis, no, don't do that," said Charlie. "Please, I beg you."

"But I have my future to think of," I said. "I cannot make a film like this, a big Hollywood film, when I know it's going to be terrible. It doesn't make sense. Why on earth would I want to do it?"

"Lewis, Lewis, you're killing me," said Charlie, "you're killing me." And down his cheeks flowed the mega tears. For all I thought and kept trying to think, 'This is acting, I'm sure of it,' I couldn't stop also thinking, 'What are you doing? Why are you are being horrible to this old man?' Old man? He was only 60. On and on went Charlie with me saying, "I'm sorry. This really is impossible," until suddenly he said, "I'll tell you what we'll do. You go and work with Ben."

"What, for another three days?" I said.

"No," said Charlie, "take your time."

"That's all very well," I said, "but any day now there's an entire film unit arriving in Malaya and they'll be wanting a script to work from."

"And they'll have one," said Charlie. "It won't take that long. Now, you and Ben should go to New York because that's where he likes to work. I'll book two hotel suites. You can leave right away. Hylda can stay here in Beverly Hills with Stephen." By now Charlie was in full flow. "You know how much they like it," he went on, "and while they're here, you and Ben will be in New York and, between you, I know that you're going to turn out a damn fine script!"

"Oh, well, I'll have a go." I said.

Ben Hecht and I then went to Los Angeles Airport where we caught the plane for New York. What I didn't know about him was that, along with his liking for the sauce, he was also addicted to pills. "May I have a glass of water?" he asked the stewardess before we'd even taken off and, from a little box, he picked out two pills. Down they went. He paused, took out two more pills, this time of a different colour, and down they went. The plane taxied on to the runway and stopped, ready for take-off. I turned to Ben. He was right out, sound asleep. 'Good luck to him,' I thought. 'He can sleep all the way to New York.'

But at that moment the captain's voice came over the loudspeaker. "I'm very sorry, ladies and gentlemen," he said. "We have a serious problem with one of the engines. We'll have to go back to the terminal. Another aircraft may be standing by but I can't guarantee it. If that is not the case, you will be accommodated in a hotel for the night and we shall take off in the morning." The other passengers harrumphed and fumed while the plane taxied back to the terminal.

Everyone got off except me and, of course, Ben. He was out, stone cold, dead to the world. "What's wrong with him?" asked the stewardess. "Is he ill?"

"No," I said, "he's taken some strong sleeping pills. What do you think we should do? Because one thing's for sure, he is not going to be able to get off this plane under his own steam."

"We need to get him to the hotel," said the stewardess. 'Oh, the hotel,' I thought. 'They knew all along there was no other plane, bloody airlines.' A little ambulance drove up and took Ben to the hotel where he carried on sleeping right through the night.

The next morning I knocked on his door, went in, shook him and told him that we had to get up. Looking at me bleary eyed he said. "Oh, we're in New York, huh?"

"No," I said, "we're still in Los Angeles. We haven't taken off yet."

When we finally got to New York we were put into the two suites and given a pretty secretary to take down this wonderful script we were going to write in three days. We set to work and soon found ourselves getting nowhere. Ben was obviously uncomfortable working with another person around. "The last time I worked with someone like you," he said, "was with Hitchcock. He was domineering with the writer too."

"I'm not domineering with the writer," I said, "I'm just trying to work with you."

"My trouble," said Ben, taking another tack, "is that I can't work here. It's impossible. Why don't we go to my house in Nyack. That's upstate New York. It's very comfortable there. We have staff. You'll be looked after and, honestly, we'd be better off there than trying to work in this cold suite."

We moved to Nyack. "What shall we do about the suites, Ben?" I asked.

"Leave them," he said. "You never know. We might want to go back." So now I had my wife in a bungalow in the Beverly Hills Hotel, two suites in New York and I was in Ben Hecht's home in Nyack.

The script we came up with was a cockamamie affair. Still, we took it back to Charlie who read it and said, "Great!" and then, "Now, who can we get for the leading woman?"

"It depends," I said. "Is she supposed to be mixed race? If she is, there are plenty of established stars who could get the look."

"I always think it's good to have a star who's on the up and up," said Charlie. "What about Capucine?"

"I honestly don't think she would be right for it, Charlie," I said, "and Bill would be very unhappy because, as you know, he did *The Lion* with her recently and that failed."

"We're not making the film for Bill," said Charlie, "we're

making it for the world. Bill will do as I tell him." In that moment I saw the steel under the charm and realised that I was heading for disaster. I also realised that I had gone too far to turn back. The contract had been signed. The money had probably been deposited in the bank. There was no way out.

The next time I saw Bill Holden was a few days later. "He won, didn't he?" said Bill.

"We might have brazened it out," I said, "if you'd stayed with me."

"No," said Bill, "I can never win with Charlie. Nobody wins with him. It's impossible. If you think you can win, forget it. Ride with the punches, Lewis. Get through the film and get home sane."

I went back to Charlie. By then I knew that John Dark had arrived in Malaya but I also knew that he would be expecting something to actually work on. "There are people out there waiting for the script," I said. "I must get it to them so that they can break it down and start working on the budget."

"There is no budget," said Charlie. "Now don't worry. It's not a problem. You really don't have to talk about budgets." He then turned to Hylda who happened to be in the room. "You know, your husband is a very strange man," he said. "I don't think I've ever worked with anyone like him. Here you are with him in Beverly Hills and soon he's going to start shooting. Why doesn't he take you to Hawaii for ten days en route?"

"Charlie!" said Hylda, perking up no end. "What a delightful idea." So now Charlie had gone and won Hylda over.

"I'm sorry, Charlie," I said, "I can't afford to spend ten days with Hylda in Hawaii. I must get on a plane and fly straight to Malaya. When I said 'People are waiting,' I meant an entire unit and it must have that script."

"Oh well, it's up to you," said Charlie shaking his head, "but I know if it was me, I'd take the ten days' holiday." And that was the beginning of shooting this film with Charlie Feldman.

The one person who had not turned up in Malaya, even by the time we were about to shoot, was the wardrobe mistress. However Capucine, who naturally had got the part of the mixed race girl, was only going to be wearing sarongs, so it was just a matter of Hylda keeping her eyes open. A woman went by on a bike wearing a sarong that was particularly beautiful. "Where did you get that?" asked Hylda and the next thing she was handing it to Capucine who was enchanted. "Just what I was hoping for."

There was another good part for a female, almost as important as Capucine's. It was that of a young English girl who falls in love with the Bill Holden character. When I suggested Susannah York, Charlie was very pleased. In the short time since the making of *The Greengage Summer* she had become quite a name and one that was known in Hollywood.

So we started and it wasn't too bad. Bill Holden was a delight. He was an old time star. If you said to him, "You've given me an idea. I think you should come in on your hands and knees, crawl across the room, climb up on to that chair and sit in it," he wouldn't say, "That's bloody silly." He would simply do it. Whatever the director says, you do it. That was how film actors were trained in his day and that was certainly his training.

We were also joined by Tetsuro Tamba, a Japanese actor well known in his own country. He was fine too. He came to play the part of a Malayan Chinese, a character who was supposed to speak English. Tetsuro didn't but he was a hard worker and learned quickly. The eventual performance he gave was a credit to him and when I made *You Only Live Twice* a few years later I remembered Tetsuro and it was he who played Tiger Tanaka.

However, a problem did arise and it was the one I was expecting. It was Capucine. Susannah York was not always easy but she was undoubtedly an actress. Capucine was not. Because she was untrained, and didn't understand what you were saying anyway, there was little you could do with her. She achieved the mixed race look easily, and she really was beautiful. That wasn't the problem. The problem was a slight dimness and the fact that she shouldn't have been there in the first place. I soon discovered exactly why she was there. She was Charlie Feldman's girlfriend. And she was Bill Holden's girlfriend. Despite all Bill had said about her, their relationship had started on *The Lion*. For a director, it was very difficult to work out who was going where and why.

Capucine cabled Charlie complaining that I was working mostly with Susannah and hardly with her. The next thing I knew, Charlie appeared. He took me for a walk and put his arm around my shoulder. Behind him was his lawyer. "Lewis, I don't know how to thank you for what you've done on this film," said Charlie. "You've saved my life." He continued in this vein until he said. "So, what I'd like to do is make you the official producer and give you five per cent of the picture."

"Thank you," I said while thinking, 'So that's the reason for the lawyer.'

"Now," said Charlie, "what do you think of Capucine?"

"She's a very nice girl, Charlie," I said, "and very lovely but she hasn't trained to be an actress and that's difficult because she doesn't know about working with other actors. When I'm doing a scene where Susannah's talking to her, I'm not just working with Susannah. I'm working with her too because I will be filming her reactions, how she listens to Susannah, that sort of thing. When I get back to the cutting room I can put all that in and even improve her performance."

"I see what you mean," said Charlie, "I'll tell her that."

"Who's on tomorrow, John?" I asked John Dark a couple of days later. He listed who was going to be needed for the next day's scene. "All those extras plus Bill Holden and Capucine."

"Fine," I said, "we'll get on with that then."

"Well no," said John. "Charlie told me that Capucine can't work tomorrow."

"What do you mean, can't work?"

"She's got the bunnies. Charlie told me she'd got the bunnies."

"What are you talking about? The bunnies? What's that?"

"You know. What women get."

"That's ridiculous," I said. "All she's got to do is ride a bike. She has no lines to say, not one. She and a gang of other people all ride along on bikes together and that's it." These people on bikes were protesters against the British government as the story was set against the troubles in Malaya.

"Charlie still doesn't want her to work," said John.

"Why not?" I asked.

"Because she won't look the same," said John. "What with the bunnies, her features might change."

"It's not a fucking close-up, we're shooting," I said, "she's on her fucking bike! We'll hardly see her face."

"You'll have to talk to Charlie," said John.

I went into Charlie's room and everything bubbled up. Like most mild-mannered people, when I lose my temper I really lose it. I screamed at Charlie for five minutes solid. When I came to an end his reaction was typical. "Lewis, why are you shouting at me? You're the director. You must do as you want. It's up to you. What you say goes and there's an end to it."

Feeling squashed, I muttered, "OK," and left the room to find John. "Don't worry," I said to him, "Charlie said it's all right. She can work."

Next day, nine o'clock came and there was no sign of Capucine. When I sent to find out where she was, a message came back to say that she wouldn't be working that day. 'Forget it,' I thought, 'I'll just change the schedule. I can't go through that again.' And that was Charlie. You could never win. I learned a tremendous amount from him and I've often used it. For example, never say, "No." You're at some idiotic script meeting with a studio executive who's coming up with a brilliant idea that would kill the picture stone dead and you simply say, "Yes, that's very interesting," and you don't do it and, what's more, he doesn't remember it. That was Charlie's secret. People don't remember. And he was clever too when he said, "You're the director. It's up to you," because he was really saying, "If you can get her to work, God bless you and good luck."

After seven days Charlie went back to Los Angeles and, in the morning, it was no longer him I saw coming out of Capucine's suite but Bill Holden.

Although Bill had a very distinguished career in films – starring roles from the age of 19 and a reputation for being a hard worker – he had a drink problem which I'd heard about. When I first met him he told me not to worry because he was going to a clinic in Switzerland to dry out ready for the picture. He did too, and afterwards told me what happened. A nurse instructed him to get into bed and then asked him what his favourite drink was. "Vodka," he answered and, thinking this rather odd, got into bed. A few moments later he heard the patter of the nurse's shoes and in she came with a glass of vodka. As he was congratulating himself at having stumbled on such a splendid cure, the nurse returned with a syringe, gave him a shot in the arm and he was violently sick. Three hours later this was repeated – the vodka, the shot in the arm and him being sick. It was aversion therapy and, for Bill, it worked. After three days with treatments four or five times a day he found that the mere smell of vodka made him feel sick and he couldn't face another glass. By the time he turned up for work on the film he was completely sober. Seeing how this man had conquered what so many others have not been able to conquer impressed me no end.

He was very funny one day. He came up to me and said, "I'm finding acting very hard now. For 30 years I've never been sober when acting, so I never really knew whether I was good or bad."

"Don't worry, Bill," I said. "You were always fantastic. Drink or no drink, you've always been a terrific actor." He seemed to be quite pleased to hear that.

Sometimes it was difficult for him. We were all invited to a Red Cross Ball with the Tonku, who was the King of Malaya, sort of. Bill was sitting at a table with some of the cast and Hylda. He asked her if she would like to dance. She was delighted and up they got. When the music stopped, Bill took Hylda back to the table, sat down and took a gulp from what he thought was his usual glass of 7UP. His face went white. He rose to his feet and tore out of the ballroom. Seeing Bill Holden running like a madman shocked the other guests, but a moment later he returned and explained. He had picked up the wrong glass. It hadn't been 7UP – it had been vodka and tonic. Fortunately for him he hadn't swallowed a drop. He had run out simply to get rid of it.

I told Bill how much I admired his fortitude. "The way you've handled yourself," I said, "is absolutely wonderful. There's something I'd like to know, though. Surely there's a time of day when you must feel 'I wish I could have a drink now', you know, midday or when you come home from work or when you're out in the evening with friends. What's the worst time?"

"That's easy," answered Bill. "For years and years, as soon as I opened my eyes my hand went out for the vodka bottle and I poured myself a stiff drink. I couldn't get up until I'd downed that drink."

"Well, Bill," I said, "your morning cup of coffee must be a big change." He laughed. Drying out hadn't taken away his sense of humour.

It was a pleasure for me to watch him getting better all the time, and when he finished the film he was still sober. In fact he was sober for quite a few years after that. One day, though, I heard he'd started drinking again. His way of handling it was quite curious, as someone explained to me. For most of the month, he hardly touched a drop, then he would go to a cottage he owned on a beach and, over a weekend, he would drink himself into oblivion.

He was always alone, inflicting this on no-one else. I had only worked with Bill for a short time, on that one film, but I had grown to admire him enormously, so when I heard this news I was greatly saddened.

Worse was to come. On one of his drinking weekends he went down to his cottage as usual and drank himself under the table, as usual, but it wasn't the same table. He stumbled, fell, hit his head on a corner of this table and knocked himself out. In so doing he cut himself and it was such a gash that he slowly bled to death. No-one was around to help. This was and still is a particular sadness for me. I think of him today as a wonderful actor but more than that, as a gentleman.

Life can be strange. A few years later I was in Geneva when I bumped into Capucine. I think she was living there at the time. Her delight in seeing me was almost startling but as we talked I could sense she wasn't happy. Some months later I heard that she had committed suicide by jumping out of a window. It was a terrible way for this beautiful woman to die. Now, I look back on the film we made together which was eventually called *The Seventh Dawn*. Bill is gone. Capucine is gone and, after only four more pictures, Charlie Feldman was also gone. I've learned that nothing in life is forever.

21
Two That Got Away

One can grumble about the difficulties of making films, but that is to overlook the films one didn't make at all. Yes, in the 1950s they came quickly one after the other. Now, in the 1960s with the films growing bigger, and with more to lose, projects came up that looked like dead certainties but which fizzled out or continued with other people at the helm.

An early one was a prison drama called *Girl in a Birdcage*, brought to me by the writer Anne Burnaby, who at the time was under contract to the Associated British Picture Corporation. Her story was based on her own experience, that of a married middle class woman who was sent to prison. Inside, this woman and a female warder strike up a relationship that leads the two of them to set up house together when the sentence is completed. Anne used to come round to the house to work, or rather that was what she was supposed to do. Often she was late but always had a good excuse. "Sorry darling, it's my period today and I've been absolutely flooding!" That was one. Over lunch in a restaurant she was recounting a prison experience when she said, "Darling, she had me up against the filing cabinet, this warder, and what she did to me, you cannot imagine!" Needless to say, these words came out just as everyone in the restaurant fell silent. As I prefer to work and save drama for the page, our writing partnership dissolved and the film was never made.

A big picture that did get made was *Khartoum*. It starred Charlton Heston as General Gordon, was shot in Egypt, and Basil Dearden (*The League of Gentlemen*, *Victim*) was the director. That is not how it started, though. It was supposed to star Burt Lancaster, be shot in Sudan, and directed by me. The producer was Julian Blaustein, an American who had known some success in Hollywood. On reaching England he installed himself at the Savoy Hotel and never left it. I began to realise what I was up against when it came to the question of Gordon's jacket. In order to be recognised at great distances and impress the Sudanese, Gordon had the back of his jacket covered with gold and silver embroidery. It made him look like the sun and he was famous for it. Therefore, it was not merely decoration but a vital part of the story. "Way too much," said Julian Blaustein when presented with the estimate for the making of this jacket. "Shoot him from the front and never show the back." Uh-oh.

I went to Sudan to look for locations with my old friend, the set designer John Stoll – he who had sewn greengages on to those fruitless trees in France. One evening, we were returning to Khartoum from Omdurman when towards us came rolling a brigade of tanks. "Military exercises," said John, who always preferred to look on the bright side of life.

"Aren't there rather a lot of them?" I said. "I mean, where do they end?" By the time, we had made our way back to the hotel, we knew that we were in the middle of a full scale revolution. Days went by during which we were unable to leave the hotel. It was very boring. Somebody told us that there was a poker game going on in another hotel. We could stand it no longer and, risking sniper bullets, dodged our way over to the other hotel as soon as darkness fell. After ten days we were told that a civilian aircraft was going to land at the airport that night. It wouldn't be stopping for long but there was a seat on board for one person. "I have to get back to let them know we can't film here," I said to John and the others who were also with us. They swallowed it.

Whoever said the plane wouldn't be stopping for long was not exaggerating. It didn't really stop at all. I stood waiting on the tarmac. The plane landed. A door opened. Hands reached out and grabbed me and off we went again. "Would you like a cup of tea?" asked the stewardess. Because of the civil unrest, the film was postponed and I went off to other work. I think, in the end, Julian Blaustein would have been more of a problem than anything else.

22

The Film That Changed My Life

Once in a while you sense that a film you are making might do well and you are proved right. Sometimes you have a feeling that it won't and you're right there too. You never have a feeling that it may change your life because that rarely happens. Hit or flop, the pattern of your life remains the same. One film, which I made in 1965, did affect my life. It was called *Alfie*.

In Hollywood, a thriller I was preparing for Paramount fell through. George Peppard, its star, was very hot at the time but was also contracted to MGM and their claim turned out to be the greater. Because I had signed a contract I was owed a full fee and that's what I was paid. It sounds good, being paid for a film you haven't directed, but curiously I didn't feel that good.

Back in London, Hylda was at the hairdresser when she found herself sitting next to the actress Margaret Courtenay. She was full of a new play she had just opened in. It was doing very well and she was sure it would make a good film. Hylda, not one to hang around, took a friend and went to the Mermaid Theatre where it was playing. She came home very excited. I had to go right away, she said. It really would make a good film. Down to the theatre in the City of London I went and there I saw *Alfie*, the story of a handsome cockney who gets what he wants, women mostly, while making absolutely no commitments. John

Neville, a leading actor of the same generation as Richard Burton, was playing the part of Alfie.

The subject fascinated me: (1) because I had never tackled anything like it before, and (2) because Alfie was a new kind of hero. Although far from admirable, he had a cockiness and an energy that was mirrored in the real life of the 1960s. Good looking men, born into the working classes, were making names for themselves as photographers, tailors, hairdressers and leading actors. That had not happened before. I knew that I wanted to obtain the rights to the play.

The author was Bill Naughton and his name was surprisingly familiar. He had contributed short stories to *Men Only*, a monthly magazine which had been very popular with us servicemen during the war. Out in the desert we couldn't wait for the next issue because it would always contain a photo of a girl posing in a swimming costume. Hot stuff in those days. Bill's stories weren't bad either. Before turning to writing full time he had been a truck driver, so he knew a bit about life and what would appeal. I rang Bernard Miles, the actor and director who ran the Mermaid Theatre, and he put me in touch with Bill. After I'd told Bill about *Men Only* being a formative part of my early reading experience, I asked him about *Alfie*. No-one had applied for the rights, he said, and if I wanted to film it he would be delighted.

I went to see his agent, Margaret Ramsay, known as Peggy. It was to be the first of four times that I would be dealing with this agent who represented almost every known British playwright in the second half of the 20th century. Her approach was unusual and always the same. "Oh darling, do you really want to make a film of this? Are you sure? Do you think it'll work? I mean, is it really right for a film?" All of this would be said while she crossed and uncrossed her legs, something she was famous for. They were very good legs, so not looking at them was out of the question. It was all most distracting. Having done her best to put me off, she would then strike a very good deal for her client and insist that he – her clients were mainly men – would write the first screenplay. In the case of Bill, I took out a year's option and set about raising the money.

Simultaneously, Bill wrote his screenplay and brought it to me. When adapting their own work for film, playwrights tend to write a scene that goes, 'Jack walks along the street, goes up to his front door and lets himself in.' The next scene is then the first scene of the play. This won't do, of course, but it was something I was used to dealing with as I had already made six films out of plays. With Bill, the problem was his second act. Alfie contracts TB and spends the whole of the act in hospital. I didn't think we needed it. Any vital information could be put into the following scene which took place in a nursing home. I called up my old writing colleague Vernon Harris and we set to, breaking the scenes up and trying to find visual ways of saying what previously had been spoken. In any case, if we had left the hospital act in, the film would have been much too long. Bill wasn't particularly pleased but he didn't try to obstruct us. At least when the characters spoke it was his dialogue that came out of their mouths.

The problem of raising the money was beginning to nag when, out in Shaftesbury Avenue, I bumped into an old friend, Leslie Grade. Leslie and I went back a very long way together. We had both been in the same class at infants' school. The story of his family was remarkable. Round about 1910 his parents, knowing no English, had come to the East End of London from Russia bringing with them his two older brothers, the eldest aged four, the younger aged two. Leslie himself had been born in London. All three had grown up to make their name in showbusiness. As their family name, Winogradski, was hard to pronounce, they had simplified it to Grade. So you had Lew Grade, Bernie, who became Bernard Delfont, and Leslie Grade. Both Lew and Bernie were made Lords, an astonishing feat considering their start in life. "What are you doing?" asked Leslie. I told him about the year's option on *Alfie*. He knew the play and was immediately intrigued. "Why don't we come in on it?" he suggested and I thought, 'Why not? The Grades are among the few people who really are in a position to organise a film's finance.'

With a lighter heart, I settled down to finish the script with Vernon. By the time we had done that the Woolf brothers, Jimmy and John, were also showing an interest. They asked to see the script, and when they had read it said they wanted to join the Grades and definitely be in on the project. This was excellent news. If any people in the country could get a film made, it was Jimmy and John. What's more, I had known and worked with them from the days of *Cosh Boy* and *The Good Die Young*.

It was time to get down to some work that was a bit more creative – casting. Who was going to play this new kind of hero in this new kind of world where the advent of the Pill meant that young men and women were free to make love to whom they liked, when they liked and most definitely did? Jimmy Woolf wanted his protégé, Laurence Harvey. I did not, and thought it was a bit of a cheek that Jimmy was trying to swing Larry on to me. If anyone knew Larry and what he was capable of it was I. Had I not directed him in three of his early films and was it not I who had introduced him to Jimmy in the first place?

My argument was that audience's ears were becoming more

On the 007 Stage built for *The Spy Who Loved Me.* Behind me are the submarines trapped inside the hull of the villain's supertanker.

Hylda and I as king and queen in a photo specially taken for the set of *Seven Nights in Japan*.

With Richard Kiel, on location for *The Spy Who Loved Me*.

In Paris for *Moonraker* with Bond producer Cubby Broccoli, Roger Moore and Lois Chiles.

Celebrating Roger Moore's birthday with Hylda in 1980. Roger added the balloons himself.

Clowning with Julie Walters on location for *Educating Rita*.

With *Educating Rita*'s author, Willy Russell, Julie Walters and Hylda.

With Michael Caine, Julie Walters and *Educating Rita*'s costume designer, Candy Paterson.

I demonstrate how the egg and chips should fall into Pauline Collins's lap on the set of *Shirley Valentine*.

With Liza Minnelli during a rehearsal for one of *Stepping Out*'s dance routines.

Liza and Julie Walters, ready for the finale.

With Julie, Hylda, co-producer John Dark and Diana, Princess of Wales, at the premiere of *Stepping Out*.

With Roger Moore in Cannes.

With Michael Caine at the British Film Institute.

Receiving the Michael Balcon Lifetime's Achievement Award at BAFTA in 1990.

Receiving the CBE at Buckingham Palace in 1997, with my daughter-in-law Joan, Hylda and John.

Carrying on the tradition – my granddaughter, Holly, is at the start of her career as an actress. She has already been in *Midsomer Murders* and played a lead in *Casualty*.

attuned to the different accents you can find in Britain, so an effortless cockney was essential. Larry Harvey had gone to drama school at a time when you ironed out your own accent, in his case South African, and learned to play the suave type of Englishman who figured in the thrillers and light comedies of the early 1950s. So his cockney accent would have to be put on. Anyway, Larry simply wasn't very good.

Jimmy, as one might have expected, was adamant, and being the creative one of the two Woolf brothers got no argument from John. Leslie Grade was content with Jimmy's choice too. I was out on a limb and had to think of something. If Larry Harvey were to do the play on Broadway and make a go of it, I suggested, he could play the part in the film. Jimmy and the others agreed to that. Two weeks later, news came through. Larry had accepted to play King Arthur in the London production of *Camelot* at Drury Lane. Surely this meant that we could start looking for someone else? That's what I thought, but Jimmy was not of my opinion. It looked like the parting of the ways.

The Woolfs and Leslie Grade made a proposal. There were still six months of my option on the play to go. I was to use the time to set the picture up by myself, they said, and if I succeeded they would bow out. They knew perfectly well that, in the UK, that would be impossible, as they were the money in the UK. It would mean my going to America and, as they rightly judged, that was a daunting prospect. I was determined, however, not to have Larry Harvey, so I signed the piece of paper I was given to confirm the arrangement, and went off wondering what on earth I was going to do. It was then that I remembered Paramount and the film I hadn't done for them. Our parting had been amicable enough but might they not want, in some way or other, to recoup their loss from paying me that director's fee?

I flew to America where two new heads had taken over at Paramount. New heads taking over Paramount is such a common occurrence I wouldn't normally mention it, but in this case the two heads were writers and that was very unusual. Scripts actually interested them and, having read *Alfie*, they wanted to finance the whole film. It would be a good start to their regime, they thought, and cheap too because when they asked me how much it would cost I said, off the top of my head, £250,000 ($625,000). I was then given a contract to the effect that Paramount would be doing the financing but would not question the casting.

Word got around Hollywood that I was going to make *Alfie* and Terence Stamp, who was filming *The Collector* there with William Wyler, got in touch. He wanted to play the part for nothing. A star wanting to play a part for nothing is music to a producer's ears and Terry was handsome, a genuine cockney and, working with a top Hollywood director like William Wyler, he was hot too. I'm very cautious, though, and I thought the young Terry needed some kind of test. Once more, I found myself saying, "Do the play on Broadway and if it works, you've got the part." To Terry's credit, he did do the part on Broadway. It was particularly courageous of him because his experience of acting on stage was almost nil. For all his efforts, though, the play closed after two days. It gave us all, including Paramount, quite a shock. Terry sensibly took his hat out of the ring.

Back in England I set up a meeting with the Woolfs and Leslie Grade. When I showed them my contract with Paramount they were so taken aback they could think of nothing to say. The next day, they did think of something. A phone call informed me that the piece of paper I had been given to sign by them was worthless. There had been no consideration. A consideration is where a token sum of money changes hands. One pound will do. That had not happened. I was desolate. 'Not quite the clever chap you thought you were,' I was saying to myself until I thought again of that script. It was so very good, I couldn't give up.

I found a top QC who specialised in the business of considerations. He wasn't cheap but he was worth it. "They've got this all wrong," he said, "and I'll stake my reputation on it. Consideration doesn't have to mean a pound. It can come in kind. Have you done any work on the film?"

"Yes," I said. "The screenplay. Vernon Harris and I wrote it together."

"That does it," he said. "That's the consideration. They have to honour the agreement."

I went back to the Woolfs and Leslie. Now it was their turn to be desolate. "But we're old friends," they said which struck me as very funny. Only a few days earlier they had been prepared to hang me out to dry. I was so happy, though, I agreed to split 50 per cent of the film equally between us, 25 for them, 25 for me, while Paramount retained the remaining 50. As Paramount had agreed not to interfere, likewise the English team, I felt that at least I had 75% of clout.

I was 44 at the time of making *Alfie*. A child of the 60s, I wasn't. Round about me, things were changing which had to be reflected in the film. My son John, by then a young man, was very much of the 60s. Music, fashion, actors, he knew about all of them and, even better, knew the people who were doing it. As he already had years of experience working in films it seemed a good idea for him to join me. He became associate producer and got off to a good start. It was he who knew that Terry Stamp had a flatmate who was also an actor, also a cockney and also good looking. His name was Michael Caine, and John thought he would make the perfect Alfie.

Michael, as it happened, had just got himself noticed. Cast against type he had played an arrogant young officer in *Zulu*. It was an important role but it wasn't the leading one and Alfie was. In fact, it was a huge responsibility and I needed something more to go on. "It's there," said John and he told me that Harry Saltzman, one of the producers of the James Bond films, had put Michael under contract to play Harry Palmer in the film of Len Deighton's book *The Ipcress File*. That was encouraging, but there was one problem. The film wasn't out yet. Its editor was Peter Hunt and Peter had edited several of my films. I asked him if he would let me see what he was working on. Yes, he said, on condition that I didn't breathe a word to its director, Sydney Furie, or anyone else for that matter.

I saw the film and it answered my question 'Do I have an Alfie?' Yes, I did. Michael was not only good, he was able to carry the film. That evening, leaving the restaurant Les Ambassadeurs, I came face to face with Sydney Furie. I wanted to tell him how good I thought his film was but that wasn't possible. I had to say, "I've heard good reports," which didn't mean so much.

Sydney, who was permanently gloomy and pessimistic, said, "Yes, that's what people always tell you before your film comes out. I don't think it's much good myself." He was wrong.

Harry Saltzman was much more up when I spoke to him. He thought Michael as Alfie was an excellent idea. It was slightly different when Paramount asked me who was going to play the part. When I answered, "Michael Caine," they came back with the classic response, "Michael who?" I reassured them by talking up Michael's certain success in *The Ipcress File* and, just as they had promised, they said no more. My picture was, after all, so cheap it was not that great a gamble. Dennis Sellinger, Michael's agent, saw very quickly how good *Alfie* would be for Michael and didn't try to ruin us when negotiating the deal.

I thought it would be a good idea to invite Michael round for lunch. With all these preparations going on I hadn't seen him for a while. He came to the house and was very quiet. During the meal he hardly said a word. Sometimes one forgets that actors can be shy and that's probably all it was. Still, I began to panic. Had I made the most dreadful mistake? At the end of the meal, Michael said that he knew of a tailor near the Elephant and Castle who would be just right for making Alfie's clothes. He had to be – he made clothes for real Alfies. I went to the fittings and, as I watched Michael walk up and down in those suits, assuming the jaunty gait of Alfie, I knew that he was going to be fantastic in the part.

The main impetus of Alfie, the play and the film, is the character's need to seduce women, not love women or care about them, merely seduce them. The conquering, for him, is all, the point being that he doesn't really like women. You can tell by the language he uses. Women are either 'birds' or, worse, 'it'. This is the way he distances himself from the female sex. He could get away with it too because, although things were changing, many women still worked as shop assistants or secretaries and rose no higher. They were yet to achieve independence.

For the women in the story, Bill Naughton wrote a series of female characters ranging from doormat to 'Don't try it with me, buster.' The actresses we found for the parts were spot on and sometimes even more than that.

I wanted Shelley Winters for the part of Ruby, Alfie's equal in tactics. He calls her the lustbox and Shelley was feminine and sexy as well as tough. Paramount did not approve. She had recently given them a hard time and they hadn't forgotten. After reminding Paramount that they had promised not to stand in my way, I tackled Shelley head on. What was all this about bad behaviour? She assured me that she would be as good as gold. She loved the part and was longing to be in the picture. When she did turn up she brought all Ruby's clothes and, looking at them, I could see that she understood her role because they were absolutely in character.

It was only a week's work for Shelley, so an ordinary fee seemed a bit unexciting. She asked for a Rolls-Royce instead. John went to Jack Barclay's car showroom in Berkeley Square, bought one and drove it to Tower Hill, where we were on location for the scene in which Alfie is 'working the smudge'. This means taking photos of gullible tourists. It's the moment he first meets Ruby. During lunchtime, John drove Shelley over Tower Bridge for a test drive. "It's great," she said, "but can you imagine me turning up at the Actors' Studio in this? They'd die laughing." She settled for her ordinary fee and Jack Barclay took the Rolls back, fortunately without a fuss.

It was four years since I had last worked with Jane Asher. She was now 19 and ready to play a grown-up part, in this case a north country girl who, for a while, keeps Alfie happy with her cooking. She has a bedroom scene with him and Jane came to me rather anxious. Her boyfriend at the time was Paul McCartney and he didn't like the thought that she might be appearing in the nude. "You don't see Alfie even kiss this girl," I said, "let alone make love to her because that's how he is. Women repel him. If a woman merely touches his shirt, he jumps back because he doesn't want it to be wrinkled."

Unflattering as this was to women in general, it was a relief to Jane.

The saddest woman in the story is a downtrodden wife who comes to visit her husband in the next door bed to Alfie while he is recovering from TB in a nursing home. The husband was played by Alfie Bass, the wife by Vivien Merchant, who at the time was married to Harold Pinter. The chance meeting between the wife and Alfie (our Alfie, not Alfie Bass) leads to the most painful scene in the film. Things start off almost in farce, though. A pretty nurse, played by Shirley Anne Field, draws the screens round Alfie's bed which, as he's feeling much better, gives him the opportunity to seduce her. The husband and wife being only a few feet away are forced to witness this and, as the nurse's legs disappear upwards behind the screens, the wife, in her embarr-assment, says to her husband, "Would you like a banana?" At a later stage, when Alfie is quite recovered, he offers a lift to the husband's wife and, with her husband's grateful permission, she accepts. Alfie stops the car by the river. It's a beautiful summer's afternoon and the two go for a row in a boat where Alfie, using the excuse that he's only cheering the poor thing up, seduces her. Some weeks later she comes to his flat, pregnant.

It's the first time in Alfie's life that he has to take some responsibility and all he can do is think of himself. As far as he is concerned the only way out of the fix is to get rid of the baby. Abortion was illegal in those days. Rich people got Harley Street physicians to trump up an excuse for a termination. Poor people found women in back streets who, for a few shillings, would do some kind of jiggery-pokery using whatever bits of equipment were to hand. It was both amateurish and dangerous. Slightly better than that was finding a doctor who had been struck off, and that is what Alfie does. He summons this man to his flat.

The part of the abortionist was played by Denholm Elliott, and what a transformation there was there. All through the 1950s Denholm had played colourless leading men in British films, frightfully decent junior officers and the like. The abortionist could not have been more different. He was down at heel, nervous, weary, suspicious, and uncaring all at once. Denholm, by then middle-aged, made a whole new career for himself from playing a part that lasts only a few minutes.

Actually the abortionist doesn't perform the abortion. He induces it, not that Alfie knows that. He's off walking with a friend because he hates all that stuff and only discovers on his return that everything is yet to come. All the doctor will say to him as he leaves, is, "Two tablets, if she sweats," which doesn't sound very reassuring.

Alfie has no idea what is going to happen next. Suddenly, the wife is convulsed with pain. She can't stop herself from crying out. Alfie puts his hand over her mouth. Even then, he can think only of his own safety. If the neighbours were to hear and investigate he would go to jail. The pain gets worse. The wife starts to scream and Alfie, now in total panic, hits her across the face.

At this moment, Vivien Merchant told us that she wouldn't be able to find the right reaction unless Michael really hit her. Both Michael and I were uneasy about this but, for the sake of the scene which, once on film would be there forever, we agreed. Vivien/the wife, started to scream again. The slap, when it came, was fearful. The wife is silenced by the shock of it but only for a moment. What happened next was so awful but so real, I couldn't say, "Cut." Vivien's screams grew worse and worse. I could feel the eyes of the crew boring into my neck. They were quite unaccustomed to real violence and were willing me to stop the whole thing. It was terrifying and moving at once. All of us were feeling this woman's pain. Exhausted, Vivien eventually stopped, and only then could I shout, "Cut." The entire crew applauded.

In the story, when the whole thing is over, Alfie goes into the curtained-off area of his flat where the foetus is lying on a table. The audience sees neither the foetus nor the table. What it sees is Alfie's face and his gaze downwards, nothing else. From his expression, it reads everything. Tears well up in his eyes. It's his moment of conversion and he can't keep it to himself. He has to get out and describe it to the friend he'd been walking with earlier. This sympathetic listener was played very well by Murray Melvin. The foetus, Alfie explains to him, was not the amorphous blob he thought it would be. It was a tiny human being, perfect in every detail. At last, he realises that sex has an end result and this is it.

Having seen the film, people come up to me and say, "I'll never forget that moment when Alfie looks down and sees this perfectly formed creature on the table."

"But you didn't see any creature," I tell them, which makes them very angry because they are utterly convinced they did.

The morning after we filmed the scene of the slap, the phone rang. It was Harold Pinter. He wanted to know what the hell we were up to because his wife had a black eye and an almighty bruise across her face. Hadn't Michael Caine heard of acting, he said. Slaps are to be faked. "Harold, your wife asked Michael for the slap," I explained. "She couldn't play the scene otherwise, and when you see it, even though Vivien is your wife, you will say that it is the most incredible piece of acting and you'll be very proud of her."

The weeks of filming flew by, not the case on every film, and all at once I was shooting the last scene. It takes place at night on Waterloo Bridge, over which lorries would drive with their loads of fruit, vegetables and flowers bound for Covent Garden Market. The police were very helpful. If they hadn't been, we would have been sunk. The drivers of those lorries were not in a mood to be co-operative and, given that we had to hold them up for over an hour, understandably not. It was hardly a pleasant night anyway, at least not for us film-makers. There was a constant, demoralising drizzle. When you see the result on the screen it's quite another matter. The rain makes the paving stones gleam and that is exactly right for the last moments of the story.

Alfie, alone and contemplating an empty future, is approached by a stray dog, who is also alone and in need of friendship. Alfie sets off. The dog, keeping its distance, follows. Alfie stops. The dog stops. Alfie turns. The dog looks up at him mournfully but perhaps a little hopefully too. Alfie gives a whistle and off they go together. We came to shoot the close-up of Alfie turning. Even at three o'clock in the morning, there were onlookers. "Blimey," said one of them, "a thousand pounds a week for whistlin' a fuckin' dog. I wouldn't mind 'avin' that job." I thought that was funny afterwards, but right then things were getting tense. There was still the last shot to do with Alfie and the dog going off together. It was vital we finished that night but the police were finding it increasingly hard to keep back the lorries. Not only that, it was summertime and dawn was not far off. If the sun had risen we would have, again, been sunk.

Moments before the lorry drivers were about to set off, police or no, we got the shot and it works very well. "Cut!" I said and sank back in my seat on the camera crane, the drizzle still drizzling. Relief and sadness overcame me. The film was shot but would it be any good? Lorries streamed by, their drivers casting me dirty looks. One lorry driver slowed down, leaned out of his cab, looked at me, damp and dejected as I was and yelled, "Why don't you get yourself a proper fuckin' job?" After all the effort and worry of that night, his words had a ring to them that was distinctly ironic.

A few days later, John and I were looking at the rough cut. "What are we going to do about music?" I asked.

"Dad, I know you've always used symphony orchestras," he replied, "but it's time for a change." Knowing that music was where John's heart really lay, I asked him what he had in mind. He told me about hearing the great American jazz saxophonist Sonny Rollins at Ronnie Scott's club in Soho. "You have to listen to him, Dad," said John. "He can be jaunty. He can be mournful, everything that's Alfie."

Hylda and I went to Soho. John rang ahead to say we were coming. With us that evening was the American actor Tony Randall, who was not only perking up Doris Day comedies in those days but was fun to know in private life. It wasn't his night, though. Hardly had he put his head round the door of the club than he was back out again, repelled by the thick haze of cigarette smoke. There was no way he could stand it. We thought he was being a bit of a fusspot. The expression 'passive smoking' was several years off. Tony's not around anymore. If he were, he'd find himself in the majority.

I wish Tony could have stayed. Sonny Rollins was as good as John said. Hylda and I were spellbound, as was the rest of the packed house. "You've hit it," I said to John afterwards, and together we went backstage. Sonny was charming and, for a jazz man, surprisingly unweird. What made him happy as much as anything was talking about his wife and the rest of his family. As a musician, he was a perfectionist. In order to rethink his playing and get some serious practice in, he had been known to take out a whole year. We were, in due course, to become lifelong friends.

The recording of *Alfie*'s score was like none I had known before or was to know again. Those three sessions with Sonny were the most exciting of my life. He hadn't written a note. In his head was a little tune, and he improvised around it while watching the story unfold on the screen. Backing him was Ronnie Scott's resident quartet, likewise jazz musicians and so able to follow where he went. Sometimes, after a few takes, I thought we'd got it, but no. "Please, one more, Lewis. I can do better," Sonny would say and go on to do perhaps 20 takes. As each one was different and interesting I could see that this was not mere preciousness but an artist at work. Now, I thank John for thinking of Sonny and I thank Sonny for giving the film the perfect aural tone.

A film goes through different stages to arrive on the screen and there's never time to relax. As you jump one hurdle, there's another one facing you. The film was finished. It had its score. It was time to show it to the censor. I was not looking forward to that. For a start, censorship in the UK isn't the same as it is in America and you have to negotiate both separately. In the UK, the censor judges the film on its own merits, makes up his or her mind and that is what goes. In America there is a written code which means that censors can think all they like but they must stick to that code.

The British censor was John Trevelyan, whom I had known for years. He was a sensible chap who understood that times were changing, and liked films anyway. He certainly liked *Alfie.* "I can see nothing in this film to censor," he said. I sighed with relief. "But," he added, "you may have a problem in America. Not only is it written in their code that scenes of abortion are strictly forbidden, so is the actual word." This was alarming because, needless to say, America was very important to us. "However," Trevelyan continued, "I know the censor over there. He's called Geoffrey Shurlock. I'm going to drop him a line to say that this is a film of exceptional merit. He may be able to do something."

And Mr Shurlock did. The film was sent to America for him to see, and out of the blue I received a phone call. It was Shurlock himself. "This code of ours, it's out of date," he said, "I'm going to use *Alfie* to help us get it rewritten. You've made a good picture, a moral picture, and standing in its way looks dumb." He set to work and, after a fair amount of argy-bargy, got the code rewritten, which got *Alfie* its certificate for America.

No time to rest, we had to think of the London premiere which was to take place at the Plaza in Lower Regent Street, Paramount's showcase cinema. Howard Harrison, the UK boss of Paramount, was right behind it. Not only that, he was also in sympathy with the style of premiere John was hoping for and, in due course, went on to organise. As a result, The Beatles, The Rolling Stones and Barbra Streisand were among those who came. Barbra was able to be there because she was rehearsing the London production of *Funny Girl*.

The invitation card to Alfie said 'Dress Informal', so instead of the usual black ties you saw silk roll neck shirts, red military jackets with gold epaulettes and an awful lot of velvet in different colours. It was the first time there had been such a premiere. The film itself got huge laughs, and when it was over there was only a short walk across Regent Street for the guests to reach The Cockney Pride tavern where the after film party was to take place. Sausage and mash and jellied eels were served while music hall songs were banged out on the piano. It was the proudest night of my life. Not only was the film a huge success but I was able to look at my son in a different light. He was no longer there just as family, but as someone who from beginning to end had made a great contribution to that success.

To keep interest alive after the premiere John, on seeing that a general election was due, got six people to join the campaigners in Trafalgar Square who were walking around with placards saying what party they were supporting. Our six walked around in sandwich boards which announced, 'I'm voting for Alfie.' Camera crews picked up on this and there, on the TV news that evening, were those sandwich boards.

The song 'What's it all about, Alfie?' by Burt Bacharach and Hal David remained a constant advertisement. It was added after the premiere, and Cilla Black sang it for the British release. Why was it an advertisement? At the time Alf Ramsey was the manager of the England football team. If anything ever went wrong during a match the crowd would chant, "What's it all about, Alfie?"

Straight after the premiere there was another hurdle – America. I boarded a plane for Los Angeles. With me was Howard Harrison. Before leaving, I sent a message to the American boss of Paramount, no longer the two writers but a man called Howard Koch, who is not to be mistaken for the screenwriter with the same name. Our Howard Koch had worked his way up from the job of assistant director. In my message, I pointed out that *Alfie*, being a comedy, would need some kind of audience at the private showing in order to make it go with a swing. I was imagining about 40 people. When

Howard and I arrived at the cinema there were 400. How would 400 Los Angeles Americans take the film, I wondered. They lapped it up, and applauded like mad at the end. As they did, Howard Koch jumped to his feet to say how glad he was that he had believed in *Alfie* all along and had been convinced that here was a picture that had to be made.

On our way home, Howard Harrison told me that when Howard Koch had been appointed head of Paramount the two of them had flown together to the UK, discussing various projects during the journey. "Drop this picture *Alfie*," Howard Koch had said, "It'll never go."

"There's hardly any point," Howard Harrison had argued casually, "they've spent half the budget already." And Howard Koch pursued the matter no further. After the showing in Los Angeles and, realising that the film stood a good chance of doing well, he got squarely behind the picture and pushed very hard.

The Paramount US distributor was another matter. American ways and the American way of speaking were all he understood. Our little British picture was a total mystery to him. "You've got to get it revoiced," he said. "Get some American actors, otherwise no-one'll understand a word."

"But the cockney is the film's appeal," I said, "That's what makes it different. We have to trust the audience." He could not see that. The film opened in New York in two cinemas. So amused was the *New York Times* that it published a glossary of our cockney terms. 'Bird' for a start, and then all the rhyming slang like 'whistle' for suit (whistle and flute, suit). It couldn't have helped us more. Everyone got interested.

"Yeah, but this is New York," said our distributor. "Here it's different. They're more sophisticated. Wait till it reaches the suburbs. They'll never get it." The film went to the suburbs where it opened in eight cinemas. All house records were broken. Chicago came next. "Not a chance," said the distributor. It was a smash. Then it was Baltimore. "Hasn't a hope." It broke all records and on it went like that right across America. The distributor insisted that no town would get it, and every town did. He was still saying the film would never go when it finally reached one-horse towns out in the middle of nowhere. And did very good business. I shall not congratulate myself by saying that I knew it in advance. I didn't. It was just very nice afterwards, to realise that *Alfie* spoke to a lot of people and they didn't have to be British. The distributor never admitted that he was wrong.

So, *Alfie* changed my life. It made me the blue-eyed boy and, all at once, I was very much in demand. Surprisingly, I felt no different.

23

Real Life: The Nephew's Story

Way back in the early 1950s, when Hylda was trying to extricate herself from that unhappy first marriage, we were helped by her brother-in-law. His name was Eric Sosnow, a brilliant businessman who was well up in legal matters. It was during the making of *Alfie* that an event in his life spread out to affect the rest of the family.

Eric was born Eric Sosnowitz in Poland where he went to university, got a degree, studied law and passed all the exams he needed to qualify for practice. Being Jewish, he then had to get out. He arrived in England with not a penny to his name, nor a word of English. There was something about this country that he had always admired, the whole English gentleman thing. However, the place he first went to was Scotland. Relatives up there were able to take him in.

As his qualifications were no use to him in Britain, he had to start again and study for the British equivalent. This he did and successfully. One of his first businesses was the importing of oranges from South Africa. He found the name of the company that he formed while on a train journey. At a station, where the train happened to pull up, he saw the sign 'Sunningdale' and that was it. Later he formed United City Merchants which became immensely successful and made him a rich man.

In due course he married Hylda's sister, Sylvia, and could not have been more delighted when she bore him a son. That boy was the apple of his eye and the opportunity to make his dream come true, which was to turn his son into the kind of English gentleman he so admired. First, he sent the child to Rugby school where Norman – that was the boy's name – was quite naughty but in an interesting sort of way. At the time of his leaving, Eric asked the headmaster, "Do you think Rugby has changed Norman?" The headmaster answered, "No, Norman has probably changed Rugby." Cambridge followed, and by the time Norman left there he was the very model of an English gentleman – tall, handsome, well spoken and blessed with the sort of easy good manners that would convince anyone his family had sailed over with William the Conqueror. Eric was grooming him to take over United City Merchants and it looked an absolute certainty that Norman would make a go of it. He was by then 22 or 23 years old.

His family, and what it was up to, always interested him, so whenever he and I met the two of us would naturally talk about films. When I told him I was making *Alfie* he was particularly interested because he had seen the play and was keen to know how the film would work out. He then remembered that he was going away on business and wouldn't be able to see it. "Come to Twickenham Studios this afternoon," I said. "We're showing the rough cut. You'll be the first person to see the film who wasn't involved in its making, so don't forget to laugh in all the right places." When the showing was over he told me that it was the best of all the films of mine he had seen and predicted that it would be a great success.

A few days later he went to South Africa to work in his father's orange business, which was still very much a going concern. Not long after his arrival he needed to travel from Port Elizabeth to Durban. "Take the company plane," said the firm's local manager, but Norman declined. His mother had forbidden him ever to go on a private plane. As a young woman she had once been engaged to a young man who had taken flying lessons at Denham airfield, where he had crashed and been killed. Norman booked himself on a commercial flight. He would reach Durban in half an hour.

I was asleep in London when the phone rang at six o'clock in the morning. "Who is it?" I said, none too happy at being woken so early.

It was Norman's distraught mother, Sylvia. She spoke in a strangulated voice. "Norman's been killed in a plane crash. This will kill his father."

I woke Hylda and told her. Staring straight ahead, as if seeing it, she said, "I heard about that crash on the radio. It was late last night." Then she burst into tears. "I didn't think that Norman – oh, this is unbearable." And it was. Norman was everyone's favourite nephew and now he was dead.

Eric was in India and flew back immediately. Someone had to meet him at the airport and that job fell to me and my brother-in-law, Sydney Tafler. It was awful. As Eric came through customs he looked a very, very old man. Suddenly his whole life had collapsed. This was something neither he nor Sylvia would ever get over.

The shock waves spread outwards hitting the whole family with a force that took me by surprise. Cousins, aunts, uncles, all were affected. However, it was only years later that I understood the precise effect of Norman's death on me. When I hear of a distant disaster where people are left dead or of a terrorist killing a hundred people with a single suicide bomb, I realise that not just those killed are the victims. The mothers, the fathers, the brothers, the sisters and the friends, they too are victims and will remain so all their lives.

My brother-in-law, Eric, tried hard to fight against the calamity but he never really succeeded. Neither he nor Sylvia saw out their three score years and ten. They had a daughter, Fiona, very much an afterthought as she was younger than Norman by 13 years. At his death she was ten and, for someone with no experience of tragedy, the blow was devastating. She remembers clearly her mother taking me to one side and asking me to look after her. I walked her away from the house, trying to paint some kind of picture of her future. A child's resilience is amazing. She grew up well adjusted, got married and had two children, one of them a boy, Richard, who looks exactly like Norman. What saddens me is that Eric and Sylvia never saw their grandchildren grown up.

As it happened, the next film I was offered was packed with death and destruction. At first I turned it down, but as this film bore little relationship to reality I could see that it had nothing to do with my family's grief.

24

James Bond – But Where's the Villain?

Soon after I finished making *The Admirable Crichton* back in 1956, Hylda and I invited Diane Cilento, who'd been in the film, round to dinner. With her came a tall, handsome, well-built young man who spoke in a broad Scots accent. He was her boyfriend. During the course of the evening I asked him if he was an actor. "Just starting," he said. "I'm in the chorus of *South Pacific*."

"What, singing 'There is Nothing like a Dame?'" I asked.

"Yes," he replied and then told me how he had got the job. "I was in a Scottish weight-lifting team up in Glasgow and we came down to London for a competition. When it was over I was on the tube going back to Euston Station, reading the *Evening Standard*, and I came across this advertisement. 'Young men with good physiques needed to play sailors in South Pacific. No previous experience necessary.'" It was the last bit that had really intrigued him. In Glasgow he had done a milk round and other humdrum jobs of the kind most young working class men around him were obliged to do but a long-term career had not occurred to him. He had certainly had no experience of theatre.

He went to Drury Lane where the auditions were taking place and the resident director asked him to take his top off. This obviously worked because the director, an American, who was really keen to have masculine-looking men in the chorus, then asked, "Have you any theatre experience?"

Since saying "No" didn't seem like a good idea, this young Glaswegian remembered that, on his way to work each morning, he passed the Glasgow Citizens Theatre. "Well, there's always the Glasgow Citizens," he answered.

"That's fine," said the director. "Go and stand over there. You're in the show." It's interesting to think that this young man, with no particular interest in theatre, joined *South Pacific* merely thinking that it sounded like an amusing gig. It turned out to be more than an amusing gig because he eventually became Sir Sean Connery.

A few years later I met the young actor again. We were both on the same side in a charity football match to raise money for an old people's home in Hornchurch. On one side was the showbusiness team, of which I was the captain, and on the other was the Hornchurch team, local amateurs. Both teams drafted in three or four footballers who were professionals to add sparkle and crowd appeal. It did the trick. Eleven thousand people showed up at the Hornchurch ground. There's a photo of me flipping a coin at the start of the match. Shirley Bassey then performed the ceremonial kick-off.

Among the professionals was Wally Barnes, right back for the Arsenal. He was just about to retire. Since I was, and still am, an Arsenal supporter, I grabbed every moment when the game was not in our part of the field to chat to Wally about life at Arsenal. The player in the opposing team who had to mark me was another great professional, the England captain Billy Wright. He was married to one of the Beverley Sisters. "Do me a favour will you, Billy," I said. "My family's in the stand. Let me go past you just once." He laughed and agreed. A moment later I caught up with him, did a clever-looking little jiggle and shot past. The crowd went wild.

"Was that OK for you?" Billy called out.

"Perfect," I said.

"Good," he said, "but don't try it again." We drew 2-2, so honour was satisfied on both sides.

Sean acquitted himself very well that day but then he was football crazy. Even when he was famous he travelled everywhere with the Scottish team. However, it was quite a while before we played together again. By then, he had starred in four of the James Bond films and we were in Japan making the fifth, *You Only Live Twice*.

It all started straight after *Alfie*. Albert 'Cubby' Broccoli, who was producing the Bond pictures with Harry Saltzman, gave me a call. "Don't you think it's time you made a Bond film with us?" he asked.

"Not particularly," I said. "What could I do that hasn't already been done before? I mean, how many is it you've made now?"

"Four," said Cubby.

"That's my point," I said. "I'd be like Elizabeth Taylor's fifth husband. I'd know what to do but I wouldn't know how to make it any different." Cubby laughed and left it there.

The next day, he rang again. "Lewis," he said, "you're making a mistake. You have the world's biggest audience and it's waiting to see what kind of a hash you make of it." That was both funny and true. It swayed me. Any other film you make, you don't know what's going to happen. A good film may die. A bad film can make money. With James Bond you know for sure. Millions of people are waiting, and if you pull it off that does you no harm. I accepted Cubby's offer and thoroughly enjoyed making the picture. Both Cubby Broccoli and Sean Connery were fine to get along with.

If there was a problem on the film, it was Sean's relationship with Harry Saltzman. This was at a critical point. In fact, it had gone past that. Sean had made it clear that he wasn't going to make any more Bond films. I don't know the full facts, but in Sean's eyes Harry had let him down. It seemed that Harry had guaranteed Sean a percentage of the film, or made some such promise. However, when Sean's agent got on to Harry, Harry denied any knowledge of it. Sean's outlook was black and white. If you were straight with him, there was nothing he wouldn't do for you. But if you crossed him, or he suspected that you were not being straight with him, then you were off his list for good and Harry was definitely off his list. Sean announced that if Harry even appeared on the set he would stop work. As Harry was one of my producers, this looked as if it was going to make for difficulties and Sean was sticking to his guns.

On location in Japan, Sean and Hylda were talking together when Harry walked past. Harry had recently been struck with Bell's Palsy, a condition where one half of your face becomes temporarily contorted, giving the impression that you have suffered a stroke. It is unpleasant, but you can live with it and in time it usually goes away. "Good morning, Sean," said Harry, but Sean turned his back on him and walked away.

"You could manage 'Good morning', couldn't you, Sean?" said Hylda, who knew nothing about missing percentages. "I mean, look at the state of his face, all twisted on one side."

"Good," said Sean, "I hope he gets it on the other side."

A more day-to-day problem for Sean was unwanted press attention in Japan. Sometimes it was frightening. I wanted to do a scene where Bond walked down the Ginza, the main street in

Tokyo. "The simple way," I said to Sean, "is to hide cameras in shop doorways so no-one knows what's going on. When I give you the cue, you get out of the car and walk down the street."

Unfortunately Sean hadn't walked five yards before a man stopped dead in his tracks and shouted, "It's Bond! It's James Bond! Look everyone!" Sean tried to walk on, but he was head and shoulders above everyone around him and his situation was hopeless. Within two minutes a crowd was surging round him screaming, "Bond! Bond!" He jumped back into the car and we were left to do the conventional thing – close down a street and hire lots of extras. Even so, a huge number of police had to be brought in to block off that street.

We set up one official press day in the hope we could keep the press away at other times. Two stands were erected, and as Japan has more film magazines than any other country in the world they were crammed to bursting with photographers. It made no difference at all. Photographers followed Sean everywhere. He couldn't even go out to dinner. There was always a crowd outside his hotel. "Come up and have dinner with me," he had to say to us if he wanted company, and room service it would invariably be. The snapping point came when he was sitting on the lavatory in his caravan on location and looked up to see a photographer trying to take a picture. He was furious.

"We'll get you a bodyguard," I said. "Twelve men who surround you all the time and keep photographers away." The following morning, six burly men were lined up on each side of his car door. As Sean walked between them he smiled, as he felt like visiting royalty. The next second, every single one of those bodyguards whipped out a camera and started to photograph him. Fortunately Sean saw the funny side of this. It was the rest of us who were furious.

This is where we come to the second time Sean and I found ourselves on the same side in a football team. To give him a break, which by then he very much deserved, someone suggested a football match. Everyone knew that he loved the game. The idea was that our crew, the 007 team, would play a local one. Getting into the spirit of things, Cubby generously sent off for football kit, shirts, shorts and boots, which arrived in a big package from London. What he didn't initially know was that Sean was insisting on playing. When Cubby got wind of this, he said to me, "You're not playing Sean, are you?"

"Of course I am," I said. "If he didn't get to play he'd be devastated. He's 007, for heaven's sake."

"That's all very well," said Cubby, "but he's not insured for that sort of thing."

"What's going to happen to him?" I said, "It's only a friendly."

"All right," said Cubby, "but this is making me very uneasy."

The match took place the next day. Fifteen minutes hadn't gone by before a Japanese player, much smaller than Sean of course, cannoned into him and over Sean went. His ankle blew up like a balloon. "You told me nothing was going to happen," said Cubby. "Now, how's he going to work for the rest of the week?"

"We'll strap up his ankle with a bandage," I said, "and shoot round him. Don't worry. He'll be fine." He *was* fine too because he was a trooper and knew about coping. Also, Bond didn't have any running and jumping to do that week.

With Harry Saltzman not around much, it was good to know that Cubby was always someone I could go to. Although I had established that I wanted to make this Bond film something of my own, whenever I had an idea I would still go to Cubby and ask if I was on the right track. He invariably said, "Yes."

A lot of the work on a picture is done before a frame of film is shot. This was particularly true in the case of *You Only Live Twice*. Obviously we knew we were going to make the film in Japan. There's nowhere else like it. So, it followed that we had to establish a relationship with the relevant Japanese authorities. Excited as they were – Japan loves James Bond – they made one important stipulation. The girls in the film had to be Japanese. They knew it was possible to use girls who were Hawaiian/Japanese but those girls, in their opinion, were virtually American. Because this stipulation seemed logical enough, Harry and Cubby were happy to go along with it. Perhaps they didn't realise what difficulties it would lead to.

Equally important as finding the right girls, was finding the right locations. Admittedly they would be for a script we didn't yet have, but that was par for the course on a Bond film. The script always seemed to arrive a few days before the film was shot. With these two main aims in mind, the girls and the locations, Cubby, myself, the production designer Ken Adam and the director of photography Freddie Young set off for Japan, knowing that we would probably be there for quite a while. That time would be needed for our thoughts to crystallise on the film in general.

The first thing I did was contact Tetsuro Tamba, the actor who had worked with me on *The Seventh Dawn* and who, by then, spoke pretty good English. He was going to play Tiger Tanaka, Bond's ally in Japan, but I wanted his help in casting other characters. He could recommend Japanese actresses who might be quick learners and pick up English in a relatively short time. While he drew up a short list to be tested at a later date in a Japanese studio, I made a start with Cubby, Ken and Freddie on finding the kind of locations that were in Ian Fleming's book.

As Bond stories go, *You Only Live Twice* is not one of the strongest. There's no plot to speak of, merely a series of incidents and that didn't make things any easier.

We decided to comb the countryside in helicopters. Harry Saltzman, meanwhile, would base himself in Los Angeles and search for an actor to play the arch villain, Ernst Stavro Blofeld, who was going to make his first appearance in the Bond series. He had been heard before but not properly seen.

The first stop for us searchers in Japan was a hotel far away from Tokyo, and so not at all westernised. It was run according to Japanese tradition which meant that, on arrival, we all found ourselves booked into the same room. Each of us had been allocated a space on its floor and on each space was laid a futon. There was no furniture. Other rooms had spaces for six futons. Our room was a four futon room. To the puzzlement of the hotel manager, Cubby said that we would like a room each. We could have that, said the manager, but we would have to pay for the other three spaces in each room whether we slept in them or not. Cubby, with his Bond film budget, was not too bothered.

In the morning we met our pilots. Two passengers per helicopter is the way we were going to travel, Freddie Young and myself in one, Ken Adam and Cubby in the other, so we had two pilots. They produced a map and, using a grid system, divided up the part of the country we wanted to look at into areas that we could view one day at a time. The next morning it was the same thing, except that we were greeted by two different pilots. This happened the next day too. 'Who are these pilots?' I wondered. 'Are they properly trained? We know nothing about them and we can't ask because they don't speak English.' I whispered my concern to Cubby. Nothing had happened so far, was his response, so what was the problem? The next day our two new pilots appeared as usual but mine and Freddie's was very, very old. He laid the map on the table, and as he pointed out our route his hand didn't stop shaking. I looked across at Freddie. He had gone rather pale. Cubby and Ken, enjoying our misery, were struggling not to laugh.

We climbed into our respective helicopters. By then even I knew how to fly one, as I had been watching every day, but our pilot didn't seem to have a clue. His hand, still shaking, wandered questioningly round the cabin. All at once a mechanic put his head into the cabin and pointed downwards. Our grizzled pilot beamed with pleasure at discovering the controls, and the next second the blades began to rotate. We rose into the air and it was the smoothest take-off we'd had so far. I felt much better. When we reached cruising height the pilot turned to me and Freddie, tapped his chest and said, "Me, kamikaze."

Freddie and I looked at each other, all confidence gone. "If he's a suicide pilot," I said, "why is he still alive? What can he have done?" At the first port of call our interpreter, who was already there, explained that this pilot had trained to be a kamikaze but had been prevented from doing his stuff as the war had ended. "I hope he has no illusions about finishing the job," I said.

The main thing we were looking for in our search was a large building on the coast that fitted Ian Fleming's description of Blofeld's headquarters. Time could have been saved if we had known in advance that no such building existed. Under attack during a war it would have been far too vulnerable. Turning inland and wondering what to do next, our eyes were caught by a volcano. Simply because it looked so interesting, we circled it and looked down. It was extinct. Where you would expect flames and white hot lava to shoot up was a shining disc of water. "Let's land," I said. We walked round the edge of the volcano, looking down into the crater itself. "Cub," I heard myself say, "don't you think that this could be the headquarters?"

"What do you mean?" he said.

"Down there, inside this extinct – " but I didn't have time to finish.

"Yes, yes!" shouted Ken. "That would be a fantastic idea. I've got it. I could build a wonderful set with a sliding roof that's the water down there, except it'll be metal to look like water, and helicopters will be able to fly down into the set. It'll be so big, Pinewood won't have a studio to hold it. It'll be the biggest set ever built in Europe." Cubby, who loved everything to be bigger and better, grinned. We had the climactic image that would make the rest of the film fall into place. This was by far the most important of our discoveries in Japan. Streets, temples, gardens – we knew we would find them. The extinct volcano was unexpected.

The screenplay, incorporating the volcano, was eventually written by Roald Dahl, famous for short stories with a sinister slant as well as children's books. We needed his storytelling skill to strengthen Fleming's plot and his dark humour to complement it. At the start of work together I was a little edgy. Roald had a reputation for being cantankerous. As it turned out I saw nothing of that. In fact years later he paid me a compliment in a newspaper article. If there was one director he could get on with, he said, it was me.

Before we had finished our search for locations in the Japanese countryside, a message came from Tetsuro Tamba in Tokyo. All was ready for the studio tests of the actresses we thought would be best for the film. I said goodbye to the boys for the time being and headed for Tokyo, still in a helicopter. It landed on the roof of a big hotel where members of staff were waiting in a kind of reception committee. As soon as I was out of the helicopter I was shown down a little flight of stairs, straight into the biggest suite I have ever seen. There were three enormous bedrooms, an enormous sitting room and a beautiful dining room. A terrace leading off the suite commanded a view of Tokyo that was panoramic.

"Would you like dinner?" asked a waiter.

"Yes," I said, as I was quite hungry. A table was pushed in, which was then positioned on the terrace. There, on a beautiful summer's evening, looking out over Tokyo, I ate a sumptuous Japanese meal, with waiters bringing dish after dish after dish. Being alone, unusual on a Bond film, I had a sudden flashback. I was in the East End of London in the little family flat where I had lived as a child with its two rooms, scullery, lavatory and nothing else. I try, on the whole, to avoid looking back. I prefer looking forward, but this time a funny sad sort of feeling was overwhelming me. In that moment I wanted my father to see me and he couldn't. What a long way I had come from the days of that cold water flat.

The next morning I went to the studio to shoot the tests. A little set had been built for us and, like all Japanese sets, it was elevated about 18 inches off the studio floor. I soon found out why I got such funny looks when I jumped onto it. Even though it was a set and not a real room, you still had to take your shoes off. I did and put them in the space between the set and the floor like everyone else. The problem was, would I ever find them at the end of the day?

With the tests over, I returned to Cubby and the boys to finish the search for locations. That done, I flew back to London.

Two actresses were chosen after that day's work in the studio, Akiko Wakabayashi and Mie Hama. Neither spoke English. The best thing we could do for them, we thought, was to send them to live with two English families where there were children. Conversation would be non-stop and simple. For three months the two actresses stayed in England, at the end of which we made another test, this time in English. My old writing colleague Vernon Harris, an ex-actor, cued them in. Akiko was fine. She could not only say the words, she could make sense of them. Mie was another matter. The three months had evidently been a struggle for her. Firstly she couldn't understand me, and when she spoke she was incomprehensible. She could make no sense of the dialogue at all. As shooting of the film was soon to start, we were facing a big problem.

I went to Cubby and Harry to explain the hopelessness of the Mie situation. She would have to go home. "Yes, but how do we tell her?" they said. It was going to need delicate handling and none of us spoke Japanese. My suggestion was to ask Tetsuro Tamba. It was the only way out. He was with us in London and he could talk to Mie.

"Good idea, good idea," said Harry and Cubby, relieved to be shot of the problem, not that it was a problem Tamba wanted either. "That's serious, very serious," he said.

"But could you not explain to Mie that it would do her no good to give a bad performance in a Bond film? It would be bad for us and bad for her," I said.

"I'll take her to dinner," said Tamba. "I don't know what I can do but I'll try."

The next morning, I rushed in to see him. What had happened? "Straight to the point," said Tamba, "if you insist Mie goes back, tonight she will jump out of her of window at the

Dorchester Hotel and commit suicide."

"What!" I said, "You're joking."

"No," said Tamba, "you have to understand face-saving in Japan. It is most important. You have a girl who has been sent to England to be in the biggest film ever made in Japan and everybody in her country knows. If you send her back, you are saying she is no good. So, for her, the only way to save face is to commit suicide." This was indeed serious, and it was not up to me to make a decision off my own bat. The producers had to be told.

"What happened with Mie? What did she say?" asked Harry and Cubby when I went to see them.

"Sit down," I said. "The news is not good." Actually I was quite enjoying myself. The two of them were always dumping problems in my lap. Now it was my turn to dump a problem in theirs. I told them of Mie's threat to jump out of her window at the Dorchester, concluding with, "It would make a splash in England and an even bigger splash in Japan," which I thought was rather funny. Cubby and Harry did not.

"What shall we do?" they asked.

"If Mie does what she says she will do," I answered, "that's the end of the film because you'll never get to make it in Japan and you can't make it anywhere else. It's that simple. So, we keep her and either carry on in the hope that her English improves or we revoice her at the end of the shoot and live with it."

In the event, several months later, the latter is what happened. Skilled voice artiste Nikki van der Zyl, who had revoiced other Bond girls, listened to a Japanese speaking English and came up with an accent that sounded Japanese but had useful English inflections. In fairness to Mie, it has to be remembered that Japanese rattles along pretty much on a level, while we tend to go up and down more. The two languages could not be less alike.

Back in Japan some weeks later, we were shooting a pearl-diving sequence when another case of doubling saved the day. The real pearl-divers, women all of them, did their jobs superbly but were tough-looking customers, which wasn't really appropriate for a Bond film. I was running out of long shots of these women and wondering how to get some closer ones when Sean happened to mention that Diane Cilento, who was now his wife, had just flown in to see him. "Why didn't you say so before?" I said. There was the solution to my problem. In Bermuda, making *The Admirable Crichton*, Diane had swum and dived brilliantly. In fact, I think she had been a champion as a teenager in Australia. Diane was sent for immediately and, once on the set, was intrigued by the whole pearl-diving business.

I asked her if she would like to help out. "Delighted," she said and, in doing those dives, got us out of the fix.

"What's your fee?" I asked when we'd finished.

"Forget it," she said, "I've enjoyed myself."

There's a mysterious female who makes her debut in *You Only Live Twice* and her success in it has made her very popular. Racing along a road in Japan, Bond radios Tiger Tanaka. "Contact M. Tell him to send Little Nellie. Suggest she be accompanied by her father." At that moment, we have no idea what Bond is on about. Does he mean a new girl? In due course, a hot and tired Q appears with four large suitcases. In them, ready to be assembled, is an autogyro – a tiny flying machine, little bigger than a go-kart. It combines features you can find in a plane, a helicopter and a glider. Wing Commander Ken Wallis, an RAF man, was its inventor and it was he who flew it for the film, doubling for Sean. This autogyro was Little Nellie.

So toy-like did she look, we wondered if she could do anything at all. The first thing we had to shoot was her take-off. This was done on a perfectly ordinary road. Once Wallis was sat in the machine, little rotary blades propelled him along from behind, while bigger rotary blades above him, like those on a helicopter, were supposed to achieve the actual lift-off. A wind blowing in the right direction was vital. It was blowing in the wrong direction. I thought of turning the camera round but that would have had us looking into the sun. I asked the Wing Commander if he could do the take-off with the wind in the wrong direction. "Very dangerous," he said. However, realising that we were in a hopeless situation, he agreed to have a go. I sat with the camera operator in the camera car and we tracked along just behind the autogyro. I wondered if we would carry on like this with no take-off or if, even worse, the machine would topple over and break. The good thing about being a pessimist is that it's all the more cheering when something goes right. In the middle of my black thoughts, the autogyro sailed up into the air.

Once airborne in Little Nellie, Bond finds the extinct volcano and flies into the crater to have a look. That was the next important scene with the Wing Commander's invention. Having chosen positions for our cameras on the edge of the crater, I told him to fly into the crater, circle the rim and fly back out again. He managed the first part all right but while he was circling I noticed that he dipped below the edge of the crater. When it was time for him to come out, he didn't. What was the matter with him, I wondered. Had he not understood me? Why was he not coming up? I signalled to my first assistant director, Bill Cartlidge. He had been taking a great interest in Little Nellie. Perhaps he knew. 'No lift,' he signalled back. The autogyro needed an updraft and there wasn't one. It could only keep circling. I did what all directors do in a situation like that. I yelled, "Keep the cameras running!" The autogyro carried on circling. We looked on helplessly. Minutes went by. For once, I think I could be forgiven for my black thoughts. At that moment, the autogyro bobbed up. The sigh of relief we all breathed was very deep. This was the start of several flights, 75 all told, that Wing Commander Wallis made with both the first and second unit over the countryside of Japan.

Most of the interior scenes in the film were shot back at Pinewood Studios after the location work in Japan. Ken Adam was quite right about his volcano. It really was the biggest set ever built in Europe and did not fit into any of the studios. It had to be built on the back lot with only a tarpaulin to cover it.

At the climax of the film, Bond pulls the lever that opens the sliding roof – the one Ken had dreamed up when standing on the real volcano. Tiger Tanaka's men, who have been waiting round the edge of the crater, throw in ropes and slide down. We had shot the first part in Japan. Now we needed to do the sliding bit. "How do we find 30 stuntmen?" I asked Bob Simmons, the film's stunt co-ordinator.

"The simple answer to that is you don't," answered Bob. "There aren't that many good stuntmen around. Ten maybe, but that's it. The rest will be ordinary guys with a lot of pluck."

Anyone who has done gym at school, knows that if you slide down a rope quickly with your bare hands you burn your palms and fingers. To prevent this, our 30 men concealed short lengths of rubber tubing in their hands. If any of them had panicked and loosened their grip on the tubing they would shoot down the rope at such a speed that the landing would break a limb. Two of the 'lot of pluck' guys did just that and broke their ankles.

What you see on the screen, however, is spectacular and exciting, which we knew it would be, even as we shot it. What I didn't know, and what was really worrying me by now, was who the arch villain was going to be. We still didn't have one.

Casting on Bond films was very often left to the last minute. Cubby and Harry were quite happy with that. "Don't worry, everything will fall into place," Cubby used to say. I did worry though, and wished all the major casting could have been sorted out before the shoot started. There we were, several weeks into making the film and there was no sign of a Blofeld.

We were days away from shooting his first scene with not even the name of an actor to consider when a man appeared in front of me, a Czech actor called Jan Werich who barely spoke English. He was introduced as our Blofeld. I couldn't understand a word he said and he looked like Father Christmas. Harry was in Los Angeles so, as usual, it was Cubby I had to turn to. This actor, I told him, was not our Blofeld. He would have to go home. Cubby agreed. Jan was disappointed but there was no threat of suicide, and he went home.

With the crucial scenes upon us, I spent all my spare minutes with Cubby, flipping through the casting directory *Spotlight*. I felt like the director of a regional rep theatre who'd lost his leading man on a Friday with rehearsals due to start on Monday. The only difference was that agents were much more obliging. They still couldn't help, though. It wasn't just stars who were unavailable, it was good character actors too. If they weren't already working they had a job in a week's time, which was no use to us. And then, an agent told me that his client, Donald Pleasence, had just finished a job that day and was immediately available. "What are you waiting for?" I said. "Send him over." I knew we were in business with Donald's menacing eyes, but when he came over I saw that he was actually quite slight in build. What we did to add even more menace may not have been original, but time was running out. Make-up gave him a scar down the side of his face. The moment when the camera pans up from the Persian cat to Blofeld's face, never before seen, is most effective.

The day came to blow up the volcano. Ken Adam and his wife, Letizia, appeared. They were near to tears. "Why do you have to blow it up?" they said. "It's so beautiful."

"But this is a Bond film," I said, "It's not a Ken Adam convention."

When the film was finished the distributor, United Artists, was thrilled with the result and said that it would go flat out to get a good premiere. The Queen, they discovered, had a pet charity she was keen to champion and so it was she who became our guest of honour. As usual, before going into the auditorium, we who had made the film were lined up with our wives to be presented. I noticed that as the Queen moved along she was not outshone by the famous and beautiful actresses she spoke to. When she reached me, she asked if I had travelled to Japan to make the film. I answered that she would have to wait and see. And so ended my first foray into Bondage. Little did I know that there would be two more, but not for another ten years.

25

The Biggest Mistake of My Career

When success comes, what follows does not arrive in a straight line. It comes from different angles and all at once. With *Alfie* established as a hit, and the news that I was directing a Bond film, I became fashionable for the first time in my life. During the making of *You Only Live Twice* offers came from all over the world. How was I to react? 'Accept everything and do the one you like best,' had always been my guiding principle. This had served me well enough in the past but the pictures had mostly been small and quickly shot. Would it be so good for the kind of offers I was receiving in the mid 1960s? These were big pictures that, once started, rumbled along like juggernauts. For those, you had to be very clear what you wanted, because the commitment was so great. I thought I was handling things well, bravely turning down offers and waiting for the right one to come along, because that's what happened. The right one did come along – a film I had wanted to make for six years.

In 1960, while adding the title song to *Light Up The Sky*, Lionel Bart told me that he was turning Dickens's novel *Oliver Twist* into a musical. I asked him to keep me posted but heard nothing until a friend of mine said that he had just seen a tryout of a new show called *Oliver!* He'd been down to Wimbledon to catch it. Realising that this had to be Lionel's musical, I asked my friend what he thought of it. "Not much," he said. "It didn't go down well with the audience at all." And that seemed to be that. A few days later I met Max Bygraves, who in 1957 had starred in a film of mine called *A Cry from the Streets*. He was full of a show he had high hopes for, *Oliver!* It was coming to the New Theatre (The Noël Coward Theatre) in the West End. As if reading my mind, he said that Wimbledon hadn't been a great success because audiences there were not keen on musicals. He was sure it would do well at the New Theatre. His enthusiasm made me want to go to the first night. "That's easy," said Max. "I've got an interest in the show. I can fix seats." When I asked what his interest was, he told me that he owned a publishing company, Blossom Music – he'd named it after his wife – and on hearing that Lionel was doing *Oliver!* had offered to publish the songs. As the two had known each other for a while, Lionel had agreed. That sounded encouraging, because if anything were to come of this musical I knew to whom I would be talking.

Hylda and I went to the first night and it was about the best and most exciting I have ever been to. As soon as I could, I went round to the stage door where I found Max. He told me that Lionel had paced up and down the alley behind the theatre throughout the performance. So sure had he been that it was going to be a disaster that he had not been in the least surprised when, at the end, he had heard a noise that sounded like "Awful! Awful!" It had been up to Max to push him on to the stage, while explaining that the audience had been shouting not: "Awful! Awful!" but "Author! Author!"

I found Lionel back-stage congratulating the cast. "Aren't you thrilled?" I said. If anything, he was in a daze. "So what are you doing now?" I asked. "Are you going to a cast party?"

"No, we didn't expect anything like this," he said. "There's nothing arranged."

"Come with us then," I said. "I'll invite Max and we can all have dinner together."

We went to the Caprice where I told Lionel that I wanted to make *Oliver!* into a film. Would he let me have it? "Yes," he said. The next day the reviews were terrific and things seemed even better when John Brabourne, with whom I had worked so happily on *Sink the Bismarck!*, told me that he wanted to produce the film. His good reputation meant that money would not be hard to find. I agreed at once, and before long everything appeared to be sewn up.

The phone rang. It was Donald Albery, owner of the New Theatre. He thought it might be a good idea if we dropped round. "I hear that you're planning to film *Oliver!*" he said, once we were sitting in his office.

"We are," I said. "Max Bygraves owns the songs and he's given us permission."

"Max may own the songs," said Donald, "but he does not own the show. I do and I'm not giving you permission. I'm not ready for that. We're going to Broadway first." I was bitterly disappointed. My chances of doing *Oliver!* seemed nil.

Six years went by, during which I directed four films, the last of which was *Alfie*. Then, during the shooting of the Bond film, the phone went again. It was Jimmy Woolf. He and his brother John, who had been part of the *Alfie* deal, had some good news. Donald Albery had released *Oliver!* to them, so would I be interested in directing it. Would I? "I was born to direct it." I said. At that, Jimmy went to Columbia Pictures who were financing the film and told them what I'd said. Since they were happy with the idea, an agreement was drawn up and, while *You*

Only Live Twice was being made, I set to work on *Oliver!*'s screenplay. Vernon Harris and I wrote it together, not a difficult job as everything was pretty much there already. It was just a question of cutting a bit and repositioning a song or two. Lionel, whose thoughts had been similar to ours, gave us his blessing.

As well as Vernon coming to Pinewood, there was also John Box, *Oliver!*'s set designer. "And which picture are we working on today?" Cubby Broccoli would ask on finding the two of us working away at the designs. I didn't feel too guilty because several hours could go by for the lighting of the big Bond sets, hours when I was simply not wanted. Anyway, Cubby knew I wouldn't let him down.

Yet again, the phone went. It was the American magnate Charlie Bluhdorn, boss of Gulf + Western. He had recently bought Paramount Pictures and was very impressed by the success of *Alfie*. From his point of view, it was a big return on a small investment. He wanted me to sign a three picture deal. I wanted me to sign it too. It was, after all, a magnificent offer. "But I have to make *Oliver!* first." I said, adding that the post-production period would not be taxing as it was the kind of film that was very carefully planned in advance. I was implying that I could start work on the first Paramount film during that period, if necessary.

"Sure, sure, you make *Oliver!* and then come to us," said Charlie. I signed his contract. Money started to come through.

"Do you know what you're doing?" asked Hylda, who loved *Oliver!* as much as I did.

"Of course I do," I said.

"Well, it doesn't look like it to me." What was she on about? I couldn't see it. Hadn't Cubby Broccoli introduced me to a top Hollywood lawyer, Norman Tyre of Gang, Tyre and Brown and hadn't Norman worked out a very good deal for me? What was the problem? There was a problem, though. I had lost touch with reality and replaced it with what I thought was reality.

In the meantime, all sorts of names were coming up for the casting of *Oliver!*, Peter O'Toole, Peter Sellers, Elizabeth Taylor and Richard Burton among them. Peter O'Toole dropped out right away as he had work elsewhere. I had misgivings about the others. I couldn't deny that their names on a poster would be very useful but they had reputations for holding up shooting on the slightest pretext. Say one of them were involved in a big production number and turned up late. Thousands of pounds – today, it would be hundreds of thousands – would be wasted on dozens of dancers doing nothing on full pay. My theory, which for the time being I kept to myself, was that the star of *Oliver!* was Lionel Bart's stage musical. The show had been a huge success both in London and on Broadway. Consequently, it could look after itself. Big stars were not required. What you required were people who could perform it well, that was all.

It was while I was looking for the Bond locations in Japan that this star hunting was at its height. Every day, telexes arrived from London with another brilliant suggestion. My son John, who was associate producer on *Oliver!*, was sent to America. His job was to get Dick Van Dyke to sing a song from the show. John went, reluctantly. You don't have to be a genius to work out that Dick Van Dyke would be a most unlikely Fagin. It didn't stop there. Towards the end of our stay in Japan, John Woolf, knowing that I was about to fly home, asked me to drop by Los Angeles. I was to link up with his brother, Jimmy, and see Julie Andrews, the latest idea for the part of Nancy. I spoke to Cubby, who was amenable as ever. Los Angeles was on his own route. He had business there. We could fly from Tokyo together. A stopover in

Hawaii allowed us go to the theatre that night. It was a production of *Oliver!* Watching that multi-national cast, none of them British, performing it very well told me what a strong show it was. I was very encouraged.

In Beverly Hills Cubby had booked me not only into the same hotel but the same bungalow as had Charlie Feldman, years before on *The Seventh Dawn*. This time, however, I was sharing it with Cubby. Jimmy Woolf was also at the hotel but he was in the main building. That evening he and I were to have dinner together and the next morning we were to see Julie Andrews. At seven o'clock I gave him a call, as we had arranged, to say that I had arrived. There was no reply. I waited quarter of an hour and tried again. There was still no reply. At 7.45 with me getting nowhere I turned to Cubby, wondering what to do. "Perhaps you'd better go over and see," he suggested.

There was a 'Do Not Disturb' sign on the door of Jimmy's suite. This was rather irritating as it left me not knowing what to do. I knocked. There was no answer. "Have you seen Mr Woolf today?" I asked a passing chambermaid.

"No, that sign has been there since I came on this morning." This I didn't understand and asked if she would open Mr Woolf's door. We could go in together, and if anyone questioned her she could say that I insisted. She refused, explaining that a 'Do Not Disturb' sign meant what it said, and that merely by unlocking that door she would be in serious trouble.

"We have to do something." I said.

"I can do nothing," said the maid. "You will have to see the manager." Together we went downstairs. I told the manager I was supposed to be having dinner with Mr Woolf but it made no impression. Growing desperate, I did what I don't like doing. I told the manager who I was and threw in names like Paramount,

United Artists and Columbia. He apologised but said that hotel policy was strict. Even he could not open that door.

"If there's any flak, I will take full responsibility," I said. "Surely you can see the seriousness of the situation?" The manager, keen to avoid a fuss, invited me to go back upstairs with him, where he used his pass key to open the door to Jimmy's suite. The first room we came into was a sitting room. No-one was there. We went over to the bedroom. I looked in. The scene couldn't have been more peaceful. Jimmy was sitting up in bed reading, only his glasses weren't at quite the right angle. I moved forward. His specs were definitely askew. The title of his book, *Valley of the Dolls*, jumped out at me but Jimmy remained very still. "Get a doctor!" I called out.

"He doesn't need a doctor," said the manager. "He needs an undertaker."

A doctor *did* come and told us that Jimmy had died some hours before of a heart attack. The manager, with all the ruthless discretion his job entailed, arranged for the body to be taken out of the hotel by the back door.

The next morning Mike Frankovich appeared in the hotel foyer, thank goodness. Between *The Admirable Crichton* and now he had remained Columbia's UK boss and was therefore behind the film, *Oliver!* I asked him if he had John Woolf's new number which I didn't have. He did. "Hallo," said John merrily. "Have you seen Julie Andrews? Was she all right?" In an extraordinary situation, it's amazing what goes through your mind. 'What a bloody silly idea Julie Andrews is,' I thought. 'She's not earthy enough.' Only then did I wrench my mind back to the matter in hand.

"John, you've got to listen to me," I said. "I've bad news. Jimmy's dead." In the silence that followed, I could feel that John was in total shock.

The next day John's father-in-law Victor Saville, my producer on *The Greengage Summer*, arrived. John, in no state to do anything, had sent for him to make all the necessary arrangements. Organising them, however, was going to take him a few days. "You're off to London right away, aren't you?" said Victor to me. When I replied that I was, I found him handing me Jimmy's plane ticket. "The return half's not much use now," he said. "You might as well take it back to the travel agent and get a reimbursement." It's funny how, in all that sadness, he was able to think of such a thing.

The death of Jimmy and what it meant didn't really sink in until I saw his brother John's face. He was utterly lost. For 20 years, he and Jimmy had made films together, some of them classics. Now that was over. This ideal partnership, Jimmy, the extrovert one who did the producing, John, the buttoned-up one, who did the distributing, was at an end. In that moment, I realised that John would be relying heavily on me to steer *Oliver!* through to its completion. I was a producer, after all, as well as a director. So, if anything, *Oliver!* took on even greater importance. I could not let anyone down.

The phone rang. It was Charlie Bluhdorn, in trouble. He had bought a big, expensive book, commissioned scripts, all terrible, and now his investors were impatient to see a return. I had to drop *Oliver!* and start work right away. So Hylda's fear was realised. I had not known what I was doing. When I told Charlie that it was imperative I finish *Oliver!* first, he only had to point out that I'd signed a contract and accepted money for me to see that I was done for. The fact that I had not yet signed the agreement with the Woolfs, and was technically free to leave Columbia, somehow made things worse. As for Charlie having said that I could direct *Oliver!*, that no longer meant a thing. I swore never to put faith in a spoken guarantee again. This was no use use to John Woolf, though. With Jimmy dead and me off the picture, things looked black for both him and *Oliver!* I spent a sleepless night.

After I had broken my news to John, I tried to cheer him up by saying that we had gone so far with *Oliver!* the script, the sets, the musical arrangements, the choreography, that any competent director could take over. "Name one," said John.

This took me aback but then I thought, 'Keep it simple. What's your favourite film? *Odd Man Out*.' "Carol Reed." I answered. The waves of indifference I felt roll over me were astonishing. "Oh, but doesn't Carol Reed have, you know, personal problems?" people kept saying. I couldn't believe my ears. Carol Reed was my idol. Fussing on about losing Lewis Gilbert while sniffing at Carol Reed seemed to me like the world gone mad.

During this period of uncertainty my son, John, came to me. "I don't know, Dad. Jimmy Woolf's gone and he was the creative one. Now you're going, I'm not sure I want to carry on. After all these upsets, I'd rather go back to music." And that is what he did, but then music was his first love. To help John Woolf out, I stayed a while to work on casting and test actors.

Since Ron Moody as Fagin and Georgia Brown as Nancy had both been excellent on stage, I thought why should they not play their parts on film? After some initial resistance from Columbia, which I managed to break down, Ron Moody was accepted. Georgia Brown was less simple. A Columbia executive in America wanted Shani Wallis, a British singer working there. It was decided that I would shoot tests of both Georgia and Shani. Could the result have been more clear-cut? No. Georgia was easily the best. The tests, both of them, were sent to Hollywood. A few days later, Hylda and I were at the theatre when someone came running over and flung their arms around my neck. "Thank you, Lewis, thank you!" It was Shani. What did she mean? She meant that she had been given the part of Nancy and was under the impression that I had fixed it for her. Since Columbia had said nothing to me, this was the first I'd heard of it but then they knew I was off the picture.

The period of uncertainty ended with Carol Reed being asked to direct, despite the reservations. Sanity had prevailed. His accepting the job, however, made Columbia anxious about the screenplay credit. They were convinced that my name remaining there caused a confusion. Carol, after all, might want to do some writing himself. As it happened, he didn't. The screenplay Vernon Harris and I had written was fine by him. Nevertheless, I had to sign a piece of paper so that my name could be removed. One good thing came of it. Vernon was given a smashing credit all to himself, and later received an Academy Award nomination.

When it came to the Oscars ceremony, *Oliver!* swept the board. Among other awards, it won Best Picture and Best Director. I have been haunted to this day, not by Carol winning Best Picture but by the thought that I was born to direct *Oliver!* and somehow or other, should have made it. Even now, I dream that I'm about to direct it but am suddenly taken off the picture. When I wake, I sigh with relief, "Only a nightmare. Thank goodness." But it isn't a nightmare. It's a fact and one that I shall have to live with for the rest of my life.

26

Real Life: Hylda

I wish I had listened to Hylda. The funny thing is, I usually did. After all, without her help and without her being the person she was, I don't think I would have reached the point that I had by that time.

Hylda was a woman of strong contrasts. A constant, though, was her beauty. She was beautiful when I first met her and beautiful ever afterwards. Walking into a room full of strangers with her on my arm, hearing the room grow quiet and seeing all eyes turn to her and sensing the question, "Who are those two?" gave me great confidence. With my humble beginnings and natural shyness, I needed it. This, of course, was nothing to do with the daily row we had, but the daily row was really our recipe for a long-lasting marriage.

It was always about something small, usually films. I'd be talking of one in particular, saying that it was directed, for example, by Carol Reed and Hylda would interrupt with, "No, Michael Powell," and I'd say, "Don't be ridiculous. It was Carol Reed," and she'd say, "Don't call me ridiculous, I'm telling you it was Michael Powell." And I'd say, "Listen, I've been in the business all my life – " "Yes and don't we all know it," Hylda would cut in, only for me to shout "Carol Reed!" one last time before storming out of the room. Twenty minutes later, I would go back and Hylda would say, "Would you like a cup of tea?" Everything else was forgotten.

She was a maddening mixture of kindness and rudeness. For instance, she could put strangers at their ease and draw their entire life stories from them after talking to them for only five minutes. At the theatre one evening, the interval came and I went off to buy us some ice-creams. When I returned, Hylda said, "This woman sitting next to me, she's had an unbelievable life."

"It can't have been very long," I said, "I've only been gone ten minutes."

"Quite the contrary," said Hylda, "It was very long indeed."

On the other hand, Hylda and I were walking along Kensington High Street when another woman rushed up and said to her. "I'm so pleased. I've been longing to meet you again. We must have a cup of coffee together."

"Fine," said Hylda, "I'll see you over the road in that coffee shop."

With gratitude shining in her eyes, the woman continued, "I took your advice on dieting. Don't you think I've lost weight?"

"Yes," said Hylda, "but you're still fat."

As the woman went away, I hurried Hylda on. "You shouldn't have spoken to her like that," I said, "It was unkind."

"But I didn't mean to hurt her," said Hylda, "I thought I was helping."

On another occasion, while I was filming in Paris and staying at the Pont Royal Hotel, Hylda flew over for the weekend. As she was tired and hungry when she arrived, I said, "Why don't you ring down and order us something. They have very good room service here."

Hylda picked up the phone. "Two small pots of caviar,

please," she said.

I groaned. "You know I can't stand caviar."

"So?" said Hylda, "We'll put one pot in the fridge. What is this place, a concentration camp?" A Mad Hatter vision of concentration camp prisoners complaining of having too much caviar to eat floated before my eyes. At least Hylda had the good grace to gasp when she realised what she had said. The point is, with Hylda words had a way of jumping out of her mouth before she could stop them.

I may appear to be against her by telling these stories but a sinner is not what I want Hylda to seem. I just don't want to make her a saint either.

A good thing was her objectivity, which could pop up when you were least expecting it. One lunchtime, she was at a popular Kensington Church Street restaurant with a girlfriend and was sitting by the window – her favourite position – when a tramp appeared outside. He peered through the window, pointed at their two plates and put his hand to his mouth, miming that he was hungry. Hylda looked down. Both plates had quite a lot of food left on them. The restaurant was good but served such large portions that neither she nor her friend were able to eat all they had been given.

Hylda summoned the waiter and asked him to put the remaining food from the two plates on to one plate and take it out to the tramp. The waiter whisked the plates away and returned carrying a tray. On it was the one plate of food, as requested, but he had added a slice of buttered bread and a bottle of Coca-Cola. The waiter had got quite carried away. Outside the restaurant he handed the tray to the tramp who hurried off, looking for somewhere to eat. A few yards up the road, he found a doorway and sat down to make himself comfortable. Some minutes later he came into the restaurant, carrying the tray on which were the plate and Coca-Cola bottle, both now empty. "Thank you for your very great kindness," he said to Hylda, "but the food was terrible." Hylda did not have to wait to find that funny.

In my eyes, her kindness and concern for others made the odd abruptness forgivable. Anyway, you only had to remember her mother for it to be understandable. Here was a woman so difficult and so jealous that she played her three daughters off against each other to make them compete for her love. She didn't do it consciously but she relished it and Hylda, being the eldest daughter, bore the brunt. Actually, her mother's real favourite was the boy, Sydney, Hylda's brother. Sydney knew this and was aware of what was happening to his sisters but couldn't protect them. Their mother was not an easy woman to stand up to. In later years, Sydney became one of my best friends, really the brother I never had, but he was no great age when he died. I always felt that something from those early days nagged at him and wouldn't let up. His relatively early death left a big hole in my life.

Here's what the mother would do. You have to know first, that of her three daughters Hylda, the eldest, and Sheila, the youngest, were outright beauties, while Sylvia, the one in the middle, had an appearance that was pleasant. Actually, in any other family Sylvia would have been regarded as the pretty one. Nevertheless the mother, when all three girls plus myself were in the room, said to Hylda and Sheila, "You two must hold off getting married. Sylvia has to have a chance. She needs the most help."

Witnessing this, I realised something about my own mother. Nearly illiterate and often with little money, she gave me and my sister what Hylda never really had – a mother's love. You gain self-confidence from it, which in turn makes you believe you can do anything. My sister and I had plenty of that. Hylda, in spite of her good looks, did not. Perhaps the people with whom she made friends easily will be surprised on reading this, but then perhaps they will remember that she never revealed her personal side to them.

Hylda's father wasn't easy either. Any tender feelings he had were kept for antiques, which was how he earned his living. He loved them so much, he found selling them torture. He handed this love on to Hylda, for whom antiques remained a constant fascination. If there was a parent she was fond of, it was him. When Hylda and I were married, he would often come round for lunch on a Saturday.

Hylda's kindness was unusual. It enabled her to put strangers at their ease, yes, but it didn't let her show love to her children. It wasn't that she didn't love them. She did. She just couldn't express her feelings. She could embrace strangers, but not her boys. Occasionally, I would try to discuss this with her but to no avail. Not a word came out. A shrug of the shoulders maybe, but that was it. I felt sad, and for her I felt sorry.

For years she was locked in conflict with our two sons, John and Stephen. The longest battle was with Stephen. The two eventually arrived at a period of calm and Steve felt able to come round to the house again. Once, as he got up to go, he said to Hylda, "I know you hate people putting their arms around you but I'm not leaving this house until I've given you a hug." He did, and when he left Hylda had tears in her eyes.

27

The Biggest Mistake of My Career: Part Two

To add insult to injury, Charlie Bluhdorn, having levered me away from *Oliver!* and thinking I had to be thrilled to be at Paramount again, wanted me to attend his wedding anniversary. The invitation came via Bud Ornstein, head of Paramount UK. Hylda and I were to join 200 of Charlie's best friends at a surprise party he was throwing for his wife in Paris.

"But we aren't his best friends," said Hylda.

"I know," I said, realising that our proposed presence was more to do with the success of *Alfie* than any friendship, "but the invitation's there and it's very generous, a suite at the Plaza Athenée and our own chauffeur for the whole weekend. It seems ungrateful not to accept."

"Oh well," said Hylda, "I'd better find something for a present." And off she went to consult her father. The antique she eventually chose was rather special and by no means cheap. She put a lot of effort into finding it.

Charlie Bluhdorn's wife was only aware of a quiet celebration, dinner with their two children, nothing more, and she wasn't happy about it. "What about all our friends?" she had argued. However, while she was walking downstairs towards this ordinary little dinner in the Plaza Athenée's restaurant, the 200 guests, Hylda and I included, were assembling in the ballroom so that, at the last second, Charlie was able to steer his wife away from the restaurant and into the room where we were. She recovered from the surprise with remarkable speed. Presents from 200 well-off guests meant that the pile on the table in front of her was more of a mountain, but she seemed to take them for granted. But if you're accustomed to immense riches, that is what happens. If the wife of a less wealthy husband had been given a party like that, she would have sent little thank you notes for those presents. Hylda heard not a word and, considering the trouble she had gone to, that was irritating. I, for my part, looked upon it as a case of swings and roundabouts. We had the suite. We had the chauffeur-driven car and we had the weekend in Paris.

The huge bestseller Charlie had bought, the one that was causing him so much trouble and the reason why I had to drop *Oliver!*, was *The Adventurers* by Harold Robbins. Charlie had bought it off the film producer Joe Levine, who had made his fortune flogging *Hercules Unchained* to the world, a cheap Italian film starring muscle man Steve Reeves.

Harold Robbins was known for taking famous real life characters and fictionalising their stories, adding lots of sex and violence. One of his best-known novels was *The Carpetbaggers*. For this, his real-life character was Howard Hughes, renamed Jonas Cord. Our real-life character was Porfirio Rubirosa, the South American playboy who, starting out with little money, managed to marry two of the wealthiest women in the world before conveniently dying three years in advance of us making the film. In 1965 his car crashed in Paris and he was killed. The story of Dax Xenos – his name in the book – contained intrigue and polo in Paris, big battles in South America and, in both places, plenty of sex and violence. I was in no mood for the sex and violence as I was still sore from not doing *Oliver!*

Among the various previously commissioned scripts was one by Harold Robbins himself, but that was only a repetition of the book and consequently far too long. The mess Charlie Bluhdorn had got into was not only with scripts, but also with dates. He had gone and committed himself and the pressure to meet deadlines was severe. On top of that, a million dollars had already been spent. He thought that the one who could sort out this mess was me.

I settled down to work with the writer Michael Hastings, who had had his first play produced at the Royal Court Theatre when he was still an East End teenager. We battled our way through the book but it was a battle that became bigger, not smaller, because our brief kept changing. At first it was going to be a two-hour film but then Charlie rang.

I thought he was calling from Switzerland since, after decades of making money, he had decided to take his very first break, a skiing holiday. All the gear had been bought, the boots, the skis and the bobble hat, and he'd been looking forward to getting out on to the slopes. However, the call was not from Switzerland. On the very first morning of this holiday Charlie had left the hotel looking quite the international champion, walked twenty yards, slipped, fallen and broken his leg. Would I therefore join him for dinner at the Plaza Athenée in Paris? He wanted to talk about the film. I flew over taking my son, John, who was back in the mood to work with me on another film.

Charlie had his leg up in plaster and, over a very grand dinner in the hotel's biggest suite, was in an expansive mood. He began by telling us how he had made his first fortune. Immediately after the Second World War, Italy was short of wheat while America had wheat in abundance. So, knowing that the staple of an Italian's diet was pasta, he had made spaghetti in America and sold it to Italy. In other words, he had carried coals to Newcastle. You just have to imagine that Newcastle had run out of coal.

Having impressed us with his business acumen, he turned to his new plan for *The Adventurers.* It was to be a three-hour blockbuster with an interval, and was to be given only two performances a day like a play in the theatre. For those performances, audiences would have to book. "But you're cutting your number of performances in half," I pointed out.

"We'll raise the price of the tickets," countered Charlie. I knew that it was possible to do this if you had a film with a heavyweight title like *Ben-Hur* or *Lawrence of Arabia* but that's what *The Adventurers* didn't have. It was a bullshit story that you could get way with at a length of two hours and with the right star. I suggested Alain Delon. "We don't need him," said Charlie. "Stars are out of date and they cost too much." He spoke with great authority but I was thinking, 'Charlie, your ignorance is beginning to show.'

We started to set the film up in Paris. I had recently seen a Roger Vadim film beautifully photographed by Claude Renoir and, in due course, Claude became our director of photography. His lineage was impeccable. Auguste Renoir, the painter, was his grandfather. Jean Renoir, the film director, was his uncle and Pierre Renoir, the actor, was his father.

Star or no star, I knew we had to surround our central character with some well known French actors, so Charles Aznavour and Louis Jourdan were cast. While this was going on, a low budget Yugoslav film opened to great acclaim. It was called *I Even Met Happy Gypsies* and the French critics loved it. The male lead was an actor from Bosnia Herzegovina by the name of Bekim Fehmiu. He had about him a brooding, earthy sexiness and it was him we chose to play Dax Xenos. Whether he could also manage the suaveness and polish of a playboy, we would have to find out.

We thought of shooting the South American scenes in Spain, partly because it was next to France and partly because it had a well established film industry. However, as the script featured a villainous dictator and General Franco was still alive, that didn't go down too well with the authorities there.

Bud Ornstein recommended Colombia. He was familiar with it and as it was the real thing, a South American country, we decided to fly there for a reconnaissance. The evening before our departure I took Bill Cartlidge, who was still my first assistant director, and his wife, Denise, out to dinner. Denise was heavily pregnant. During the meal, we heard rhythmic chanting and saw a large group of students advancing down the centre of the street. It was a demonstration but not like one in London. This was more aggressive. Waiters at the next-door restaurant climbed on chairs and unscrewed the light bulbs attached to the awning. I pushed Denise and Bill into a back room and we didn't come out until the marchers had gone past.

The next day, without realising what that march was leading up to, I boarded the plane for Bogotá. Colombia looked fine but what we were hoping for, its own film industry and actors, we did not find. We realised everything would have to be imported. While we were there, we kept in touch with Paris via telex and telephone. The latter was only a radio line, so voices would come and go. It was therefore with difficulty that we heard of the worsening situation in Paris. Then we saw it on TV – riots. Masked State Security Police were firing off tear gas grenades as students on the Left Bank threw cobblestones at them. It was

1968 and it looked frightening.

Claude Renoir was worried about his family. France ground to a halt – the Cannes Film Festival, among other major events, was cancelled and I was worried that our production might be cancelled too. What we saw looked like a revolution.

I rang Paris to find out from our production manager, Geoffrey Helman, what was going on. "It's hopeless," he said. "We can't even find any bread."

Invoking the spirit of Marie-Antoinette, I said, "Let them eat cake," which he didn't think was very funny.

I flew back to Paris and Geoff was right. It was hopeless. I rang Charlie Bluhdorn and told him that if he wanted the film finished by the date he had specified, we would have to move to Rome at once, lock, stock and barrel. He offered no argument at all.

It was only when we arrived in Rome that it dawned on us that everything had to be rejigged. For a start, most of the parts being played by French actors had to be recast. Thus Louis Jourdan was replaced by Rossano Brazzi. At least we were able to use that rarely invoked clause known as force majeure. It let us off the hook when it came to paying the French actors who had already been contracted. We didn't have to.

Many films were being made in the late 1960s and all Rome's studios had pictures in them, some of them big. Each of the four major ones – Cinecittà, Centro Sperimentale, Incom and Dino de Laurentiis – had some space, but not much. We took the lot, basing ourselves at Cinecittà which had given house room to *War and Peace* once, *Ben-Hur* twice and *Cleopatra.* There, in one long corridor, you could see cigarette smoke billowing, sometimes 18 hours a day, out of our production offices. It was typical of the trance-like state we found ourselves in when I, walking down that corridor, felt the need for a pee and turned into the gents. At the time, I was surrounded by 19 men desperate for decisions without which they couldn't proceed. All of them followed me into the gents. We fell about, laughing hysterically.

On this film, Vernon Harris's job was script editor. New pages were coming at him from different writers every day because there was also Clive Exton and Jack Russell working on the script as well as Michael Hastings. Each was an experienced screenwriter but none knew what the others were doing. They were just rushing to have the script finished on time. Vernon, who was simultaneously turning French names and places into Italian ones, must have felt he was in *Hellzapoppin*. It was an utter mess. We were clutching at straws and I thought I had drawn the short one.

Counting my blessings seemed the best answer. First there was Claude Renoir. At least the film would look terrific. Then we had some good senior actors. As well as Rossano Brazzi, there was Olivia de Havilland, Ernest Borgnine, Fernando Rey, Alan Badel and Charles Aznavour. Of the French actors, Charles was the one who didn't have to be replaced. Young actors, just making their names, were also in the cast, Thommy Berggren from Sweden and Candice Bergen. Bob Simmons of the Bond films was going to be the stunt arranger. None of that sounded too bad, and indeed when we came to the end of the Rome shoot and were about to fly to Colombia, we felt surprisingly optimistic. Not only had we finished on time but the rough cut, including, as it did, a polo match, fashion shows, fast cars and pretty girls, had rhythm and bounce.

After that, Colombia came as a shock. Italy, with its creature comforts and long tradition of film-making, had been easy. In

Colombia we had to travel all over the country to find the variety of landscapes we needed, driving hours out into the middle of nowhere each day to find our locations. It wasn't only out either. It was often up. Some actors' agents had insisted on posh cars for getting their clients to work. "They'll have a horse and count themselves lucky," I had said, only to find negotiations abruptly terminated. Maybe they thought I was joking. They were wrong. To reach lonely hillsides where we were to shoot a hacienda on fire and a rebel camp being overrun at night, a horse was by far the best means of transport.

For a scene where our villainous dictator reviews his troops, we went to a small town called Villa de Leiva, at the heart of which was one of the biggest squares in the whole of South America. It's called Plaza Major. As there was only one hotel, and as that hotel had only four bedrooms, most of the crew had to be billeted elsewhere and that included me. The location manager's suggestion was someone's home, in this case, a ranch. At first I wasn't keen, as the owners had seven children, but when I realised that they were grown up and living in Bogotá, I changed my mind. The children did appear, but only at weekends. It was at this ranch that Hylda joined me. Typically, she adapted to her surroundings in no time and became lifelong friends with the lady of the house, Emma Botero.

The reviewing of the troops in the square needed not only people to do the marching and riding but also people to look on and cheer. As the population of Villa de Leiva was quite small 6,000 extras were needed, and they had to come from elsewhere. Each day, they walked from their homes far away, setting out at three o'clock in the morning to be on time. For the caterers, it was the toughest test of the whole film. Lunch had to be provided for every one of those 6,000.

The weather was often against us during those days and once, while waiting for a break in the clouds, I joined the crew for a kickabout. One of them tackled me and knocked me into a ditch. I landed with a loud *klump*. Bill Cartlidge ran over to find me lying with my foot at right angles to where it should have been. "Quickly, Bill," I said, "take hold of my foot and turn it the other way." Reluctantly he did, and we listened to it creak back into place. One of the Colombian assistants told me that I would have to fly to Bogotá for an operation. "But that would bring the film to a halt," I said.

"There'll be a halt if you don't go," said the assistant. "You won't be able to walk."

That evening I explained this to my hostess, Emma Botero, in whose hacienda I was staying, when she interrupted. "Don't worry. My husband's a surgeon," she said, "and he's coming back for the weekend."

That night he looked at my foot. "It's not broken. You've torn some ligaments," he said. "All you have to do is keep the foot in the same position for a month. I'll put it in plaster."

"How do I walk?" I asked.

"You don't," he answered. "You ride a horse, the same as the rest of us."

And from then on, all outdoor scenes were directed by me on horseback. It was the right time for it to happen. Up there, I gained more respect not only from the unit but also from those thousands of extras. I felt like a great old time director in the days of silent films. It was not something I would try at a British studio, though.

The South American scenes, though spectacular in themselves, didn't help the scenes shot in Rome. They weighed them down and the picture lost its bounce. Much, of course, rested on the shoulders of Bekim Fehmiu but he never found the suave playboy and it wasn't his fault. He was miscast. It was as simple as that. Had Alain Delon played the part, he would have found the hero's easy manner as it was natural to him. That would have taken a lot of pressure off and perhaps lifted the picture on to a different level.

Paramount Pictures wanted a sensational venue for the film's press show and came up with the idea of a Boeing 747, a Jumbo Jet. It was to be the very first flight for this kind of plane, so this was indeed a sensational idea. But it was terrible for the film. Four hundred nervous journalists and critics climbed aboard to become, almost at once, four hundred drunk journalists and critics. The screens they had to watch were only small, so the effort that had gone into getting all those thousands of extras to turn up, all that spectacle, was wasted. It was a fiasco and one from which the film never recovered.

The Adventurers was a big picture but it was a big picture about nothing and big pictures about nothing usually make nothing. There was one good thing about the event on the plane, though – it was the only press show where the critics couldn't walk out.

28

Real Life: It's an Ill Wind . . .

The Adventurers took four years out of my life, not something to be repeated and it wasn't. Now, with the passing of time, I can relax and pick out the better parts of that period. Rome, for example, and one particular moment there. It was a coincidence and coincidence has always fascinated me, its effect on people's lives, how far reaching it can be. My seeing Hylda a second time at Lime Grove Studios, there's an example. It led to our marriage. The one in Rome was not like that but it too was good.

The evening after I arrived there to set up *The Adventurers* I found myself pretty much alone. Dinner time was approaching and the thought of eating by myself held little appeal. I left my hotel, the Excelsior, and walked along the Via Veneto. The least I could do was sit outside at a café and watch the world go by. That is what you do on the Via Veneto, after all.

I ordered a glass of Cinzano and, while I was sipping it, looking up and down the street, I was amazed to see Eric, my brother-in-law, and his wife, Sylvia, walking towards me. 'This is crazy,' I thought, 'Eric's in India. He told me so and Sylvia's supposed to be in England.' I looked at my glass of Cinzano to see if someone had slipped me something extra. However, when I looked up there they still were, now whooping away because they had just spotted me.

"But you're not meant to be here," I said.

"We know," they replied. "It's just that we fancied a break and decided to rendezvous here in Rome."

"What a delightful coincidence," I said. "And what are you doing for dinner?"

"Nothing," they answered. "Good, you can have dinner with me," I said.

After drinks, we decided to go back to our hotels for a wash and brush up. "Where are you staying?" I asked.

"The Excelsior," they answered. "That's where I am," I said. "We can walk together." At the hotel, by the lift door, I suggested that we meet again in the foyer at eight o'clock. However, when we stepped into the lift, Eric pressed the button for the fourth floor, my floor. 'How very amusing,' we thought.

When the lift stopped we got out, but instead of going our separate ways found ourselves walking down the same corridor in the same direction. When we stopped outside the same suite, we looked at each other in amazement. "But this is my suite," I said.

"Ah," said Eric, "I think I can explain." He then told me that he and Sylvia had arrived late the night before and been put in a poky room up at the top. The manager had been unable to do anything about it, the hotel being completely full at the time. The next morning, Eric had spoken to the manager again. Was there really nothing he could do? Eric was an habitué of the Excelsior and a valued one too, so the manager, having thought for a while, said, "There's a film director staying here. He has a suite with two bedrooms but he's only using one. You could have the other."

Eric unlocked the door to his bedroom and we all went in. The coincidence was so incredible, we laughed and hugged each other as if we'd been given the freedom of the city. I went over to the door which connected the room to my sitting room and turned the key. "We can both share this now," I said and flung the door open. Eric went in and looked across at my bedroom. Its door was wide open and, through the doorway, he could see a double bed chastely turned down for one person. What he said next I have never forgotten.

"Boy, are you lucky!"

Delirious with this piling up of coincidences, we found it hard to stop laughing. For a moment I saw the sadness, ever present since the death of their son Norman, melt away from Sylvia and Eric's eyes. I could not have been more delighted. Now, what was the chance of that coincidence happening? It must have been not a million, but *millions* to one.

29

Making *Friends*

After the nightmare of *The Adventurers* I needed to regain my sanity. Another big picture was Paramount's aim but I had a different idea. Left to myself, I had done well with smallish pictures and that's what I wanted to do next. To be specific, I had in mind three short love stories to be called *Morning, Noon and Night. Morning* was to be about two 14 year-olds. *Noon* was to be about two middle-aged people and *Night* was to be a romance between two elderly people. Nowadays, it's not something you could do on the big screen because it's regarded as television's department. In the late 1960s Fellini, Vadim and Malle had just put together a triptych, so it was acceptable.

With Jack Russell, who had worked on *The Adventurers*, I sketched out the first story, the one about the 14 year-olds, and to make sure I was on the right track I showed it to Paramount's head of production, Bobby Evans. He was so delighted he wanted me to go no further. "Expand it," he said. "Make this one story the whole picture. Nobody's done anything like it before." I didn't argue. It was a good idea of his, and right away I began to see it forming in more detail. The story should start in a town, cold and unfriendly, then move south to a countryside that was both warm and unusual. I chose Paris for the town, and for the countryside the Camargue, with its wild horses.

In 1970, 14 year-olds were more like children than they are now, so trouble with the censors was on the cards. As soon as the script was finished, which by then Vernon Harris had also worked on, I sent it to our censors and they cleared it.

The story was simple but slightly transgressive. A 14 year-old boy and girl, both for different reasons unhappy at home, meet in Paris and become united in their hatred of what life has handed them. To pass his lonely hours the boy has been stealing cars and, wanting to amuse the girl, does it one more time. The ensuing crash makes up their minds. They travel south to a cottage in the Camargue, once owned by the girl's late grand-mother. Since it has only been empty a little while it is quite habitable. There, as friends (*Friends* is the title of the film) they set up house together.

The boy goes out looking for work and finds various jobs, one of them in a bullring. As time goes by, the teenagers' feelings for each other turn from friendship to desire and it overwhelms them. The girl becomes pregnant. If this were to be known, though, all would be lost. It has to be kept secret. While the girl regrets the lack of professional medical help, the boy heads for town to look in the local bookshop. There, an elderly English lady (Joan Hickson), who is trying to buy a book on French cookery, overhears the boy ask for a book on how babies are delivered. Puzzled, because he is after all only 14, she asks him if he plans to become a doctor. "No, it's for now," says the boy, sailing out of the shop to the elderly lady's amazement.

Nothing goes wrong with the pregnancy, so when the baby starts to arrive the boy has to use the book in earnest. It's a nerve-racking, sweaty time, not to mention painful for the girl. However preparations, though basic, have been made and the boy delivers the baby safely. It made for a powerful scene. When the baby is a few weeks old, the boy and the girl have a bath together in front of a crackling fire and blow bubbles, enough bubbles to fill the whole room. The young lovers with their baby have found an idyll, even if only for a few moments, and it looked beautiful.

The scenes when the boy and girl make love had to be handled delicately. On the days of filming them, the set, which was in a Paris studio, was closed. Anyone who didn't need to be there had to stay outside. Anicée Alvina and Sean Bury, who played the girl and boy, were over 14 but were both nervous. Anicée showed it in her behaviour, while Sean asked lots of questions. I answered them as discreetly as I could. The crew, I was interested to note, were totally unconcerned by the passionate lovemaking of two teenagers. What did concern them, a lot, the next day, was the frying of two sardines. It was a different scene in which the boy, at a low point, tries to make the best of a meagre dinner. This time, no member of the crew held back. Everyone knew how best to cook those fish and delighted in giving me advice. Do not believe those stories about the French being obsessed with sex.

The idyll in the bath is only short-lived. Photos of the missing boy and girl are printed in all the papers, and gradually a couple of detectives track the two teenagers down. The baby is taken away and they themselves are separated. What to them was innocent, to the outside world becomes a crime.

Knowing that the Camargue's stark but beautiful landscape and its most famous feature, the wild horses, would be vitally important to the film, I realised that we were going to need a second unit. The first unit and myself would be going to shoot scenes with the actors but I needed more. Once again I turned to my son John, and this time I sent him, as director, to record all that we might need. He took his young cameraman, Ray Steiner, and together they produced really beautiful shots that, when threaded through the film, gave it an enormous lift.

During the entire shoot I was thinking about the music. I knew it was going to be crucial. I didn't know precisely what was needed, but I knew we needed something different. My son, still very much involved in the music business, was by then back in London. I put a call through to him. "Can you think of someone up and coming?" I asked. "Someone who could go with the story of these two teenagers?" On my return, John handed me an LP. It had a dark cover and, at its centre, a moody profile of a young man in glasses. *Elton John* was its title and Elton John was the artiste who had composed and sung all the songs. I listened to it and heard melody after melody. "Do you think he would be interested?" I asked John as soon as the record had come to an end. "Do you think he might see the film?"

"We'd better find out," said John, and a few days later he invited me to his house for tea and a talk with Elton. Just after I arrived, a young man whom John addressed as Reg came in. We sat and chatted, our conversation remaining utterly general. Never once did it touch on music. After a while, this Reg chap stood up and asked John where the lavatory was. After he had left the room I turned to my son and asked him rather impatiently when Elton John was going to arrive. "He's here, Dad," said John. "That's him."

"But why do you keep calling him Reg?" I asked.

"Because that's his real name," explained John. "Reg Dwight."

When Reg/Elton, returned, I asked him how he had come by his new name. "It belongs to a bass player I used to know when I was starting out," he answered.

"But won't he object?" I asked.

"Oh no," said Elton, "he retired ages ago. Anyway, it wasn't his name either. He got it from someone else."

The film opened at the Plaza, Lower Regent Street, in the summer of 1971, by which time the cinema had become a duplex. Even so, the run of the film was only a few days. The magic, and there was magic, happened elsewhere, in the Far East. Japan and the Philippines took the film to their hearts. In fact, in Japan it was Paramount's biggest hit of the year.

Meanwhile, all sorts of things had been happening to Elton John. Just after recording the score with its string arrangements by Paul Buckmaster and lyrics by Bernie Taupin, he performed at a club in Los Angeles and was taken up by America overnight. Paramount, having not realised they were on to something, woke up and started pushing both the score and the film like mad. That's when the picture took off in all those unexpected places and found success in other countries too, right round the world.

Twenty-five years later heads of Paramount, tough men in their 40s, became misty-eyed when they met me. "Ah, *Friends*," they said, "we saw it when we were teenagers and so did all our friends. It was our favourite film of the year. We were crazy about it." And that's who it appealed to – not the critics, just lots of teenagers. After *The Adventurers* it made me feel much better. Normal service could be resumed.

30

Jetskis and Jaws

Ten years after *You Only Live Twice*, Cubby Broccoli was setting up his next James Bond film, *The Spy Who Loved Me*, and he wasn't happy. The series was healthy enough – this was number ten, after all – but, for the first time, Harry Saltzman was no longer by his side. Why was that?

Over the years, success went to Harry's head. He turned into an old time movie mogul. His office was so stuffed with tailors, barbers and stenographers that no-one else could squeeze in. If you did, any conversation was impossible because Harry was on the phone all the time. Not only that, he had gone mad buying up companies, Technicolor, for instance, and Debrie Cameras (heyday 1922), plus a load of small firms that turned into big failures. The debts were massive, and for Cubby to continue working with Harry proved impossible. He bought Harry out but a problem remained. His custom had always been to work with a partner. During the 1950s it had been Irving Allen, with whom he had run Warwick Films. Now, for the first time in decades, he was alone.

At this moment *Operation Daybreak*, the seventh and last of my war films, opened. I was still a client of the lawyer Norman Tyre, and it was he who suggested to Cubby, also still his client, that he see the film. All being well, Cubby might then ask me back on board and so feel less bereft, since I had experience of producing. Without my knowing this Cubby saw the film, liked it and showed it to United Artists. They liked it too and so Cubby gave me a call. By then I had made so many films away from England that I had settled abroad. In fact I was sitting out in the sun, which I adore, when Cubby's call came through.

Of course things had changed over those ten years, chiefly the actor playing James Bond. Roger Moore by then had played him twice. While watching him, I'd had the feeling that Cubby and Harry wanted him to be Sean Connery. This was no use. Roger didn't have Sean's animal grace. However, he was at ease in light comedy. It therefore seemed to me much more sensible for Roger to play to the strength he had, rather than the one Sean had.

Another thing that had changed was the way the script was produced. By the time Ian Fleming wrote *The Spy Who Loved Me* he was running out of steam. His book, little more than a novella, was a romance told from the woman's point of view. There wasn't much there for a Bond film. There was no alternative but to start from scratch. Anyway the Fleming estate, probably mindful of that woman's angle, had given permission for only the title to be used.

Cubby had a script by Richard Maibaum, the American writer who had been with the Bond films since the start. His solution was a megalomaniac who wants to dominate the world, and the plot was the good old standby in which the arch villain sets Russia and America at each other's throats, then steps in to claim the prize. For this one, he had come up with a tanker that swallowed submarines and one of the best henchmen villains ever, the mighty Jaws, whose steel teeth could bite through anything. That was fine, and for Jaws we found the seven foot four American Richard Kiel who, though playing a merciless killer, had the sweetest of natures in real life. For all that, the tanker and Jaws, I wanted another ingredient – humour, which seemed to be lacking in the script. I discussed this with Harry Saltzman before he left and also with Cubby. They agreed to my suggestion of bringing in Christopher Wood, a writer best known for comedy. While Cubby went to Switzerland to sort out his split from Harry, Christopher and I were left alone to start work.

In the meanwhile Ken Adam, who had not done the previous two Bond films, was back in his element, planning to outdo himself with the tanker that could swallow submarines. His set would be its interior, containing water, submarines, lifts going up and down and all the other realistic touches he was famous for.

Experience on *You Only Live Twice* had taught Ken and all of us a lesson. Ten years earlier, with only a tarpaulin to cover the volcano set, we had frozen. For this tanker a special sound stage, the biggest in Europe, was built. It was called the 007 Stage and the former Prime Minister Harold Wilson came to open it. Later, it was used to house other big sets on other big films. In 1984 it caught fire and burned down. It was rebuilt, even bigger than before, and put back to work immediately, this time called 'The Albert R Broccoli 007 Stage'. Back in 1976 Ken's tanker set took people's breath away. It took my nerve away. I wasn't at all sure how I was going to film it.

I prefer to cast the main parts at an early stage, and with Harry Saltzman no longer trawling the world for unknown actors to play the arch villain it was easy for me to think back to one of my films, *Ferry to Hong Kong*, and one of its stars, Curt Jürgens. He was a big name in Europe and, being also tall and handsome, made a perfect adversary for Bond. He became Stromberg, our arch villain.

There's a tradition of trying to find new faces to play the girls in Bond films, and while we were in the middle of searching I was approached by one of the heads of United Artists UK who had a photo of his girlfriend, a beautiful but inexperienced actress called Barbara Bach. Perhaps we could find a small part for her, he wondered. After Cubby and I had looked at the photo, met Barbara and saw a test she had done for Tony Richardson, we began to think she could play the female lead, Anya. In terms of acting, it wasn't such a huge stretch. So, Anya was the part she was asked to play and she accepted.

The basic plot was an old one, so needed a new angle. Ours was to have the villain obsessed with oceans. His lair was a palace under the sea, another good set for Ken to design. From that idea, came two good Bond gadgets, a Wetbike and a car that could change its purpose. The Wetbike was the first example of a jetski and even I liked it because when I climbed on I didn't fall off. The car was a Lotus Esprit. In the film it runs along a pier, plunges into the sea and disappears from sight. All is up with Bond, or so it seems. The car, however, does not sink to the bottom. Air is pumped in, its wheels retract, fins emerge and propellors drive the transformed vehicle forward. It's no longer a car but a submarine.

Sitting next to Bond in the passenger seat, marvelling at all that's going on around her, is Anya. The Soviet Union has assigned her as a special operative to help Bond kill Stromberg and obtain the microchip on which is printed Stromberg's program to destroy the world. What the Soviets don't know is that she is playing a double role. Because Bond has killed her boyfriend, she secretly plans to kill Bond as well as keeping the microchip for her country.

Once the Lotus Esprit is converted into a submarine it is attacked by Stromberg's crew, who fire torpedoes from menacing underwater vehicles. Bond wins the day with skill and superior fire power – his amphibious car has torpedoes too. When the battle is over he drives the Esprit, a car once again, out of the water up on to a beach crowded with holidaymakers. They cannot believe their eyes, particularly as Bond, to their even greater astonishment, winds down his window and delicately drops out a tiny fish. Poor Cubby, with all his experience of keeping a tight grip on what Bond would or would not do, hated this, but it suited Roger Moore so well we managed to persuade Cubby to let it stay in. In cinemas the holidaymakers' reactions raised big laughs, but the biggest laugh was for the fish.

Who thought of that fish gag? Not I, nor Christopher Wood, nor Richard Maibaum. It was Roger Moore himself, and that makes a point about Bond films. They are collaborative efforts. One person, not necessarily the scriptwriter, says, "Wouldn't it be brilliant if…" and someone else says, "Yes, but wouldn't it be twice as brilliant if…" and so on. For our pre-titles sequence, quite one of the best stunts ever filmed came about that way.

Cubby's stepson Michael G Wilson had trained as a lawyer in Norman Tyre's office but, while working alongside Cubby, had become a Bond nut. In fact, he still is. He learned well, became a tower of strength and now produces the films himself with Cubby's daughter, Barbara Broccoli. It was Michael who became Harry Saltzman's long-term replacement, and it was he who showed me a certain magazine with a certain photo in it. The magazine was *Playboy* and the photo was an advert. It showed a young man skiing off the edge of a mountain, out over water. "Wouldn't that be fantastic for us?" said Michael.

"If it's possible, yes," I said. "It would be an incredible stunt."

We contacted *Playboy*, who gave us the telephone number of

Rick Sylvester, a young man living in Canada. Would he come to England to discuss this stunt, we asked. On arrival he told us, "That photo was a fake. I didn't do it. They photographed it and printed me in over the sea." Disappointing as this was, we cheered up considerably when he added, "I can do it for real, though. I know how and I know exactly the mountain where I could do it from. You have a ski chase. Bond goes over a precipice which has to be dead vertical – "

'Of course,' I thought as he talked, 'you can't jump off any old mountain. There wouldn't be far enough to fall before you hit the side again. It would have to be a very special place.' This turned out to be Asgard Peak on Baffin Island in the Canadian Arctic, and that's where the second unit went to film just this one stunt. The start of the chase was shot elsewhere, Switzerland in fact, but that sort of thing was common on a Bond film.

When it was time to leave for Canada I was already at work on scenes that involved the actors, so I had to stay behind. The second unit director was John Glen. He was also the film's editor and, in that capacity, I knew him well from other films I had directed. With John, I worked out where the cameras should be positioned and off he went with his unit and Rick to wait five weeks until the sun and wind were doing exactly what they wanted them to be doing. One gust of wind in the wrong direction would have meant, quite simply, an end to Rick and the stunt. Even so, with perfect conditions Rick still had to reach the right speed in order to project himself clear of the precipice. He did, and down he tumbled until, at the last moment, he pulled the cord to a parachute concealed on his back and that is where the collaborative bit comes in. It was Christopher Wood's idea for the parachute to be a Union Jack. This was the cherry on the cake and it brought the house down, even in America.

As soon as the parachute opened, Rick had to jettison his skis. What he didn't bargain for was the skis shooting straight upwards. They missed the parachute by a matter of inches. If they had become entangled, the silk would have closed over them and that again would have meant an end to Rick, who was only 24. He was contracted to do two jumps but everything that was needed was there in the first one. John Glen had prepared well and done an excellent job. We had one of the most memorable openings to any film.

Later in the picture, Bond and Anya's search for Stromberg takes them to Egypt, and the temple of Karnak is spectacular on screen. Its timeless grandeur, however, belies the day-to-day troubles a film producer and his unit can face. Cubby, Bill Cartlidge and I were out looking at a desert location in advance of the crew. Apart from sand all you could see were three tents, put there to give us a little shade. In this lonely spot we had a rendezvous with George Crawford, maverick caterer. He was travelling from England to meet us, his refrigerated truck filled with food and ice-cold drinks for at least a hundred people. It would tide us over that first difficult day's shooting. When the big moment came, three perspiring film men whooped as they saw the truck coming towards them across the desert. At the thought of delicious drinks, ice-cold lagers, perhaps even a vodka tonic, we all embraced each other.

When the truck finally came to a halt, George jumped out and we shook his hand, congratulating him on his navigation. Bill, unable to hold back, flung the truck doors open. Out came a delicious, cool breeze. We breathed it in. At first, we couldn't see anything because our eyes were still dazzled by the sunshine. When they did become accustomed, what they saw left us speechless. The inside of the truck was completely bare.

Somewhere on George Crawford's long and – we began to think – foolhardy journey, some person or persons unknown had stripped it of everything except the cooking unit.

That evening, Cubby, Bill and I roamed Luxor looking, not just for a meal, but a substantial quantity of food to feed the crew at lunchtime the next day. We found nothing. When the next day came, that first morning's work was hard to get through. The thought of lunchtime and no lunch was making me so nervous. Mutiny was not out of the question and where was Cubby? There was no sign of him. At one o'clock, I headed reluctantly for the lunch area but then what a sight I saw. Behind giant pans on Calor Gas rings stood Cubby in a chef's hat, pushing sheaves of spaghetti into boiling water. Only a few hours before lunch was due to be served, Cubby had been told by a local guide about a store of pasta and naturally, being of Italian origin, had known exactly what to do. After that, the tomatoes and onions for the sauce hadn't been so difficult to find. Not a word of this had come through to either Bill or myself because Cubby had wanted it to be a surprise. When the crew heard the whole story, Cubby's stock – and he was already a popular producer – rose even higher.

Cubby and I had taken a chance on Barbara Bach. We knew that she was inexperienced but that was a chance we were prepared to take. Other people's reactions we had not considered. First of all, there was her boyfriend, the chap at United Artists. He was nervous. "I only asked if you could give her a small part," he said. "I never meant to push her into this."

"It's all right," I said. "I'm quite clear on the matter and I'm sure everyone understands. It's my decision and Cubby's."

Then there were the actors. What would their reaction be? Not only did we have Roger Moore and Curt Jürgens, both of whom had been in front of cameras for decades, but also some experienced character actors, types who could rapidly become impatient on sensing a weakness in a fellow performer.

Roger, having taken to my idea of lightening the character and making him more fun, had Bond pretty much sewn up, so I didn't have to say much to him. What was I going to do, then, if I had to keep stopping to talk to Barbara? The best thing, I thought, was to enlist Roger's aid. "I need your help," I would say or, "I need you to be kind and understand."

This worked pretty well until Barbara, more nervous on one occasion than usual, simply couldn't take in what I was saying. We did 15, maybe 20 takes, and Roger was becoming visibly fed up. Barbara burst into tears. "No, I can't do it. I'll never get it," she said.

I took her to one side. "It looks like I'm bullying you, I know," I said, "but really, I admire you. Taking on a part like this took courage. OK, it's making you unhappy right now but when you see the film at a big premiere, you'll thank me and say, 'Yes, I was much better than I expected.' The point is, don't think about it. Just do it. The number of takes doesn't matter. Film's cheap. Keep going and you'll get it." And keep going she did and she got it. Bond girls are not noted, on the whole, for giving good performances and so tend not to get good reviews. Barbara *did* give a good performance and *did* get good reviews.

When I'd finished the film I was quite pleased with it because it contained certain elements not seen in a Bond film before. The Soviet Anya playing off the English Bond with Anya winning one round, Bond fighting back and winning the next, made for a good structure. It leant itself to both comedy and romance. Although you could tell the two were physically attracted to each other, at the same time the two scoring off each other created a double image which was good for the film. Of the three Bond pictures I made, I think this one was the best. And I've read lists that put *The Spy Who Loved Me* among the top three of the Bond pictures. Bond purists were a bit nervous about it because of the comedy and lightness of touch. They hadn't been used to it in the Connery Bond films. However, it was a big hit at the box office right around the world, so I suppose the risk had been worth taking.

One of the biggest hits in the film was, of course, Jaws. The steel teeth that bit through anything gave him an identity that was immediate. It was just a pity that Richard Kiel who was playing him had such difficulty wearing them. They went over his own teeth right to the back of his mouth where they touched that part of the throat which makes you gag. He had to take them out after every take.

It was the decision to make Jaws indestructible, though, that really fixed him in audiences' minds. They found that so funny. He could fall off a roof or out of a car or have building works fall on top of him and invariably he would extricate himself, dust himself off and walk away unscathed. It provided a marvellous end to the film. The arch villain's lair, in the sea this time, is blown sky high and nothing is left. However, up bobs Jaws who is seen glancing backwards and swimming away, off into the next picture, as it happens. Not only did that raise a huge laugh, it had a further effect on audiences which led to an unexpected consequence.

Working with Richard was an unusual experience. I expected him to be very strong. He wasn't. His feats of strength in the film, just as they would have been for any other actor, were illusions. His height, though, had an effect that was quite odd. After my first day of working with him I went home with a fearful stiff neck. I couldn't figure out what the hell had caused it until I remembered that I had spent the entire time with my head tilted back, looking up at and talking to a man who was taller than me by nearly two foot.

When Richard lost his shoes on location, going to a shoe shop and buying a new pair was useless. His feet were far too big. Production staff had to stay up two nights, ringing round to find someone who could make shoes that were 16 inches long. At airports we would take him to the VIP room where, in due course, a member of ground staff would come to announce boarding for the flight. We would jump to our feet, but not Richard. He'd had far too many bad results doing that. Firstly, he would look at the ceiling and then he would slowly stand up. Banging his head was no longer something he was prepared to risk. As he walked along the airport corridors he provoked the most extraordinary reaction which was nothing to do with him being Jaws. People would stop dead in their tracks and, as he passed, turn their heads, trying to work out whether what they had just witnessed was real. They couldn't help themselves. Once on the plane Richard needed two seats, and at night had to sleep in a special bed that went everywhere with him. An ordinary bed would have been too uncomfortable.

He was married, to a girl who was five foot two. Their first meeting had been an oddball one. He described it to me. On location in a remote part of America, where nothing but a garage and a greasy spoon were to be found, he had gone into the greasy spoon and had instantly fallen in love with the young waitress there. Would she come out for dinner, he had asked.

"Yes," she had said, "but first you must meet my father. He's very strict about meeting boyfriends before I go out with them."

Richard, like the good boy he is, went to this man's house and knocked on the door. It amuses me to imagine what happened next. The girl's father goes to the door, expecting to meet some ordinary, tallish young fellow, opens up and is confronted by a waistband. Still, Richard eventually married the daughter, so it couldn't have done him any harm. Over the next four years the two of them produced four children. "Not surprising," said Roger Moore. "At your size, Richard, you could have been in one room, your wife could have been in another and conception would still have taken place."

Maybe it was something in Richard, rather than Jaws, that made audiences write masses of letters asking for the character not only to be in the next film but to be a goody. If so, their judgment was right and that was the consequence I knew nothing of when filming Jaws swimming away at the end of *The Spy Who Loved Me.*

United Artists were so delighted with the film they wanted the next Bond picture right away. This was *Moonraker* and its chief novelty was, indeed, Jaws becoming a goody. After a fight between him and Bond on top of a cable car thousands of feet up in the air, the car goes out of control, careers towards the landing stage and knocks it to smithereens. Bond and his girl jump clear but Jaws goes with the car and is next seen trapped in the wreckage. A sweet little girl with blond plaits and surprising strength comes to his rescue. Tchaikovsky fills the air and both immediately fall in love. That's the moment Jaws starts to become a goody, just as several children and quite a few adults all over the world had asked for.

Fun though it was working with Roger Moore and Richard Kiel again, the mixture, storywise, on *Moonraker* was pretty much as before. As I came to the end of making it, I had a strong feeling it was time for a change.

31
Real Life: Tam's Story

Films have been my life. All my waking hours and sometimes my sleeping ones too, the making of them has obsessed me. Very occasionally, though, something happens that shatters that world entirely.

On Christmas Eve 1977, Joan, the partner of my son John, gave birth to her second child, Tamasine. She already had a son, three year-old Cass, and was bringing up John's two children from a previous relationship, Nick and Justine. Together, they all lived in an airy Holland Park flat and, with John working hard in the pop music world, all seemed to be bouncing along very pleasantly.

One Saturday morning, exactly three months after Tamasine's birth, Joan woke up, her head abuzz with a little tea party she was going to throw for the other children that afternoon. They were to celebrate Tamasine's first quarter year. As John set off for work, Joan busied herself around the flat, preparing Nick and Justine for their Saturday morning judo class. That done it was time for Tam's feed, but on entering the baby's room Joan found her lifeless. A slap elicited only the feeblest of twitching. She rang the doctor. The child had to be taken to hospital at once. Having shepherded Nick, Justine and Cass into the car, Joan set off for St Stephen's Hospital (The Chelsea and Westminster) in the Fulham Road. The children, seeing their baby sister in her carrycot, pale and hardly breathing, grew quieter and quieter. The journey was hell. Even though it was early in the morning, fans for that afternoon's Chelsea football match at Stamford Bridge were already abroad, parading along the streets, waving flags and singing.

At the hospital, a nurse took Tam away. Joan went to a payphone to ring John. He had not reached work yet. She rang David Hentschel, a composer who was working with John. All David could do was leave a message for John to call him. When John reached his office he picked up this message, rang David and drove at once to St Stephen's. By then, Tam was in a small room with a tube in her mouth and another one coming from her arm. Beside her was a nurse who had given her a heavy dose of Valium. John asked how long Tam had been in this state and whether she had brain damage. The nurse could not answer. It was the weekend and there were no consultants on duty. John's younger brother, Stephen, arrived to take Nick, Justine and Cass round to my house, where Hylda was waiting.

On Monday evening, John and Joan were at home when the phone rang. It was the hospital. Tam had been having convulsions and was being rushed by ambulance to Great Ormond Street Hospital for Children as the facilities were better there. Tam had been given too much Valium. By the time John and Joan arrived at Great Ormond Street, Tam had been taken for a brain scan. John asked a doctor what was going on. The doctor said that he would explain after he had eaten his dinner. John went mad. He didn't care about the doctor's fucking dinner. He wanted to know what was happening to his baby daughter. The doctor walked away, leaving Joan and John alone in a waiting room.

The surgeon, Mr Till, appeared. He was a warm, friendly man who told Joan and John that they could stay overnight in a room next to Tam. Nourishment was going to be needed for the baby, he said, but as breastfeeding was not possible he asked Joan to express some milk, which she did. John wanted to know Tam's chance of survival. Mr Till said that it was too early to say.

That night John and Joan slept fitfully and were awoken by the sound of running feet and shouting. Equipment was being wheeled into Tam's room. She had suffered a cardiac arrest. The staff revived her and put her on a life support machine.

Back in Holland Park, John rang me. I was in New York at United Artists discussing *Moonraker*. "I'll be on the next plane home," I said. John, having put down the receiver, felt useless. What could he do that was practical? He prepared a cassette of the songs Tam had heard in the three months of her life and took it to the hospital. He found her on a ventilator in a little plastic tent. Would it be all right if the cassette player were placed next to Tam and switched on, he asked. The nurse looked at the doctor. He nodded.

Joan's own doctor, a woman, arrived and went off to talk to one of the nursing sisters. On her return, she said that Tam had suffered considerable brain damage and that there was little chance of the baby having any kind of life. The best advice she could give was to turn the ventilator off. Joan could not believe her ears. This woman, her doctor, had not seen Tam. She had not spoken to a consultant. She was going on the word of the nursing sister and nothing else. Scared but angry, Joan told her doctor that the ventilator would not be turned off and that John would back her up in this.

Joan and John left to go and see Mr Till. When they reported to him what the doctor had said, he was shocked. "If the time comes to make that decision," he told them, "we will talk it through and make it together."

The phone rang. A nurse passed it to John. On hearing who was on the line, he put his hand over the receiver. "It's our doctor," he said. Removing his hand, he then said, "Please don't call again. In fact, we don't want to hear from you again ever." Mr Till nodded and smiled as if to say, "Well done."

Round about then, I arrived at the hospital. For Tam there was nothing I could do, while to John and Joan there was little I could say. The only comfort I could give was simply being with them. Together, we looked silently through the glass at Tam on a ventilator.

Five days later the decision was made to turn the ventilator from 100 per cent support to 50 per cent. Tam had started to breathe by herself, if only weakly. Mr Till and the hospital staff were amazed. They could not understand it. John could. He was sure it was the music on the cassette. Even in the first few weeks of her life, Tam had always reacted to those songs.

A new face appeared, consultant paediatric neurologist Dr John Wilson, a kind and gentle man whose concern was for Tam's survival, of course, but even more for the quality of her life. John asked him if going private would make any difference. He said that it would not. Great Ormond Street was the best and there was a long road ahead.

The anaesthetist decided that it was time to take Tam off the ventilator. John and Joan were terrified. What if she stopped breathing? She didn't and they were elated, at least until Dr Wilson told them that Tam had viral encephalitis. Although it was too early to come up with a long term prognosis, she would in all likelihood be unable to walk or talk. Remaining in a vegetative state was a possibility, maybe for years, maybe for ever. Joan and John took Tam home, where they discovered she could not see. This was only one of her many problems.

A few days later, Joan and John were at the flat in Holland Park when Tam started to have spasms. They took her to Great Ormond Street Hospital where they were told by the weekend registrar not to worry but to come back on Monday for their regular appointment. That Monday, Tam was immediately put on Epilim, a drug used for the treatment of infantile spasms. Perhaps it was those spasms that caused the problems that were to follow. Babies with viral encephalitis have been known to recover, not that it seemed likely in this particular case.

For the next five years, Tam ran high temperatures at the slightest infection, and on those nights slept in John and Joan's bedroom. The two of them spent long hours sitting up with their daughter, sponging her down, taking her temperature and becoming really scared when she went floppy. On one occasion, an X-ray revealed that Tam had contracted pneumonia. Because they had grown so used to those high temperatures, sometimes over 104 degrees, they had not realised it. Joan did, however, remember that it had been extremely hard to get her temperature down that night.

During those years life had to go on. Livings had to be earned and the three older children had to be brought up. At the same time, John and Joan did not let matters rest. As with anyone facing a big problem, their antennae were constantly on the alert for a solution. A friend mentioned cranial massage. It was not widely known then. They tried a series of treatments. On hearing about this, Dr Wilson said that he was not against it but that it was mainly used for tired businessmen.

Homeopathy was in the news. The royal family was keen on it. Today doctors of allopathic medicine, the ordinary kind, dismiss it, but when you're desperate you explore every avenue. John and Joan consulted Dr Blackie, the Queen's homeopathist, and she turned out to be quite sensible. She believed in both types of medicine and combined them. For Tam she prescribed some white powder that came in little paper wraps, like cocaine. Up until then, Tam's head had lolled from side to side, but within weeks she was able to raise it.

At Dr Wilson's suggestion, Joan took Tam to the Paul Sandifer Clinic at the Great Ormond Street Hospital. There, twice a week, children with problems were brought by their mothers for physio, speech and occupational therapy. The last of these could mean threading beads, very difficult, or singing, which an elderly lady volunteer accompanied on the piano. While this was going on the mothers had coffee, talked about their children and managed to find humour in the reactions of the ignorant. "I hear your baby has cerebral palsy. Is it catching?" That sort of thing. It was therapy for them. They felt less isolated. In fact some of those mothers became firm friends. To start with, Tam could only sit propped up in the therapy room, taking no part.

Her nearest relative in age was her brother, Cass. The two were very close. However at five years of age, like every other child, Cass had to go for his first day of school. On his return, he ran upstairs, yelling, "Tam! Tam!" and at the sound of his voice Tam's face lit up.

Around this time, the combined stress of worrying about Tam and working in the pop world sent John into hospital. He needed an operation. Although it was successful, it made him think. Working with pop bands he had been living life in the fast lane, which meant heavy drinking, smoky clubs, all night recording sessions and sleep warded off by artificial means. Long distance journeys and the consequent absences didn't help either. He decided that it all had to stop. At any moment there could be an emergency with Tam and it was vital that he and Joan tackle it together. It would mean a loss of earnings but it was a sacrifice he had to make. He and Joan would manage.

One day, at therapy, while the elderly lady volunteer was plonking away at the piano and the children were singing away and doing their arm movements, Tam reached down to pick up a small object from the floor. In that moment, Joan realised that she could see. It gave Tam such a lift that she learned the words of the songs off by heart and was even able to attempt the arm movements.

At the age of three, Tam was taken by Joan to the Cheyne Centre for Spastic Children on the Embankment. There, a Dr Foley asked Tam how you could tell the time from the kind of watch which had a big hand and a little hand. Tam could do it. What she could not do was identify a certain picture the doctor showed her every time she came. This was a lesson, however. From it, the doctor could work out that Tam's sight was like a jigsaw puzzle with half the pieces randomly missing. What Tam could see, she could see clearly, what she could not see, she could not see at all. When the doctor had got to know her better, he came to the conclusion that Tam was very bright but would never be able to take a bus or a train or work out money. Her brain injuries were too serious for that. Eye to hand co-ordination was minimal. He agreed to send a physiotherapist to the flat each week to work with her. He also recommended that she wear splints to help her walk. The apparent progress she made when she held on to the edge of a sofa and walked along it gave John and Joan a big thrill.

However, the fact that Tam, when not wearing splints, had to be carried everywhere until she was four, was an indication that this progress was not progress at all. At a school which used the Glen Doman method for teaching brain-injured children, Joan and John were told that the natural order of development had to be maintained. Tam had to learn to crawl before she could learn to walk. The splints were not to be used. John bought a long scarf, put it under Tam's stomach, lifted her gently, and every day for several weeks walked round the room until Tam had no alternative but to crawl.

Tam took her first steps while still four. Belinda Humphries, a friend of Joan's who ran a nursery school, invited her to come to it. To start with Tam could do little except sit and try to take in all the activity around her, but gradually she began to interact. She came to love going to nursery school.

Christmas came, and back at the Paul Sandifer Clinic Dr Wilson appeared dressed as Father Christmas. The sight of him transfixed and terrified Tam. When he handed her a present she screamed her head off. At home, as Joan laid out empty stockings at the end of the children's beds, Tam made it clear that she did not want Father Christmas to come down the chimney. In fact she wanted nothing to do with him at all. John put through an urgent call to Lapland. Would Father Christmas please leave the presents outside in the street?

Tam was talking by now, but her articulation was not good. It wasn't helped by a stammer, aggravated at moments of nervousness or tiredness. Dr Wilson made an appointment for her to see Mary Lobascher, a clinical psychologist who worked at Great Ormond Street. This small, charismatic woman ignored John and Joan totally. Tam was the only person she would speak to, which she did in a woman-to-woman way. There was no patronising sing-song. She asked Tam to help her feed her goldfish and held out her hand. Tam took it and tottered over to the aquarium. As Mary talked and pointed to each of the goldfish she watched Tam carefully, gauging her sight and the tiniest of her hand movements as she pointed jerkily with her right hand towards the fish swimming about. At that point in Tam's life, no-one knew what was going to happen.

32
Rita in the City

"Time for a change," I thought as I finished *Moonraker*. It came during the summer of 1980. Under the auspices of the Royal Shakespeare Company, a play called *Educating Rita* opened at the Donmar Warehouse, near Covent Garden. It was by Willy Russell, who lived and worked in Liverpool. He had previously written a musical called *John, Paul, George, Ringo … and Bert*, which had been such a big success there at the Everyman Theatre that it had transferred to the Lyric Theatre, Shaftesbury Avenue, where it had won the Evening Standard Award for the Best Musical of 1974. It hadn't, however really caught on there. *Educating Rita* was another matter. The Royal Shakespeare Company obviously thought it would catch on because when Hylda went to see it at the Donmar she noticed that the set was realistic and solidly built, in other words ready for a speedy transfer. The Royal Shakespeare Company was proved right because the reviews were immediately good, hence Hylda being tempted to the Donmar. So when she came home saying that it was absolutely up my street and that it was transferring to the Piccadilly Theatre the following week, I thought I'd better hurry along there before someone else snapped it up.

The play is about Rita, a 26 year-old hairdresser who, having taken no exams as a teenager, discovers an immense desire to learn. Before the play starts she enrolls with the Open University and then we, the audience, follow her relationship both with English literature and with her tutor, Frank. In fact, Rita and Frank are the only characters on the stage, which caused my mother-in-law, who was sitting with Hylda and me at the Piccadilly, to call out after 20 minutes, "Oh, don't tell me this is a play with only two people in it!"

Fortunately I was already enjoying myself and, amid all the shushing going on around us, was able to quieten her with, "Yes, but what people!"

You can see Shaw's *Pygmalion* in *Educating Rita* – the professor who transforms his pupil into a different kind of human being – but you can also spot a balance that is not so even. Henry Higgins and Liza Doolittle are well matched whereas Rita is all giving out and Frank, for the most part, is all taking in. It is as if Willy Russell, in finding the voice of Rita, wants nothing to get in her way because she has the ability to put over what Willy himself wants to say. Both actors, Julie Walters and Mark Kingston, played their parts very well, but up on that stage it was Julie's show. I thought it was wonderful and knew I had to get in touch with the author right away. First, though, I went backstage to tell Julie Walters that if ever I was able to make a film of *Educating Rita* I would do my damndest to see that she played the part. Julie was savvy enough to know that I couldn't make it a promise because the financing of films is tricky, depending as it often does on a star name. At that time, she hadn't made any films at all.

The next day I tracked Willy Russell down and invited him over to the house. He was thrilled at the idea of his play being turned into a film, particularly as the thought had never crossed his mind. It meant that I could look forward to seeing Peggy

Ramsay's legs again because Peggy, inevitably, was his agent.

"Oh darling, do you think so?" Peggy was crossing and uncrossing her legs – business as usual in other words. "Do you think you can make a film out of this? I'm not at all sure. Actually, I wasn't sure about it as a play." Most agents suck their cheeks in and say, "Ooh, well, I don't know. There are so many people interested in it." That's the hard sell, but the hard sell was not Peggy's style. She still made a deal, though, a sensible one, thank goodness. I was keen to have the play, she knew that, but she didn't crucify me. Perhaps the reason for her giving me such a fair price was explained by her reaction when I told her I was off to America to find the money. "You don't have to hurry, darling," she said. "I doubt if anyone else will be wanting it." I told her I'd call from America.

When I arrived, I went to United Artists. Since I had just made the two Bond films with them, they seemed the obvious first port of call. That is not what they thought. The Bond films were big and international. *Educating Rita* was small and British. Why on earth was I bothering with it, they wondered. This was an unpleasant surprise but Norman Tyre, who seemed to know everything, suggested I try Columbia. Remembering that I had made three films and set up *Oliver!* with them, I did and they were much more enthusiastic. Right away, they wanted to pay me for the option I'd taken out with Peggy and draw up a contract for me to produce and direct the film.

"We're in business," I said to Willy as soon as I was home. "Now we have to write the script." As with Bill Naughton on *Alfie*, Peggy Ramsay had stipulated that Willy would write the screenplay's first draft but the whole business of opening out a play is not that easy and more than one head can be useful. I explained to Willy that I usually worked with Vernon Harris, but that all three of us could make a team. Vernon was an old hand who would listen to both of us and only do what we wanted. If Willy wished to go off and write scenes, that was fine too.

"I'll work with you," said Willy.

I had a flat in Cannes – still do – and that is where all three of us went to start the process. Our task was to take the play out of Frank's study and, by so doing, also strengthen his character.

In the play, Frank is divorced from his wife and lives with a girlfriend, Julia, who is impatient with him and with his consumption of alcohol. This girlfriend went altogether. In the screenplay, Frank is still married but his wife is having an affair and he knows it. This, coupled with his unruly behaviour caused by the drink, makes him a more desperate man. At the start he is the one in the superior position, but as things proceed Rita rises and he falls. His only hope is her energy and optimism. When it looks like Rita may miss her exam, his drunken search round town to find her is pathetic, yet full of suspense.

As soon as the script was finished I went back to America. Four days passed during which it felt like everybody at Columbia, including the janitor, read the script. After the four days I was summoned to the office of the studio's head, Frank Price, the man in charge of production. "It's great and we're going to do the picture with you," he said, which oddly didn't sound encouraging, "but we've kind of changed our minds about something. We think the movie should be American."

"That's crazy," I said, "The characters are so English."

"You can adapt it," he said, "I'm sure, you can. Set it in the States and then you have Dolly Parton as Rita and Paul Newman as Frank. Think about it. Why would we want to do a little British picture when we can do a big American one? We don't know who you've got for yours yet but it can't be anyone good.

You have so few British stars and Dolly would be great."

I nearly said, "Give me two reasons," but I stopped myself. I didn't want to give him a chance to smile. Instead, I said, "This is out of the question. I'm not going to do it that way."

Frank thought for a moment and said, "In that case, the best we can do is release the property to you for six months. If you don't set it up in that time, we will take it over and you need have nothing more to do with it. If, in six months, you have set it up, the whole thing, providing you pay for what we've laid out, that will be fine by us."

'Easy,' I thought as I left Frank's office. 'It's an English subject. The play couldn't be more successful. I'm bound to be able to raise the money in the UK.'

Nevertheless, my experience with Frank Price had been bruising, so I thought I'd go and torture someone else and not suffer alone. I rang Willy Russell and said that I was seriously thinking of going with Dolly Parton. There was a pause followed by a thud. I honestly think he fainted.

"It's not true?" he said a moment later.

"No, it isn't," I said. "I was joking. There'll be no Dolly Parton and, for that matter, no Columbia. We're going to set the picture up in England." He was very relieved because the idea of the film being made by an American company had never appealed to him. "Yes," I went on, "and if we raise the money in England we can put up a really good fight to get Julie Walters into the film. She's so good in the play, it would be a shame not to give her the part." Willy was delighted. Julie knew nothing of this, which was probably just as well.

I started to take the script round all the British companies and that is when I had the biggest surprise I experienced in the making of *Educating Rita*. Nobody wanted to do it. Everyone found something wrong with it. Of the big companies, my last port of call was Thorn EMI, the former Associated British Picture Corporation. The guy in charge sounded enthusiastic. I went to see him.

"Yes, I liked the play and I liked the script," he said, "but we won't be doing it."

"Why not?" I asked. "Since I spoke to you," he said, "I sent my two teenaged daughters to see the play and they hated it. So it looks as if the film won't be liked by young people and you know how they make up such a large part of our audiences."

"Since when did teenagers run Thorn EMI?" I said. "In any case, when I go to the cinema I see lots of different age groups, not just young people." The man at Thorn EMI did not shift his position.

And so it continued with everyone I saw. They all had a niggle, usually to do with the play having only two people in it. Telling them that our script opened the play out and was consequently not the play made no impression. During this time I would occasionally see Julie. She wasn't a bit worried about getting the part because, listening to what I had to say, she was certain the film was never going to be made in the first place and, even if it was, it would be without her.

Then, one night – it's funny how these things always come out of the blue – Hylda and I went to dinner at a friend's house, where sitting between us was a man who began talking to Hylda about the picture business. "Do you know?" I heard him say, "I've always wanted to get into films. I'm an investment banker."

Suddenly, my ears became the two largest things in the room. "Oh really?" I cut in, "It's funny you should say that because I have a subject that I think would make a very good film. It's a play and the notices were wonderful for it but I'm having a bit of difficulty setting it up."

"Why don't you do it with me?" he said, "I know everybody in the City. Maybe I could take you around to meet some of them?" Well, this angel was called Herbert Oaks, a delightful man whose wife was the actress Sheila Fearn, very recognisable from television. She too was at the dinner party and, being already familiar with the business, was keen for her husband to move into films and make ours in particular.

Herbert Oaks meant what he said and very soon we were doing the rounds of all the different investment companies, city bankers and money people in general. It was at the Prudential that we had our lucky break, though things there didn't sound too great at first. The Man from the Pru started by quizzing me on how and where I was going to do it. "You see, I have a problem," he said. "Not with you because I know your track record and, as it happens, I know of the play. It sounds really good. No, it's not that. It's the past. We had dealings with film people years ago and they were catastrophic. Before the war, we backed Alexander Korda. He built Denham Studios, you know, and made lots of films with our money. It was all right for him. He seemed to do quite well but we lost every penny. So, the Prudential's not too keen on films these days. In fact, since Korda we haven't invested in them at all."

'Which would make it about 40 or 50 years,' I thought, keeping this and all my memories of Korda very much to myself. I was right to because the Man from the Pru was still talking.

"However," he said, "leave it with me for a few days and I'll see what I can do. After all, it's not that much money and I'm curious to see how things work in the film world today." This was good news indeed because raising the rest of the money would become so much easier. The Prudential was quite the most conservative company in the City, so if they became involved with our film we hoped others would follow.

During this rather uncertain period I was offered a picture with no financing problems. No problems at all, in fact. All I had to do was turn up. It came about in a rather odd way. Bill Cartlidge and I were invited to a screening of a film that had been made by a distinguished director who had seen better days. The producers were unhappy with the way it had turned out and were wondering if I might come up with a rescue plan.

Our presence at this screening, which was held for us alone, was to be an absolute secret. No-one was to know we were there. We went to Twickenham Studios where the showing was to take place. Beforehand, Bill and I went for a cup of tea in the canteen where we bumped into our old friend, the production manager John Dark, now a producer in his own right and a man well known for his practical jokes. After we had traded the usual insults, Bill and I left John and made for the projection theatre.

The film had been running only a few minutes when the telephone rang, or rather a flashing light told us that there was a call waiting. Bill picked up the receiver and, a second later, handed it to me, saying in a rather awestruck tone, "It's Dino de Laurentiis for you." Obviously I knew that Dino de Laurentiis was an internationally known Italian film producer, but I wondered how he had found me here.

I listened for a moment and then remembered John Dark out in the canteen. "Fuck off, John," I said. "That's the worst Italian accent I have ever heard," and handed the receiver back to Bill, adding, "It's John Dark, winding us up."

When I got home that evening Hylda, who knew that I was at Twickenham Studios for the afternoon but not why, said, "Did Dino de Laurentiis get through all right? He rang just after lunch. It sounded urgent." And that was the offer of the easy-to-do picture.

Obviously, I had a proper conversation with Dino later but it came back to me that he had been asking around if I was often drunk. Luckily, his assistant was a British guy who had once been my production manager. "Oh no," he said to Dino, "if anything, Lewis is maddeningly sober."

During the proper conversation, Dino told me that he had something he wanted me to direct that I would really enjoy. I thanked him and told him that I was trying to get my own film going. "All right," he said, "let us leave it like this. I shall give you two weeks and if you don't find your money, come straight here to Rome and you can start work on this film." It was a comforting thought.

In London, the day arrived when all the money for *Educating Rita* was supposed to come through. It didn't. Not one cheque appeared. Two weeks passed and then I had to ring Herbert Oaks. "I'm sorry, Herbie," I said, "but I can't go on like this. I've been offered a film by a very reputable Italian producer. I could start immediately. You've got to tell your people that there's a deadline. Tomorrow afternoon, all six companies have to be at the Prudential with their cheques. If they're not, the deal is off and I'll be on my way to Rome."

"Oh, don't do that," said Herbie.

"But I can't keep on waiting," I said.

"All right. I'll ring round," he said. The next morning, he called back. "They're all coming at three o'clock this afternoon with their cheques." That was an hour before I was due to call Dino with my final answer.

I went to the offices of the Prudential and suddenly all the cheques were in my hand, enough money to make the film. It was a wonderful moment for two reasons: America and Julie Walters. First of all, I was able to ring Frank Price at Columbia. "We will be returning your money because we've got the go-ahead to make the film here," I said, to which he replied, "Oh dear, is that so?" having evidently been convinced that I would fail. "Yes," I said, "As soon as you send us your account, you'll receive a cheque."

Next, I was able to settle down to casting, which the men from the City interfered with not one bit. In fact, from then onwards they never came near us, except for a short visit to Ireland when two or three flew over during the shoot and that was only because they were curious to see how a film was made. I was able to ring Julie Walters with news that was not only good but surprising. "After all I've been through," I said, "you'd better bloody want to play this part because it's yours." I can't remember her exact response but striking the deal with her agent the next day was not hard.

The business of casting the part of Frank was a different kettle of fish. Rita in the play and Rita in the film are pretty much the same. Frank, after all the work we had done on the screen-play, was not going to be the same in the film. We had a part we could offer to a major British male star, which was very handy given that Julie Walters was unknown. My son John, who would be producing the film's music score, had a brainwave. "It's too obvious, Dad. Michael Caine. He's just the right age now."

'Well,' I thought, as John dialled Dennis Sellinger, Dennis still being Michael's agent, 'it would certainly be one in the eye for Frank Price. He may have been right about us having few stars of any value but one of those few is Michael Caine.'

In the event, Dennis thought the part was exactly what Michael needed and quickly agreed a fee, one that was reasonable too. Then Michael changed his agent. Sue Mengers, a high-powered Hollywood type, took him over. "I've read the script and I'm appalled," she said to him. "What do you want to do this little British picture for? I didn't take you over for that. I took you over to put you into big American pictures ... OK, have it your own way," she went on as Michael didn't seem to be saying anything. "If you won't change your mind, at least we can double your fee."

Michael, in his favour, was very apologetic when he next saw me but he knew he'd burned his boats. "Don't worry," I said. "We'll pay it."

Before a make-up test with Michael, I talked to him about his look for the part. Maybe Frank would have a beard. As we sat there chatting, we related so well to each other it was as if the 17 years since the making of *Alfie* had not gone by.

During my hunt for the film's funding I had made a quick trip to Dublin and walked round Trinity College. It was perfect for our university. It had the dreaming spires feel that would have been Rita's idea of a university, she never having been near one in her life. I decided that if I ever succeeded in raising the money we would shoot the film there and that is how it turned out. We shot during the summer break, so there were plenty of young people on holiday who were prepared to lay around on the grass creating the mood of academia that Rita longed to be part of.

On the first day of shooting, Julie Walters seemed a little nervous. The scene involved her and Michael Caine and there he was, a big star, and there she was an unknown. I could understand the way she felt. After the first rehearsal I led her to one side. "This is going to get you nominated for an Academy Award," I told her.

Michael Caine, who was listening, gave me a funny look. "I

see," he whispered, "so that's what you say to everybody, is it? Because that's what you said to me on day one of *Alfie*."

"No," I said, "I meant it. And weren't you nominated?" He was too and so, in some months' time, Julie would be. And Michael, again.

Of course, it being midsummer there had to be a winter scene in the script and, of course, this had to mean snow. The artificial variety was sprinkled along a whole street. Tam, aged four, on a break from her therapy with Mary Lobascher, was over in Dublin on a visit. She was making progress but life was still a struggle. At that point she could walk but she had to hold her mother's hand. She could make neither head nor tail of what she saw. No other street had snow in it. Why had it fallen only on this one? It made no sense. Putting her question was not easy for Tam but I understood and tried to explain that the snow was not real. The look she gave me was sceptical.

It was a happy shoot but the moment that touched me almost more than any other was when the prop man, Irish (we being in Dublin) walked over to my chair and said, "You've got a good one here, gov'nor." Winning the approval of a prop man, and he being prepared to say it, is very rare.

The score that my son, John, produced was written by David Hentschel, a protege of his. Actually, David didn't just write it. He performed all of it too, electronic music being his thing. Once more, taking a risk paid off.

When the film was finished the first company we showed it to was the Rank Organisation and wasn't it cheering when the boss, Fred Turner, at once asked to distribute the picture in the UK? Naturally, came the moment when Frank Price at Columbia rang. "I understand you made the picture and it's now finished," he said.

"Yes, it is," I replied, "and, funnily enough, I'm leaving today for America to hold showings."

"Ah yes, well, you'll show it to us first, won't you?" he said. "After all, we were the ones who started the ball rolling."

"That's fine," I said. "We'll do that but I have to warn you, you'll need to make up your mind quickly. I have lots of other people waiting to see this film." I was not using the Peggy Ramsay technique, you will notice. This was the straight hard sell. "One other thing," I said. "I don't want you to see the film and then say, 'I like it but I want publicity to see it and accounts to see it and then every other department to see it.' Have them all there tomorrow evening at five o'clock in your screening room and I will bring the film."

I did and got quite a surprise. The screening room was packed. There must have been 400 people there. Herbie Oaks, who was with me, had never seen anything like this. Actually, we were both in a state of shock. "Herbie, my heart's pounding," I said. "The whole studio's here and there's every chance they won't like it. We're trying to sell them back what they turned down in the first place." Frank Price appeared. I told him that I would wait five minutes to make sure the sound level was OK but would then leave and come back in the morning to collect the film. "Yes, we can talk tomorrow," said Frank, "and I'll let you know."

Herbie and I returned to the hotel, had a drink and tried to behave normally. Considering it to be sound psychology, I said after a while, "At this moment, Herbie, the lights are coming up and they're saying, 'What a load of rubbish. Thank goodness we didn't carry on with this film. We were right all along –'"

The phone rang. A voice said, "Lewis Gilbert? Frank Price wants to speak to you."

I put my hand over the receiver. "This is it, Herbie," I said, "We're in," and when Frank came on the line he wasted no time.

"Lewis, we're sitting here with egg on our faces. We must have this film. Come tomorrow morning with Norman Tyre. I know Norman, and we'll do a deal." I was on the phone to Norman at once.

"Sharpen the razor, Lewis," he said, "we're going to cut him down to size. They will not want to make the same mistake twice and they know you're seeing other companies."

The next morning Herbie, Norman and I went to Columbia. As Norman started to perform, Herbie went quiet. This was a way of doing business he was not familiar with. Norman's point of leverage was that the other studios had already got wind of the film, which was perfectly possible. Hollywood is not that big and the chance to spread the news had been given to 400 people. In that place, it's very hard to keep a secret. What's more, Frank Price knew it and realised he had a problem on his hands. Suffice it to say, Norman went on to do a fantastic job. He fixed it for our company to receive a percentage, not of the net, which is what usually happens, but of the gross.

With business over, I said to Norman, "I must show the film to the other companies."

"You don't have to," he said.

"I know," I said, "but they've all been very nice about it and, after all, it won't do any harm." Norman left me to get on with it.

The phone rang. It was Sue Mengers, Michael Caine's agent. "I hear the film is very good," she said. "May I see it?"

"I'm showing it to Fox tomorrow," I told her. "Why don't you go along and see it there?"

The next day, Herbie and I arrived at the Fox screening room just as the lights were coming up. Someone leapt to their feet. It was Sue Mengers. She looked round the room and then said, "I'm so pleased I persuaded Michael to do this movie. It took all my guile to make him see that it was a much better idea than coming to Hollywood and making any old American film. I knew I was right." I could do nothing but look at her in amazement and even a little admiration. She carried it off so well.

That was the start of *Educating Rita*'s worldwide success. The American Motion Picture Academy nominated it for three Oscars, for Julie, Michael and for the script. This was good going for a small British picture. At the Bafta Awards in London it was nominated not only for Best Actor, Best Actress, Best Script and Best Film but for other categories too. At the big gala evening a British film, for once, swept the board. We got Best Actor, Best Actress and Best Film and all of us were there to accept our awards, Michael, Julie and myself. When I went up to accept the award for Best Film, I found myself being handed it by Diana Ross. This was something of a coincidence as I was supposed to be seeing her the next morning to talk over a film she wanted me to do with her.

In all those months of excitement, a highlight was the premiere in Hollywood. Columbia pulled out all the stops and the party they laid on afterwards was marvellous. A huge marquee was put up in the grounds of the studio and everyone came. The day before I'd seen a film that I had particularly liked, *Risky Business*. In it was a young actor who had been given his first starring role. He was about 21 and his girlfriend, Rebecca de Mornay, was also in it. At the party, he was among the guests and he came up to me. With a touch of awe in his voice he asked if I was the director of the film. "Yes, I am," I said.

"Oh," he said, "my girlfriend and I, we absolutely loved the movie. We thought it was wonderful. May I ask you a favour?

Do you think you could introduce me to Julie Walters?"

"I'm sure I could," I said, "but you'll have to give me your name first."

"Tom Cruise," he answered. Tom Cruise, asking in awe to meet Julie Walters, has become an accolade in retrospect.

33

The Shirley Valentine Effect

After the glamour of the Lord Mayor's Show comes the horse-shit. What happened next felt like that.

Cheered by the success of *Educating Rita*, I was soon back in Peggy Ramsay's office. I was buying the rights to another play, *Not Quite Jerusalem*, confident that I could successfully transfer anything to the screen. I should not have been. That isn't the way of showbusiness. The film was a flop. Nobody was to blame except me. I had made too many mistakes to save the day. At least it taught me a lesson. No-one's infallible.

When I was at my lowest ebb Willy Russell rang, and I count myself very lucky that he did. He was abuzz with a new play that he'd written. It was about to open at the Everyman Theatre in his home town, Liverpool, and its title was *Shirley Valentine.* Knowing nothing more than that, Hylda and I booked ourselves into the Adelphi Hotel and set out for Liverpool. Willy had thrown me a lifeline.

To start with, however, that's not how it felt. When we arrived in Liverpool we discovered that, on that very day, the actress playing the part of *Shirley Valentine* had fallen ill, and worse, the play had only one character. In regional theatre, where under-studies are out of the question, any actor being off is bad enough, but in this case it looked fatal. Inventiveness saved the day. To a packed house, Willy Russell read from a lectern and acted out the part himself. It worked brilliantly. Hylda and I were enthralled and I couldn't wait to get back to Peggy Ramsay's office.

Peggy gave me the "Are you sure?" treatment and, for good measure, "It only has one character," before giving in and saying, "Well, it's your problem and you seem to know what you're doing. The last one with Willy was a success, which frankly I didn't expect, so I suppose we'd better come to an arrangement." I can't say she screwed me down but nor was she ultra kind. The price was fair enough, I suppose, and at least it meant we could make a start.

Round about then Willy was quite busy, probably rejigging his musical *Blood Brothers*, which was eventually to become a big success in the West End. Anyway, he was not immediately available to work on the screenplay. I asked Vernon Harris round with his wife, Joan, to listen to Willy's recording. They laughed all the way through, which was a good start. From that tape, Vernon and I came up with a preliminary screenplay, typed out, as always, by Joan, who, as always, adjudicated when Vernon and I differed. We handed the finished result to Willy. He was not happy. It was the first time we hadn't seen eye to eye. I suggested that he take what we had done and see what he could come up with. The end result, which we were all happy with, was achieved with no bones broken.

The story is of a Liverpool housewife who has been married for nearly 20 years and whose children have grown up and gone away. The marriage is not wretched, but with the children gone it's empty. Her husband isn't cruel but he treats his wife as little more than a piece of furniture. He's polite most of the time, but occasionally he loses his temper. There is nothing in Shirley

Valentine's life and the play's title encapsulates her dilemma. Shirley Valentine is her maiden name, not her married name. The rebel schoolgirl has never had a chance to fulfill her dreams. Stuck at home, she is so lonely that she talks to the wall. This was ingenious, by the way, because it was both believable and a way for her to address the audience.

Her best friend, Jane, wins a competition. The prize is a holiday for two on a Greek island. Perhaps Shirley will go with her? At first she refuses, but then she serves her husband egg and chips instead of his usual Thursday night steak. He pushes his plate, food and all, into her lap. She walks out on him to go for that holiday.

Everyone thinks that middle-aged women, holidaying on their own, are only after one thing. Jane, who has previously announced herself a feminist, proves them right by letting herself be picked up before the plane has even landed. By the time Shirley Valentine reaches the Greek island she is alone again, left to sit on a beach and talk to a rock. That evening she goes to a taverna run by an amiable, not to say good-looking man called Costas. She asks him if he wouldn't think it too silly if he were to carry her table and chair to the water's edge and leave her there at sunset with a pitcher of wine. When he asks her why, she answers that it's always been a dream of hers. He, sounding very practical, says that it is his task to make dreams come true and does as she requests. Seeing that she is only saddened by having her wish come true, he suggests that he accompany her back to her hotel, only a short walk away. It leads to a brief holiday dalliance. Both know it's not serious but it is, nevertheless, the first time Shirley has a sexual relationship outside marriage. While knowing that she's not in love with Costas, she realises that she has fallen in love with the idea of living.

At the end of the two weeks when Jane, who has reappeared, is trying to chivvy Shirley on to the airport bus, Shirley tells her that she is not going home. She is staying in Greece. She wants a life quite different from the one she has known in her Liverpool street. That is the basic premise of *Shirley Valentine*.

Remembering the success of *Alfie*, I sent the finished script to Paramount. They liked it but, of course, wanted to know who would play Shirley. For once, they did not hit me with a list of American stars. It was a question they were leaving up to me, which I very much appreciated. I had an answer too, one that would keep everyone happy. Julie Walters. She was right for the part and, after *Educating Rita*, was known in America. There was only one snag. Julie was pregnant with her first child, which made jumping into a Grecian sea with no clothes on an unlikely proposition.

By this time, 1988, the play had arrived in the West End where it was running successfully at the Vaudeville Theatre in a new production. The part of Shirley was now in the hands of Pauline Collins, and her performance was a revelation. Until then, the public had not been aware that she had been brought up near Liverpool. The press thought she was terrific. I thought she was terrific too and also thought that she should play the part in the film. It would mean a battle though, or so it seemed, because in Hollywood she was not a name. "Please," I said to Paramount, "before you make any suggestions, come over and see Pauline."

"It's not exactly round the corner," they grumbled.

"Do it for my sake," I said, "and if you think Pauline is not for you, we'll carry on talking, OK?" By then Paramount had a certain faith in my judgment, as Michael Caine had similarly not been well known at the time of casting *Alfie*.

Three of their top brass flew over. I rang Pauline's agent.

"Should I tell her?" I asked, "Or would it put her off?" As the agent seemed unconcerned, I rang Pauline. Having told her how good she was in the part and how magnificent it would be if her performance could be seen worldwide on film, I told her about the Paramount top brass. She too was unconcerned.

"I don't mind them coming," she said, "because I know they'll find any excuse to say they must have an American actress."

"Over my dead body," I said.

As soon as the Paramount three had arrived, I went to the Dorchester Hotel to let them know about the seats I had booked for them at the Vaudeville that night. "Fine," they said. "Come and have breakfast tomorrow and we'll talk it over." The next morning I set off, ready to do battle, but as soon as the three saw me they said, "Take her. She's brilliant. She'll be a knockout." They must have felt even more confident when, soon afterwards, Pauline won not only the Laurence Olivier Award for Best Actress in the West End but also the Tony Award for Best Actress when she took the play to America. On Broadway she became the toast of the town with all the stars you can imagine cramming into her dressing room each night.

While all this was going on we were continuing to set up the film. Now that the play was opened out, the characters Shirley Valentine talks about on the stage were going to have to appear. There was a fair amount of casting to do, chiefly for the Greek bar-owner.

Our aim was not to have an actor who was English – that could have sounded phoney – but to look for a foreign actor who could speak English well enough. With that in mind we tried Greece, Italy, Spain and France, all without luck. Meanwhile, Pauline Collins had been talking to her neighbour, the Scots-Italian actor Tom Conti. She'd been telling him about the film.

Next thing, I was at the theatre with Hylda when Tom came up to me in the interval and started talking to me in a Greek accent. I was most impressed. It was also good to know that he wanted the part. By then, he was a highly regarded actor who had starred in American films. I suspect Willy had different ideas about who should play Costas, but I think I convinced him that Tom would give a fine performance and, when the film came out, the opinion of the critics was that he had, thank goodness.

A character in the film I particularly like is one that starts out as the head girl of Shirley's secondary school. Her name is Marjorie Majors and everything she does, she does well, if rather smugly. All the qualities that a school could expect of a prize pupil are hers, and for that reason the teachers consider her a great asset, unlike Shirley, of whom they think very little at all. Worse still, Marjorie is beautiful and Shirley can't help secretly looking up to her.

Years later, out shopping in the rain and looking an absolute mess, Shirley is splashed by a passing limousine. An elegant woman steps out and apologises. It's Marjorie, the onetime head girl. Joanna Lumley plays her with great style. The two go up to Marjorie's hotel suite for tea and a chat. Marjorie asks Shirley what she does. Shirley is forced to say that, apart from having two children, nothing. At the same time, she is looking round the suite and thinking that Marjorie, by contrast, must have done very well for herself. Beautiful as she still is, constantly travelling and staying at top hotels, she has to be an air hostess on Concorde. "What on earth gave you that idea?" says Marjorie. "I'm a hooker, I'm a whore," a line that caused audiences to erupt with laughter. It leaves Shirley able to settle down for a nice afternoon of reminiscing with Marjorie, her new friend.

We began shooting in England where an early scene took

place between Shirley and her neighbour, who was played by Julia McKenzie. On Julia's first day I went to see her in make-up, where she told me that she loved the script but added that it was a long time since she had played such a small part. "Don't worry," I said, "you'll feel right at home because I shall treat you like a small-part actress." This was to be our joke for the day.

We began with a tracking shot of Pauline and Julia crossing the road. I was looking through the viewfinder, lining this up, when I stopped and said to Julia, "You dear, what's your name?" and Julia, playing along, answered, "Julia McKenzie, sir."

"Well, Miss McKenzie," I said, "you'll have to concentrate harder. If you don't keep close to Pauline, we can't see you. Have you not done a picture before?"

Most of the unit was in on this joke. What I had not bargained for was a camera crew from Barry Norman's *Film '88* programme, recording the prank. The following Sunday up it came on television, but with no explanation. I was watching and the pain of my embarrassment could not have been more acute until Barry, after the piece was over, said, "I can't imagine Julia McKenzie being too pleased with that." Then, it was worse. The best I can say is that it taught me to check for hidden cameras before making jokes on a film set. Whenever I meet Julia she always laughs at my discomfort, while her friends still say, "Wasn't it awful when that director forgot your name?" Try as she may to explain that it was a joke, they will not have it. They prefer the insult version.

After Pauline Collins had shot her first scene I told her that she would be nominated for an Academy Award. As she didn't believe me, I told her that, precisely at that moment on day one of *Alfie* and day one of *Educating Rita* I had said the same thing to Michael Caine and Julie Walters respectively, and both times

I had been proved right.

While we were shooting the scene where Shirley's husband pushes the egg and chips into her lap, Pauline came to me with an unusual request. It started with her recounting a story about herself that went right back to the beginning of her career.

As a young actress, she told me, she had been seduced by a fellow actor and become pregnant. She had not, however, had an abortion. Instead, to avoid unwanted attention, she had gone to Ireland and been delivered of a baby girl which she had put up for adoption. This period of her life had haunted her from then onwards. Though not seeing or hearing from the child, she dreamed of the baby often. Then the law changed. Adopted children were entitled to know who their biological parents were. The girl, by then a young woman, had got in touch with Pauline and that had given her quite a shock. Having spoken to John Alderton, her husband, she then had invited the girl to her home. "Even though it was the first time we'd met," Pauline said to me, "it was remarkable how quickly we were at ease with each other." The daughter, nevertheless, had not settled down in England, but instead had accepted a very good job she'd been offered in Australia.

Naturally, Pauline wanted to keep this story private but she was only too aware that the press would soon get wind of it. If she wanted to scotch rumour and speculation, decisive action was necessary. Her best bet seemed to be to give an exclusive interview to a trusted journalist. She therefore asked me to allow this journalist, a friend of hers from *The Daily Mail*, to visit the studio for the interview. In such a sensitive situation all I wanted to do was lighten the atmosphere a bit. "Of course she must come," I said of the journalist, "but don't forget to give *Shirley Valentine* a plug."

The Greek island which, in Willy's stage play, could be anywhere, had to be somewhere specific for the film. I rang the Greek Arts Minister who turned out to be the former film star Melina Mercouri, who in the early 1960s had become famous in the picture *Never on a Sunday*. As it happens, during the late '50s Melina had made a film at Pinewood Studios, *The Gypsy and the Gentleman*, and during that time had come round for dinner with Hylda and myself. She remembered this, so suddenly the business of where to go and who to apply to for permissions became very easy. She suggested the island of Mykonos and set to work, smoothing our path for us to shoot there. As soon as I saw it, I knew that I wanted to enrich the film with more local colour than I would have time to shoot myself. As with *Friends*, I decided on a second unit but on this occasion, instead of asking my elder son, John, to direct, I turned to my younger son, Stephen. He'd already made himself useful on a couple of my films. For *Educating Rita* he had written a song that Rita's family sing in a pub. Giving him the second unit would be a way of both stretching him and providing us with some very helpful material.

It was on Mykonos that most of the scenes between Pauline Collins and Tom Conti took place, and how gratified I was to watch the two working and hitting it off so well together. I could feel Tom rejecting any part of himself that was remotely English. My favourite moment between them is when Costas and Shirley make love in a boat out at sea. The boat rocks from side to side. The prow goes up and down. The sea rushes up the beach, then down again, all of it in time to the climax of Stravinsky's 'Firebird Suite'. We were not taking it too seriously, and when Shirley says, "Where did that orchestra come from?" you realise she isn't either. Of her stretch marks, Costas thoughtfully says, "Don't hide them. They are the marks of life." Shirley just looks up at the camera and says, "Aren't men full of shit?"

When the film came out, Mykonos itself became something of a star. Years after filming there, I turned on the television to see two middle-aged American women climbing aboard a plane. "And where are you going for your holiday?" asked an interviewer.

"Greece," they answered, trying not to giggle.

"Why Greece?" asked the interviewer.

"We saw *Shirley Valentine*," they said, "and we're hoping to meet some nice Greek fishermen."

'You'll be lucky,' I thought. 'There aren't too many Greek fishermen who look like Tom Conti.' Still, today Mykonos is known as Shirley Valentine's island and the taverna where Shirley at one point finds work is now called Shirley Valentine's Taverna. Similarly, the beach, where she first goes to sunbathe is known as Shirley Valentine's Beach. So Mykonos has been a good advertisement for Shirley, while she has been a good advertisement for Mykonos.

When the film was finished, the head of Paramount was so excited that he did something we in the UK always complain big American companies never do for small British films. He got behind it and publicised it like mad. If anything, he went too far. He took out an advertisement in *The New York Times* that covered two pages. Bond films usually only had one. As a result, readers were convinced that this was the next *Gone With the Wind* and were rather puzzled when they heard that it was a small film from England.

It was not long before Pauline Collins was nominated for both an Oscar and a Bafta. At first I was just pleased that my prediction about the Academy Award had come true, but then a thought struck me. Pauline had won the Laurence Olivier Award and a Tony. Could she go on to a clean sweep? This had only happened once before, when Rex Harrison won a West End award, a Tony, an Oscar and a Bafta for playing Professor Higgins in *My Fair Lady*. Could Pauline do the same thing with *Shirley Valentine*? If she could, she would be making film history as the first woman to do it.

What happened next comes from Pauline. Paramount flew her to Hollywood and booked a table for ten before the start of the show. Nine of the most important people at Paramount surrounded her and they could not have been more charming or attentive. However, at the Oscar ceremony itself, the envelope was opened and the usual pause was followed by the words, "Best Actress, Jessica Tandy for *Driving Miss Daisy*." With hypocritical enthusiasm, the Paramount team clapped away while Pauline just clapped. From that moment onwards, none of those people from Paramount either looked at her or spoke to her again. It could only happen in Hollywood.

Pauline told me this over a drink at her house. After that, she showed me to her study. I was amazed. It was lined with her awards for *Shirley Valentine* from right round the world. I was only annoyed that the British film industry had never been able to offer this attractive, talented actress the work she deserved.

Up came Bafta night. For the evening Paramount, presumably having forgotten about the Oscar business, came over in full force. It was a remarkable effort and I was impressed. The wait for Best Actress was a long one, so when it finally arrived our nerves were at snapping point. Pauline may have been hot favourite but there was no way we could be sure. She won though, and we were thrilled.

We were also rather exhausted. As no other prizes looked like coming our way, I said to Hylda, "Let's slip out. I'm sure we won't be missed." In the middle of edging our way towards the door, we heard the last award being announced. It was the Michael Balcon Lifetime Achievement Award. Princess Anne, who was giving out the prizes, was talking about a director who had been making films for 50 years. "Quick," I said to Hylda, "some old buffer's going to get up and drone on forever. If we don't shift, we'll be here until three in the morning."

"*Reach for the Sky ... Sink the Bismarck!*" I heard Princess Anne say. 'That's funny,' I thought. 'I directed those.' And then the penny dropped. Princess Anne was talking about me.

"Do you know anything of this?" I said to Hylda.

"Absolutely not," she said, "I have no idea what she's on about."

"... Lifetime Achievement Award goes to Lewis Gilbert!" concluded Princess Anne. In a total daze I walked down the aisle and up on to the stage. What on earth was I going to say? I had nothing prepared. Fortunately, a montage of films I'd made was shown. It gave me a couple of minutes to arrange my thoughts.

"I'm so tired," I said to Princess Anne, "I was just about to slip out."

"You wouldn't have got far," she said. "We have people on the doors for that."

When the lights came up I was able to thank Willy Russell for being such a good writer and making my job so easy and to mention Martin Davis from Paramount, whom I'd known for ages, and his team who had come over from Hollywood with him. By then, it was clear to me why they had come in such numbers. They had been in the know. So in the end I didn't trip up or make a fool of myself but, great evening as it was, I was glad it was all over.

Not so long afterwards I was awarded the CBE, Commander of the Order of the British Empire. On the day of the actual presentation the Queen was away visiting India with the Duke of Edinburgh. Her deputy was Princess Anne.

"This is the second time you've given me an award," I said. "The first one was that Bafta."

"Ah, yes," she said with a wry smile, "but this one is much more important."

34

One More That Got Away

When I mentioned earlier that I had an appointment with Diana Ross, you may have wondered, what was the appointment for? She wanted to make a film about the life of Josephine Baker, the American cabaret star who became famous in France during the 1930s for dancing around in nothing but a belt of bananas.

Diana and I had several meetings. One of them was in Paris. I flew there with Bill Cartlidge and met her at the Ritz. "I'm sorry, I can't come out with you," she said. "I've just fired my chauffeur. I sent him to find a flat and it was terrible."

"Why didn't you ask me?" I said. "I know plenty of Parisians who could have helped." I should point out that the fired chauffeur was an American who had never been to France before, let alone Paris, and spoke not one word of French. I felt sorry for him, that is until I began to feel sorry for myself. I had not had lunch, nor had Bill, and we were dying of hunger.

"Have you fed the dogs?" said Diana to her maid, interr-upting our conversation.

"Not yet, ma'am," answered the maid. Diana rang down to room service and ordered two hamburgers which soon appeared, wheeled in on a trolley. They were sitting on a silver salver. This the maid lifted and placed carefully on the floor for the two dogs to start their meal.

Looking at the hamburgers as they rapidly disappeared, I explained my plight and Bill's to Diana. "Oh, I'm sorry," she said. "I've only just arrived. Go down to the restaurant and sign with my room number." We did and, like two naughty schoolboys, ordered a very expensive lunch.

"Let's meet tomorrow," Diana said, some time later when I was still in Paris and she was back in New York.

"Isn't that a bit tight?" I said.

"Take Concorde," she said, so I did.

The life of Josephine Baker was a long one, and to do her justice you needed plenty of time. Too much for a feature film. "This should be a television series," I said to Diana.

"No, I want an Academy Award," she said, and that is why the film was never made.

35

Stepping Out With Liza

Stepping Out was a stage comedy by Richard Harris and directed, as it happened, by Julia McKenzie. It was already running very successfully in the West End when Hylda and I went to see it. As we both thought it would make a good film, I rang Paramount. To be frank, I don't think they were all that crazy about the idea, but after *Shirley Valentine* they were in a mood to oblige. Their objection was not to the play itself. It was to what it would become – a little British film, and little British films are hard to sell. Paradoxically, it would not have been a little British film had it been financed in the UK. With dancing in it and a period of rehearsal required, it would have been quite a big picture for a British financier.

Aware of this little/big problem, Paramount suggested that the film be set in America. As the play wasn't rooted in a specific town, like Willy Russell's Liverpool, I thought, 'Why not?' In fact, I thought the transfer would work admirably. I suspect Richard was not of my opinion, but even he could see that everything would be easier in America. Also, Paramount had rather a good idea for the lead character, who is an ex-dancer in musicals – they suggested Liza Minnelli. She not only had star presence but, with her sense of comedy and talent for dancing, was actually right for the job.

Having made the decision that America it would be, I rang Liza's agent. He thought the idea was so good, he gave me Liza's home phone number and told me to speak to her directly. I rang with some trepidation, but she knew who I was at once and what films I had made, and altogether sounded very jolly. Having asked to see the script she read it in no time, and before two days were out she had accepted.

As a matter of fact we shot the film in Toronto, but one has to stress that both the play and the film are to do with a group of people, rather than where they live, and Toronto was a perfectly acceptable double for an American town. All these different influences were reflected in the cast, made up as it was of Americans, Canadians and one British performer, Julie Walters.

The story tells of eight women of differing types, and a lone man who all attend evening classes for tap-dancing. They aren't very good, but their teacher is convinced that she can galvanise them if she enters them for a competition. Many would think she was pushing her luck. How she copes, how her pupils cope and how they resolve their private problems is the film's story. The climax takes place in a real theatre where this disparate bunch of near no-hopers perform a dazzling routine and win the day.

Liza Minnelli was to be the teacher, who for the film was an ex-Broadway dancer. During shooting I was able to get very close to her and she would often tell me stories of her past life. Being the daughter of Judy Garland and the gifted film director Vincente Minnelli meant that plenty of talent had come her way, but so had plenty of problems. Her mother's life had been wrecked by MGM. There, from the age of five onwards, at the studio which boasted more stars than there are in heaven, Judy had grown to become one of its brightest and most successful.

However the studio's boss Louis B Mayer, a father figure merely because there was no other, took no real interest in the child's life. To him she was a commodity to be pushed into one picture after another. When the little girl became overexcited she was given pills to calm her down, and when she found it difficult to get going again she was given pills to perk her up. The main thing was to keep her working. Judy's mother, a product of vaudeville, was only too relieved at Judy's financial success and was content to go along with this exploitation. There were 14 years of overwork, drug abuse and no proper love.

After some youthful affairs Judy married Vincente Minnelli, the director of *Meet Me in St Louis* and later *Gigi*. Liza was the result but the set-up was not happy. Both parents were impossible and divorce followed a few years later. For different reasons, Liza didn't receive family love from her mother or her father. Her mother was incapable of giving it because she had never received it herself. Her father didn't have the chance. Liza adored him and he adored her, but under the terms of the divorce he was only allowed to see her for one weekend a month. If he was more at ease being gay than straight, it was something that didn't bother her. It was, if anything, a side of him that she found attractive – witness her relationships with homosexual men in later life. Back at home Liza realised that her mother, cocooned by MGM as she had been, was incapable of looking after herself. It meant that by the age of nine Liza had become the mother, while Judy was the daughter.

When Liza was 15 or thereabouts, an incident occurred that did not improve matters. She described it to me. On a train from Chicago to Los Angeles, she and her mother were in one of those sitting room carriages you see in American films when she caught sight of herself in a mirror and burst into tears. "Good

God, what's the matter?" asked her mother.

"I'm so plain," said Liza, "I'll never get married. How could any boy ever want me? I'm ugly! Look at my nose!"

"What are you going on about?" said Judy. "We'll get it fixed." It was the last thing Liza wanted to hear. What she wanted to hear was, "Don't be silly, darling. You're beautiful now and you'll be even more beautiful when you're grown up. Now, really, that's not the sort of thing you should be thinking about at your age." A typical mother's reply. However she didn't get that and I don't think she ever forgave her mother for not giving it. Perhaps it explains why I had this feeling during the making of our film that Liza was always in search of parental love. Between set-ups, she often sat on my lap and hugged me like a little girl would hug her father. I adored her.

Before the start of the film I met John Kander and Fred Ebb, who were great friends of Liza's having written the first musical she had starred in, *Flora, the Red Menace*, not to mention *Cabaret* and *Chicago*. They were going to write our title song. "Have you worked with Liza before?" they asked. When I told them that I hadn't, they said, "You're in for a treat. She's a phenomenon in showbusiness because she's not only talented, she's lovable and she works really hard to create a good feeling in the company." This turned out to be quite true. As I watched Liza work I came to the conclusion that, if anything, her talent was greater than her mother's because she could dance terrifically as well as sing and act. Unlike her mother, however, she wasn't difficult.

After work she would often take the girls out to dinner, which led them to call her the headmistress, that and one other thing. As her role was that of their teacher, she came in three weeks early to master the routines because she wanted to be utterly on top of things, like a real teacher. Later, when it came to the rehearsals for the rest of the actors, she was still there working alongside them, even though she didn't need to be. All this time, both her hip joints were giving her hell. She was in constant pain. A stand-in dancer was provided for every member of the cast who had to dance, so that it was possible for them to relax while scenes were being lit. At the same time, these stand-ins were useful for trying out any changes necessary in the choreography. You would have expected Liza to have taken full advantage of this. She didn't. Invariably, she jumped up and joined the stand-ins. It got to the point where I became quite anxious. However, I needed to think of something silly rather than serious to solve the problem. I asked one of the prop men to bring some handcuffs and leg irons. When Liza next tried to jump up, he and a mate simply plonked her back in her chair and clicked the cuffs and irons. It worked. Liza had to stay still, but at the same time everyone, including Liza, was laughing.

Her sense of discipline, she told me, came from the time of rehearsing *Flora, the Red Menace.* It was directed by George Abbott, the doyen of Broadway musical comedy directors. One morning she was late for rehearsals, and on arrival found another girl rehearsing her part. Liza, having apologised, said she was ready to take over. "No," said George, "that's fine. If you're not keen to work, you can sit there at the back and someone who *is* keen can carry on rehearsing." She was not late again.

Naturally, before anybody could do any dancing at all in our film we had to find a choreographer. I asked Liza if she knew someone good. It was the end of the 1980s, so when she told me that she knew lots of good choreographers, she also had to say that most of them had died of AIDS. The one she recommended was Danny Daniels, who proved to be a godsend. He was a brilliant choreographer, a tough disciplinarian and, as it happened, married.

The eight women pupils and the lone man were all cast primarily for their acting ability. Fortunately for Danny, most of them had some dancing experience – most but not all. Julie Walters had none and, by her own admission, had little aptitude either. The routine involved hats and sticks and, during the weeks of rehearsal Julie's hat and stick, as like as not, ended up on the floor. This was the cause of much merriment but I think there were times when Julie wondered what she had taken on. Danny showed no sign of worry at all. "Keep going, keep going," he said to her. "You *will* get it." In the event, learning the routine turned out to be the least of Julie's problems.

I knew that she had a two-and-a-half year-old daughter called Maisie, and that Maisie was with her in Toronto. Another of the girls in the film had a small child too, and occasionally brought her to the studio. Why didn't Julie bring Maisie to play with her, I suggested. Julie thought this was a good idea. The man in her life was Grant Roffey, who had met her in a pub and chatted her up without knowing who she was. Theirs was a splendid relationship because Grant was utterly devoted to both Julie and Maisie, on hand for both of them at all times. The following day, it was he who brought Maisie to the studio.

When it comes to small children I'm an old hand, as I've been through all that several times what with having not only children but grandchildren. I know that a child can appear to be at death's door and frighten the life out of you but, an hour later, can be as right as rain. I also know that a child can be nervy and clingy to the point of driving you nuts when there is actually something wrong. Maisie was Julie's and Grant's first and only child, so they had no such reference point. Maisie was nervy and clingy, which was made all the more obvious by the bounciness of the other small child on the set.

That night, Maisie had a terrifying nosebleed. Grant took her to hospital. Next morning Julie came in, but she wasn't really there. Not long afterwards she was called to the phone, and when she returned she was in tears. Grant had told her that she should come to the hospital as Maisie had been diagnosed with leukaemia. I told Julie to get changed, go at once and forget the film.

I rang the man in charge of production at Paramount, not as confident as I had sounded when talking to Julie. Men in his position have a tough job. For them, the film always comes first. His reaction gave me a big surprise. I had never heard anything like it before. "Tell Julie to take a week off," he said. "We'll reorganise the schedule around her. She's not to worry about money. Paramount will pay all her expenses." At last, a studio with a heart, I thought. It was such a relief.

If Maisie had any luck at this frightening time it was in the hospital that Grant had taken her to. By sheer coincidence, it was the pioneer for treating childhood leukaemia. Soon, its techniques would be copied all over the world.

Three days after Maisie had been admitted, members of the cast went to visit and to offer Julie support. I went too, unsure of what I would find. What I found was a bright-eyed Maisie sitting up in bed, bossily lecturing her roommate, a little boy, on his forthcoming treatment. "You'll have dial-assist and intervenus dips," she said. "The nurse brings those. She's very good. You'll be better after that." The next day, it was with a much lighter heart that I set off for work. After a week, Julie came back positively happy to be dropping her hat and stick.

Another member of the dancing class was played by Jane

Krakowski, who was yet to become famous in the TV series *Ally McBeal* and visit London to star in the musical *Guys and Dolls.* When someone is talented and you have confidence in them, you can build up a special relationship. Teasing can be involved. Jane was very talented and I did tease her, not that I got away with it. She was smart and witty and came back at me every time.

Dance classes must have music. Nowadays, it's often on a CD but the traditional way is to have someone bang out the beat on an out of tune upright and that's what Richard Harris had in his play. His pianist is a crotchety old woman, quick to shift the blame on to the dancers when accused of playing wrongly. For the film she was played by Shelley Winters who, in 1965, had been the lustbox Ruby in *Alfie.* In those days she had been a sexpot in real life, able to turn men's heads with ease. Twenty-five years had elapsed and there she was, an elderly woman surrounded by girls who were attracting the kind of attention she had once been used to. It wasn't easy for her. Nor did it help that during close-ups her lines sometimes eluded her. On those occasions she would stop dead and say the first thing that came into her head.

"Have you ever thought of making love to a very mature woman?" she once said, looking at a male stand-in dancer.

"No, thank God," he replied, "I don't have to." In finding this frightfully funny, Shelley avoided having to admit that she had forgotten her lines. "I've made a hundred B-pictures!" was another off-at-a-tangent remark.

"No, Shelley," I said, "it's now 101." She didn't stop laughing for ten minutes.

The end of shooting came all too soon but at least we finished on a climax, the big finale where the dance class emerges triumphant. The routine went superbly. I was proud of what the cast had achieved in its own right, not just of how it looked on film. When Julie got through the whole lot without once dropping her hat and stick we all burst into spontaneous applause. Maybe her experience with us proved useful when she came to make *Billy Elliot*.

It was when the film was finished and hardly anyone had seen it that we hit real bad luck. At that moment, the top distribution brass at Paramount and its entire publicity team moved to another major studio. They had been with the production since the beginning and their move was a disaster. The new broom swept us to one side. It was a big disappointment, particularly for Liza. The agency that represented her, one of the grandest, was furious. They were convinced that *Stepping Out* was going to put her back on top. I just remember Liza as she was then, hard working, lovable and terrific at creating a good feeling in the company, just as Kander and Ebb had described her. I can find no resemblance between her then and the Liza we know now with all the ridiculous marriages. I would be glad if she found her old self again.

36

Real Life: Tam's Story Continued

When I last spoke of my granddaughter Tam she was a four-year-old child in Dublin, incredulous at the sight of snow in only one street. At home, she was still hard at work with Mary Lobascher, learning scanning techniques to compensate for her incomplete vision. The ability to read was not expected to be within her grasp.

Five is the age when all children start full-time education. What was Tam going to do when she reached it? John and Joan, her parents, wanted her to lead a life as near as possible to that of any other five year-old. They needed to find a school but knew that it could not be one that was ordinary. The school they found, Parry House, was on the surface rather formal. A uniform was required and the girls' hair had to be pulled back into a ponytail. Underneath, however, Parry House was way ahead of its time. All the ages were put together and the children were of mixed ability. Tam liked it.

During the term, some of the children rehearsed an excerpt from *A Midsummer Night's Dream*. It was the scene between Titania and Bottom. This was going to be performed for the parents at the end of term. Tam was fascinated and watched every rehearsal. She couldn't read so she didn't take part, but she discovered that she could memorise every word. When it came to the day of the performance a child dropped out. Tam stepped in to save the day.

Activities that are considered good for children, like riding, swimming and dancing, took on extra importance for Tam because they improved her co-ordination. Dancing was admittedly a bit much, but she eventually got the hang of riding and swimming. These activities were done after school, as was her therapy. One day, during her scanning sessions, she looked at a printed page, made out a single word and read it aloud. Joan was in a muddle of smiling and crying all at the same time.

By the time she was seven, Tam had become a voracious reader. Even so, a Professor Charles Bedwell, consultant in visual technology and visual sensing, warned that things were not going to be that easy. Those missing jigsaw pieces, those holes in Tam's vision, were never going to come back, so reading would always be a physical effort and Tam would be tempted to guess words she could not immediately see. Still, her academic ability was deemed above average. By then Tam had a younger sister, Holly. In the relaxed atmosphere of home with no pressure, Tam loved to read her stories.

In 1990 it was time for Tam to go to secondary school. There wasn't a suitable one in London so, in a massive upheaval which changed all the family's lives, a move was organised to Dorset where Croft House, a posh girls' school, seemed to fit the bill. After all, did it not have horses? It was a disaster. The girls in her year looked down on her and gave her no help when she needed it. An older girl tried to make her feel at home until a teacher said that she did not encourage older girls talking to younger girls. One night, Tam was on her way to the lavatory when a teacher stopped her and told her to put on her dressing gown. Tam said that she was not able to, not by herself. The teacher told her to go back, fetch the dressing gown and carry it. Another time, she was asked to sing a song. Tam, thinking there was nothing in this request, sang away. Only then did she realise that the others wanted to laugh at her, which they did. Back in London, Tam reached the national finals in a swimming competition for disabled children. Her team won but not a word of this was mentioned at Croft House. It was time for Tam to leave but where would she go? There was no obvious choice and GCSEs were coming up.

Against all professional advice, John and Joan sent Tam to a state school with 1500 pupils. Everyone thought that the rough and tumble of such a large place would be too much but things turned out quite differently. Unlike the staff at the posh Croft House, the teachers at the Queen Elizabeth School, Wimborne, made a real effort to understand Tam's problems. There she was able to make friends, and later gain a distinction in word processing. In the case of any other teenager that may sound a bit ordinary, but in Tam's case it was far from it.

When it was time for GCSEs, Dr John Wilson stepped in by writing a letter to the exam board listing the obstacles that Tam had faced in her life, particularly the problem with her sight. As a result she was given extra time to take the exams and an amanuensis, someone to help with the writing down which Tam found difficult. She got four As and four Bs, enough encouragement to consider university.

She went on holiday to Poland with the RNIB (Royal National Institute of Blind People). A partially blind Polish boy gave her a kiss. He was none too handsome but as Tam said to her sister, Holly, when she got home, "It didn't matter. It was my first kiss. That was the important bit."

A social services worker, Marje Hall, came to the house to

teach Tam the rudiments of the kitchen, how to make tea and prepare simple meals, that sort of thing. She also took her out into Blandford so that she could get the hang of moving round a busy place by herself. A lady from the RNIB recommended a white stick. Marje did not agree. By actually being with Tam, she could see that she couldn't use it. She needed all her strength and co-ordination to handle a shopping bag.

Tam applied to the University of Kent to read English Literature. A place was available but the A level grades she had to reach were high. Again, when it came to actually taking the exams, extra time was given. On this occasion, however, it had an adverse effect. All the exams had to be taken in one day and the extra time – each exam took four hours – only served to wear Tam out. Also, because of this extra time she had to be put in a room on her own. It was next door to the staff common room. The sound of constant chatter coming from it was not an aid to concentration. On the day when the results were given out Joan found Tam in tears. She had done badly.

Joan and John got on to the therapist, Mary Lobascher. Mary sent a fax to Dr Wren, the registrar at Kent University, explaining what Tam had had to overcome and how hard she had worked. Dr Wilson chipped in too. 'Against all odds,' he wrote, 'she has made impressive progress and is a delightful young lady.'

Professor Innes, head of English at Kent University, asked to see Tam's course work. He was impressed. A fax arrived in Dorset. Tam was being offered an unconditional place to read English Literature at Kent University.

The problem of practicalities took over. Tam had little experience of looking after herself. At the same time, the university put her in a room for the disabled and she said she didn't want it. Instead, a keypad and a telephone line were added to an ordinary room. The keypad was for avoiding problems with fiddly keys. The telephone was there in case of emergency. Even so, the university was unaccustomed to a student with Tam's disabilities and consequently did not offer enough help.

An advertisement in the paper was the only solution. Out of the sifting process, which Tam took part in, came Teresa Drayton, a graduate of Kent University. Her job was to take notes at lectures when Tam couldn't keep up, type them out when she tired and fetch books from the library to save on physical effort. It's good to say that, in every sense of the word, she stayed the course.

In the middle of Tam's studies the government changed the rules of the Disability Living Allowance. It believed that too many people were conning it, Tam among them. How could someone disabled be attending university? She was summoned to a tribunal headed by a government representative assisted by three other people, their job to be impartial. The prospect of it was nerve-wracking. The interview was held in a large room and the tribunal sat behind a long table. Joan led Tam in and guided her to a chair on the other side of this table. After much paper shuffling, a woman started to explain to Tam why she had been summoned. The government representative interrupted. He was stopping the interview right away. Deeply embarrassed, he said that Tam would continue to receive her Disabled Living Allowance and that he was sorry to have put her into this position.

As Tam left the building she said to Joan, "I would have preferred not to have been eligible for the allowance. It is a strange triumph to be found disabled enough to deserve it."

One day in the university bar Tam met Kevin, a young man

who was quite unfazed by her disabilities. The two formed a relationship. "Is he your carer?" asked a girl student.

"No," she answered, "he's my boyfriend."

In 2001, in front of her parents, Tam received her degree for English Literature at a ceremony held in a packed Canterbury Cathedral. John and Joan, as they remembered the long battle that they and Tam had fought and won, were bursting with pride.

Afterword

Hylda died in 2005. With her no longer there, I don't know how I would have carried on were it not for my family. When I'm visiting London my son, John, comes up to town to take me out to lunch, and every evening my son, Steve, and I talk on the phone about football. At other times he presents me with labour-saving gadgets in the hope that I will learn to live in the 21st century. For that, I owe him my heartfelt thanks. Nick, my grandson, not only takes me out to eat when I'm in town, he drives me up to the Arsenal football ground where we watch matches together.

Which reminds me of how Michael Winner – he who can't stand football – revealed an unexpected side. During the weeks after Hylda's death he rang regularly to see how I was and to take me out for meals when I was especially low. This is stuff that he won't like me saying, I know. It ruins his Mr Horrid reputation. Still, I was very grateful to him.

At the time of *A Cry From the Streets* and *Carve Her Name With Pride* I mentioned the appearance in our lives of a young woman called Tessa Hodgson. Tessa came round one afternoon because we needed help with clerical work and the running of the house. I didn't know it but that was our lucky day. 51 years have passed, during which she became like a daughter to my wife. Today Tessa Bloy, as she now is, still manages, with all her other work, to make sure the family doesn't get in a muddle. I can't imagine what we would do without her.

Hylda and I were lucky in another way. We had five grandchildren and were able to watch them grow up. It has been fascinating to see each one become their own person, quite different from any of the others. Number three is Cass. When he was a very little boy, Cass picked up a guitar and plucked some notes with such immediate understanding that it was clear he had talent. John, his father, always the music lover, set about organising lessons so that by the time Cass had reached his teens he was being taught by some really distinguished guitarists, among them Paco Peña. In his summer holidays he would further his studies by travelling to Spain to be taught by other great guitarists. However, it was always Paco Peña who believed in both his playing and his compositions.

At 18, and by then very accomplished, he went to Manchester University. All of a sudden he stopped playing and never touched the guitar again. He also stopped composing, and we in the family thought he really had a gift for it. Seeing that he had invested so much time and effort in the guitar, I could not resist asking him why he had set it aside. "If you want a career playing the guitar," he said, "you can't join a quartet or a chamber orchestra. You have to play solo, and for that you have to be great. I'm not great. I know that and I don't fancy spending my days picking out tunes in pubs and cafés." When he left Manchester he seemed to have no idea which way his life would go. The only thing he liked was cycling.

With all the confidence of youth, he decided to cycle from Sydney to London. To make it mean something he obtained sponsorship from the charity Children with AIDS. Quite alone, he rode through jungles and up mountains, living off the land and sleeping where he could. Many a time, out in the middle of nowhere, he would arrive in a village to be greeted by its entire population. It can be imagined that a white man on a bike was quite a novelty. From these brief halts he learned that the poorer the village the more generous was its hospitality, and parting from such kind people was always painful. Again, all the villagers would turn out but this time there would be hugs and tears, Cass weeping along with them. Having waved goodbye, he would then set off to struggle through the next jungle and up the next mountain. The journey took him two years and he raised a very large sum for Children with AIDS.

Cass had discovered a new career without realising it. With his recent experience, he could make a living by accompanying groups of other nuts who wanted to cycle round faraway places, the Himalayas for instance. Such trips were becoming very popular. "That's fine," I said to him, "but what if you want to marry? There can't be many women prepared to go with their husbands over the Himalayas." How wrong could I have been? Not long afterwards, Cass introduced me to a pretty American girl who was prepared to do just that and to go to even remoter places. I hadn't realised how many cycling enthusiasts there were, and magazines too. Cass, who writes for these magazines, is now well known in the cycling world and has been asked to edit some of those publications.

Not so long ago, he and his girlfriend made a trip to Edinburgh for a cycling convention. As soon as it was over they cycled down to Manchester, as Cass was due to be interviewed there. The girlfriend couldn't stay because she needed to be in London to renew her visa. "What did she do?" I asked Cass when next I saw him. "Put the bicycle on the train?"

I shall never forget the pained look on his face. "Put the bicycle on the train?" he said. "That is bizarre. She cycled to London, of course."

Nick, who is his older brother, expressed an interest in joining one of Cass's excursions but was anxious that he might tire. "Don't worry," I said. "They always travel with a Jeep behind them in case of emergency. You could go and ride in that when you get tired."

Cass, who had been listening, was having none of it. "Absolutely not," he said, "because then if anyone else got tired they'd want to travel in the Jeep too. It's only there for emergencies and for storing sleeping bags and cooking gear." What a far cry from playing the guitar in the world's most famous concert halls.

Cass has a sister, Holly. She is the youngest and has just started to act professionally. This means she can look forward to a fair amount of advice from me, whether she wants it or not. My relationship with John's wife, Joan, works so well that I look upon her not so much as a daughter-in-law but as the daughter I never had. She has been a tower of strength to me and to others too, I suspect, because I've heard people refer to her as Saint Joan. To us in the family, she's known as Joannie.

I have two great grandsons now, Harper and Lucas. My granddaughter Justine, who lives in Vienna with her husband Roman, is bringing her son Harper over next week. Lucas, the son of Nick and his new wife Shirley, lives where I can see him pretty much whenever I like. It's all part of looking forward, which I have always preferred to do.

After *Stepping Out* I directed two more pictures, the second of which was *Before You Go*. It fulfilled an ambition that first came to me when I was 12. While acting in the film *Dick Turpin* back in 1932, I was interviewed by Roy Nash of *The Evening Star*. "Do you want to be an actor when you grow up?" he asked.

The reply I gave was, "I want to be working in films when I'm 80." Admittedly I didn't imagine that it would be as a director, but when I finished *Before You Go* I was 82.

As time has gone by, however, I have come to realise that my children and grandchildren mean more to me than any film I have made, or award that I have won. After all, what film can match the transformation of Tam? She is able to live in a flat by herself, go shopping by herself and, what's more, hold down a job – that of directing a company of disabled actors in plays. Although I am 89, her example encourages me to think that there is one more film ahead. Or, as she herself puts it, "We're looking forward to you being the first 100 year-old film director."

Filmography

As actor

1933 **Dick Turpin**
Directors: John Stafford and Victor Hanbury
Leading players: Victor McLaglen, Jane Carr, Frank Vosper

1935 **Boys Will Be Boys**
Director: William Beaudine
Leading players: Will Hay, Gordon Harker, Jimmy Hanley

1937 **Good Morning, Boys**
Director: Marcel Varnel
Leading players: Will Hay, Martita Hunt, Peter Gawthorne

1938 **The Divorce of Lady X**
Director: Tim Whelan
Leading players: Merle Oberon, Laurence Olivier, Binnie Barnes, Ralph Richardson

As assistant director

1938 **Vessel of Wrath**
Director: Erich Pommer
Leading players: Charles Laughton, Elsa Lanchester, Robert Newton

1939 **Jamaica Inn**
Director: Alfred Hitchcock
Leading players: Charles Laughton, Maureen FitzSimons (Maureen O'Hara)

As second unit director

1944 **Target for Today**
Director: William Keighley

As writer

1949 **Marry Me** (*with Denis Waldock*)
Director: Terence Fisher
Leading players: Derek Bond, Susan Shaw, Patrick Holt, Carol Marsh, David Tomlinson

As producer

1961 **Spare the Rod** (*uncredited*)
Director: Leslie Norman
Leading players: Max Bygraves, Geoffrey Keen, Donald Pleasence

As director

1944 **The Ten Year Plan** (*also as writer*)
Leading player: Charles Hawtrey

1946 **Arctic Harvest** (*also as writer*)

1949 **Under One Roof** (*also as writer*)

1949 **The Little Ballerina** (*also as co-writer*)
Leading players: Yvonne Marsh, Martita Hunt, Anthony Newley
Guest stars: Margot Fonteyn, Michael Somes

1950 **Once a Sinner**
Leading players: Pat Kirkwood, Jack Watling, Joy Shelton, Sydney Tafler

1951 **Scarlet Thread**
Leading players: Laurence Harvey, Kathleen Byron, Sydney Tafler, Arthur Hill, Harry Fowler

1951 **There is Another Sun**
Leading players: Maxwell Reed, Susan Shaw, Laurence Harvey, Hermione Baddeley

1951 **Harmony Lane**
(*as Byron Gill, also as producer*)
Leading players: Max Bygraves, The Beverley Sisters, Svetlana Beriosova, David Paltenghi, The Television Toppers, Dora Bryan

1952 **Emergency Call** (*also as co-writer*)
Leading players: Jack Warner, Anthony Steel, Joy Shelton, Earl Cameron, Freddie Mills, Sidney James, Thora Hird, Sydney Tafler, Dandy Nichols

1952 **Time, Gentlemen, Please!**
Leading players: Eddie Byrne, Hermione Baddeley, Dora Bryan, Thora Hird, Sidney James, Sydney Tafler

1952 **Cosh Boy** (*also as co-writer*)
Leading players: James Kenney, Joan Collins, Hermione Baddeley, Hermione Gingold, Johnny Briggs, Sidney James, Ian Whittaker

1953 **Johnny on the Run**
(*also as producer and co-writer*)
Leading players: Eugeniusz Chylek, Sydney Tafler, Michael Balfour, Jean Anderson, Moultrie Kelsall, Mona Washbourne

1953 **Albert RN**
Leading players: Anthony Steel, Jack Warner, Robert Beatty, William Sylvester, Anton Diffring, Eddie Byrne, Guy Middleton, Paul Carpenter

1954 **The Sea Shall Not Have Them**
(*also as co-writer*)
Leading players: Michael Redgrave, Dirk Bogarde, Anthony Steel, Nigel Patrick, Bonar Colleano, James Kenney, Sydney Tafler, Griffith Jones, Jack Watling

1954 **The Good Die Young**
(*also as co-writer*)
Leading players: Laurence Harvey, Stanley Baker, Richard Basehart, John Ireland, Gloria Grahame, Margaret Leighton, Joan Collins, Robert Morley

1955 **Cast a Dark Shadow**
Leading players: Margaret Lockwood, Dirk Bogarde, Kay Walsh, Mona Washbourne, Robert Flemyng, Kathleen Harrison
Guest star: Lita Roza

1956 **Reach for the Sky** (*also as writer*)
Leading players: Kenneth More, Muriel Pavlow, Dorothy Alison, Lyndon Brook, Lee Patterson, Alexander Knox, Sydney Tafler, Jack Watling, Michael Warre, Howard Marion Crawford

1957 **The Admirable Crichton**
(*also co-adaptor*)
Leading players: Kenneth More, Diane Cilento, Cecil Parker, Sally Ann Howes, Jack Watling, Gerald Harper, Martita Hunt, Peter Graves, Miles Malleson, Eddie Byrne

1958 **Carve Her Name With Pride**
(*also as co-writer*)
Leading players: Virginia McKenna, Paul Scofield, Jack Warner, Denise Grey, Maurice Ronet, Alain Saury, Avice Landone, Anne Leon, Nicole Stephane, Bill Owen, Sydney Tafler, Noel Willman, Billie Whitelaw

1958 **A Cry from the Streets**
Leading players: Max Bygraves, Barbara Murray, Colin Petersen, Dana Wilson, Kathleen Harrison, Eleanor Summerfield, Sean Barrett, Mona Washbourne, Toke Townley, Avice Landon, Dandy Nichols

1959 **Ferry to Hong Kong**
(*also as co-writer*)
Leading players: Curt Jürgens, Orson Welles, Sylvia Syms, Jeremy Spencer, Noel Purcell, Marjorie Withers, John Wallace

1960 **Sink the Bismarck!**
Leading players: Kenneth More, Dana Wynter, Carl Mohner, Laurence Naismith, Karel Stepanek, Maurice Denham, Mark Dignam, Michael Goodliffe, Jack Gwillim, Michael Hordern, Geoffrey Keen, Esmond Knight, Jack Watling
Guest star: Edward R Murrow

1960 **Light Up the Sky** (*also producer*)
Leading players: Ian Carmichael, Tommy Steele, Benny Hill, Sydney Tafler, Victor Maddern, Harry Locke, Johnny Briggs, Cyril Smith, Dick Emery, Cardew Robinson, Susan Burnet, Sheila Hancock, Fred Griffiths

1961 **The Greengage Summer**
Leading players: Kenneth More, Danielle Darrieux, Susannah York, Claude Nollier, Jane Asher, Elizabeth Dear, Richard Williams, David Saire, Raymond Gérôme, Maurice Denham, André Maranne

1962 **HMS Defiant**
Leading players: Alec Guinness, Dirk Bogarde, Maurice Denham, Nigel Stock, Richard Carpenter, Peter Gill, David Robinson, Robin Stewart, Ray Brooks, Peter Greenspan, Anthony Quayle, Tom Bell, Murray Melvin, Victor Maddern, Walter Fitzgerald

1963 **The Seventh Dawn**
Leading players: William Holden, Susannah York, Capucine, Tetsuro Tamba, Michael Goodliffe, Allan Cuthbertson, Maurice Denham, Sydney Tafler, Beulah Quo, Hugh Robinson, Tony Price

1965 **Alfie**
Leading players: Michael Caine, Shelley Winters, Millicent Martin, Julia Foster, Jane Asher, Vivien Merchant, Eleanor Bron, Shirley Anne Field, Denholm Elliott, Alfie Bass, Graham Stark, Murray Melvin, Sydney Tafler

1966 **You Only Live Twice**
Leading players: Sean Connery, Akiko Wakabayashi, Mie Hama, Tetsuro Tamba, Donald Pleasence, Teru Shimada, Karin Dor, Bernard Lee, Lois Maxwell, Desmond Llewellyn, Charles Gray

1970 **The Adventurers**
Leading players: Bekim Fehmiu, Alan Badel, Candice Bergen, Ernest Borgnine, Leigh Taylor-Young, Fernando Rey, Thommy Berggren, Charles Aznavour, Olivia de Havilland, John Ireland, Delia Boccardo, Sydney Tafler, Rossano Brazzi

1971 **Friends**
Leading players: Sean Bury, Anicée Alvina, Ronald Lewis, Toby Robins, Sady Rebbot, Pascale Roberts, Joan Hickson

1974 **Paul and Michelle**
Leading players: Sean Bury, Anicée Alvina, Keir Dullea, Cathérine Allegret, Ronald Lewis, Toby Robins, Peter Graves, Georges Beller, Anne Lonnberg

1975 **Operation Daybreak**
Leading players: Timothy Bottoms, Martin Shaw, Joss Ackland, Nicola Paget, Anthony Andrews, Kika Markham, Anton Diffring, Carl Duering, Diana Coupland, Ronald Radd, Kim Fortune

1976 **Seven Nights in Japan**
Leading players: Michael York, Hidemi Aoki, Charles Gray, Eléanore Hirt, Anne Lonnberg,

Peter Jones, James Villiers,
Lionel Murton, Yolande Donlan

1977 **The Spy Who Loved Me**
Leading players: Roger Moore,
Barbara Bach, Curt Jürgens,
Richard Kiel, Caroline Munro,
Geoffrey Keen, Walter Gotell,
Edward de Souza, Vernon Dobtcheff,
George Baker, Bernard Lee,
Desmond Llewellyn, Lois Maxwell,
Michael Billington, Shane Rimmer,
Sydney Tafler, Bryan Marshall

1979 **Moonraker**
Leading players: Roger Moore,
Lois Chiles, Michael Lonsdale,
Richard Kiel, Corinne Cléry,
Emily Bolton, Geoffrey Keen,
Toshiro Suga, Bernard Lee,
Desmond Llewellyn, Lois Maxwell,
Walter Gotell

1983 **Educating Rita**
Leading players: Michael Caine,
Julie Walters, Michael Williams,
Maureen Lipman, Jeananne Crowley,
Malcolm Douglas, Godfrey Quigley

1984 **Not Quite Jerusalem**
Leading players: Joanna Pacula,
Sam Robards, Todd Graff,
Kevin McNally, Bernard Strother,
Selina Cadell, Ewan Stewart,
Kate Ingram, Gary Cady, Libby Morris

1989 **Shirley Valentine**
Leading players: Pauline Collins,
Tom Conti, Alison Steadman,
Julia McKenzie, Joanna Lumley,
Sylvia Syms, Bernard Hill,
George Costigan, Anna Keaveney,
Tracie Bennett, Gillian Kearney

1991 **Stepping Out**
Leading players: Liza Minnelli,
Julie Walters, Shelley Winters, Bill Irwin,
Ellen Greene, Carol Woods,
Jane Krakowski, Robyn Stevan,
Sheila McCarthy, Andrea Martin

1995 **Haunted**
Leading players: Aidan Quinn,
Kate Beckinsale, Anthony Andrews,
Anna Massey, John Gielgud,
Alex Lowe, Liz Smith,
Geraldine Somerville

2002 **Before You Go**
Leading players: Julie Walters,
Joanne Whalley, Victoria Hamilton,
Patricia Hodge, Tom Wilkinson,
John Hannah, Hugh Ross,
Dermot Crowley

Index